BLOOD IN THE SEA

HMS Dunedin and the Enigma Code

STUART GILL

CASSELL

Cassell Military Paperbacks

Cassell
Wellington House, 125 Strand
London WC2R 0BB

Distributed in the United States by
Sterling Publishing Co. Inc.
387 Park Avenue South
New York, NY 10016-8810

First published in 2003
by Weidenfeld & Nicolson
This Cassell Military Paperbacks edition 2004

British Library Cataloguing-in-Publication Data.
A catalogue record for this book is available from the British Library.

ISBN 0 304 36691 9

Printed and bound in Great Britain by
Cox & Wyman Ltd, Reading, Berkshire

www.orionbooks.co.uk

Stuart Gill is a career diplomat. His father, William Gill, still alive and well, signed up for the Royal Marines as soon as the Second World War broke out, and intending simply to tell his father's story Stuart Gill soon found himself drawn into the wider history of an unglamorous but happy ship, her crew and her sudden loss. It is a story somehow representative of all the tragedy of war at sea. A website dedicated to HMS *Dunedin* is available at www.hmsdunedin.co.uk.

To the men of

HMS *Dunedin*

On the seas and far away,

On stormy seas and far away;

Nightly dreams and thoughts by day

Are aye with him that's far away.

On the Seas and Far Away (1794)
ROBERT BURNS (1759–96)

Acknowledgements

I am grateful to many people for their support, without which this book would not have been written. I thank Lieutenant-Commander Chris Broadway, RN, and Daniel Morgan for becoming my new friends and for displaying levels of dedication, ingenuity and resourcefulness beyond any reasonable expectation. Chris pushed me with a potent mixture of naval insight and brilliant humour, cajoling and encouraging me in equal measure just when I needed it. Daniel's habit of turning up new sources and fresh information rightfully earned him the title of Chief Ferret. He provided a never-ending flow of surprises and, as a German speaker, gave me invaluable assistance with the German language and in Germany itself. I shall remain honoured for the rest of my life to have met, in addition to my own father, men who served in *Dunedin* without whose help this book would not have been possible. They are Harry Cross, Jim Davis, Les Barter, Tommy Handley, Keith Mantell, Andrew Prideaux, Charles Embury and Alan Jarvis. I corresponded with, but did not have the pleasure of meeting, Raymond Harris and Harry Hunt. At the time of writing I had not met the fifth known living survivor, John Miles. Sadly, since the publication of the hardback edition, we have lost Harry Cross.

Unless the many relatives and friends of *Dunedin*'s ship's company had come forward, the book would have lacked the vital ingredient of many more human stories. When I began this project in 1995, I knew of only one person who had any connection with HMS *Dunedin*, but now

I have had the pleasure and good fortune to meet and correspond with many wonderful people who have willingly shared stories, information, photographs and memorabilia. I am also indebted to Barry Holmes at Weidenfeld & Nicolson for his wonderful support, without which this book would not have made it to the book shops.

No words can adequately express my thanks to my family for allowing me to use precious spare time to research and write this book. Balancing a career and a family is one thing, spending all my spare moments glued to the PC, sifting through papers or disappearing to the Public Record Office is another altogether. To my wife, Maggie, I say 'thank you' for her patience, ceaseless support, love and unending encouragement. To my daughters, Elizabeth and Claire, I thank them for their understanding of why 'Daddy is in the office again'.

My father's role goes almost without saying. As a survivor, his recollections and stories are undeniably central to the book. As my father, his contribution is indescribable. I wondered constantly whether I had any right to reopen old wounds and to rekindle painful memories and I relied often on the unseen supportive hand of my mother. My father did not always find it easy, but he insisted from the beginning that the book should be completed as a memorial to the men who served in *Dunedin*. I shall be eternally grateful to him for allowing me to glimpse into the past.

Contents

Introduction

When I started to write this book I intended it to be no more than a private account for family consumption, a placing on the record of my father's war experience in a minor warship. It was a natural thing for a son to do. It soon became clear to me, however, that this would not be enough. The history books were largely silent about the loss of a British light cruiser and over 400 of her men in November 1941. It was a gap I wanted to fill.

HMS *Dunedin* was no glamour ship. Her frontline role in the Second World War consisted mostly of intercepting German and French merchant vessels. Her anti-submarine capability was virtually non-existent, she was showing her age even when the war began and she became a mere pawn on the chessboard of the Battle of the Atlantic. If ever a ship sank without trace, *Dunedin* was it. Until now.

After several years' research, the ship, which – in my father's words – was a bit player on a large stage, can be seen to have been very much more. She was a workhorse, pulled into service beyond her time and often beyond her capabilities. Between September 1939 and November 1941 she sailed the hostile waters of the North Sea, the Arctic Ocean, the Caribbean and most of the central and south Atlantic in pursuit of enemy surface vessels or escorting Allied convoys. She often spent weeks on end at sea, grinding away on patrol or with convoys. For most of the time she was overcrowded and even overrun with rats and cockroaches. The ship's company suffered the same deprivations as *Dunedin*'s more illustrious compatriots and as a coherent group of men the '*Dunedins*' missed home and their families as much as anyone. The long periods at sea or in foreign ports were punctuated for them, as for all others, by occasional deliveries of mail but, more likely, by the disappointment of no delivery at all. Too often, the sight of land and the approach of a harbour brought the exciting expectation that mailbags would be waiting, only for the men to be disappointed and have to set sail once more, with only the hope that next time something would be waiting for them.

And yet, we should not conclude that *Dunedin* was an unhappy ship. Far from it. Just as in all other Navy ships, her ship's company lived and fought together, carving friendships and having fun. For the vast majority of the men on board, especially the younger ones, this was a time of great adventure. Despite the long periods away from home and the discomforts and deprivations, the men of *Dunedin* forged unique bonds beyond the usual bounds of camaraderie.

This 'bit player' was unknowingly wrapped up in the greatest wartime secret of all – the breaking of the Enigma code. In *Dunedin's* story we see the effects on real lives of the brilliance of the men and women of Bletchley Park and the Admiralty's Operational Intelligence Centre. Few knew anything about this at the time, certainly no one on board *Dunedin*, and it remained a massive secret until well after the war had finished. Now it is an oft-told story and the secret of Bletchley Park is in the open. For a forgotten ship like *Dunedin*, however, we now know that the Bletchley Park secret was ultimately the do or die, the success and failure, of her life. In her last months, most of what *Dunedin* did had some connection with the intelligence gleaned from breaking Enigma. Ironically, both her biggest success and her ultimate downfall happened as a result of the Admiralty's use of Enigma-based intelligence. First, in June 1941, she captured a valuable tanker in a joint operation with the carrier HMS *Eagle*; and then, in November, U-124 stumbled on her and sank her while she was searching for a surface vessel known – through the Admiralty's reading of decrypted Enigma messages – to be in the area.

The writing of this book has uncovered more information and more memories than I could possibly have imagined and, by putting them together, we can no longer maintain the fiction that *Dunedin* sank without trace. Too many people have come forward to offer their insights, their

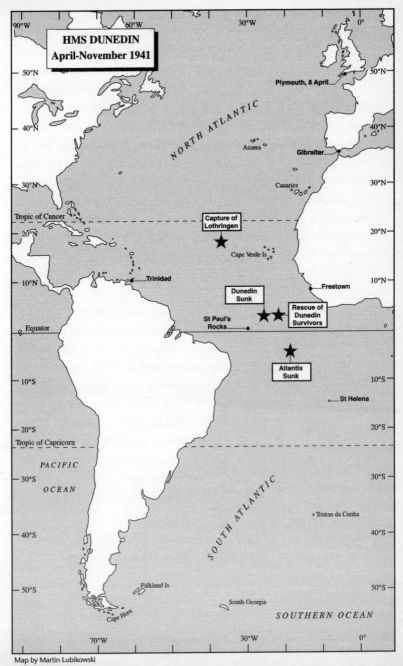

**HMS DUNEDIN
April-November 1941**

90°W   60°W   30°W   0°

50°N

NORTH ATLANTIC

Plymouth, 8 April

40°N

Azores

Gibraltar

30°N

Canaries

Tropic of Cancer

Capture of Lothringen ★

20°N

Cape Verde Is

Trinidad

Dunedin Sunk ★ ★   **Rescue of Dunedin Survivors**

Freetown

10°N

St Paul's Rocks ●

Equator

★ **Atlantis Sunk**

10°S

St Helena

Tropic of Capricorn

20°S

PACIFIC

OCEAN

30°S

SOUTH ATLANTIC

Tristan da Cunha

40°S

Falkland Is

South Georgia

50°S

Cape Horn

SOUTHERN OCEAN

70°W   30°W   0°

Map by Martin Lubikowski

research and their memorabilia for that to be the case. At the first ever reunion for veterans of HMS *Dunedin* in April 2001, a crowd of over 150 relatives and friends of *Dunedin*'s ship's company squeezed into a pavilion at Henley-on-Thames to pay their last respects and to hear what had happened to HMS *Dunedin*. The remaining four known survivors proudly and sadly told their stories to a hushed and sombre audience.

One of the hardest problems in writing this book was to decide how to tell the story, so I need to give the reader some explanation of the way it is set out. When I began to write it, I used the first person of my father as the narrator. I was convinced that it was important to express things from the point of view of someone who was there. I interviewed him in great depth about his life and his time on board *Dunedin* and built up a picture from his perspective. As the research developed and it became clearer that it would be possible to write not just a series of memories but also a history book, I found that I needed to adapt the narrative technique into three strands. The first, which the reader will find in italics, is in the first person of my father and relates an eyewitness account and genuine personal reflections. The second strand is the verbatim extracts of some of the letters of members of the ship's company. The third is written from the author's standpoint and relates the historical facts. In this way the book is a historical narrative interlaced with personal memories of those who were there. Everything described in this book happened.

Undoubtedly yet more remains to be uncovered and told, notably about the many other men, Captain Lovatt included, who went down with the ship or who died in the water or on the rafts after the torpedoes hit. This is a first step in uncovering the true story of what happened to *Dunedin* and the men in her. More than sixty years after the loss of over 400 men, the story deserves to be told.

CHAPTER 1
Beginnings

27 November 1941, South Atlantic

The early-evening sky hinted at the arrival of a fourth night afloat. The only sounds were the lapping of the sea against the sides of the Carley float and the occasional words from the two other men in the raft. We had nothing to say, except silently to ourselves, and to God. The sun had beaten down on us all day, turning our skin a parched red and drying the last vestige of moisture in our mouths. Our tongues were swollen, our legs bitten by fish, our minds hanging on the precipice of sanity. I cupped my hands in the sea and splashed water on my face, telling myself over and over again not to drink it. I wanted to close my eyes, I wanted to sleep, to drift away to peace.

Pictures flashed before my eyes, pictures of faces, people I knew, places that were familiar. I saw my mother crying, my father talking, but I could not hear them. They were pleading with me, cajoling me, but I could not hear them. My brothers stood in the background, quizzical, quiet, bemused. Then I was in the park, on the pond, rowing – a girl's face smiling. I was laughing, running silently.

The images faded and I awoke with a start, water splashing in my face, another wave trying to tip us out. I wiped the water from my eyes and heard sound again, but it was only the sea and the faint creak of the raft, gently buffeted by the swell. I rested my head on the side of the raft and saw the sky turning a deeper blue.

I looked at my two remaining comrades. How long had we been together? Three days, four days, three weeks? I tried to remember. How many nights? I tried to work it out, but all I saw were the faces of the men who had been with us in the beginning. I remembered now, remembered that I had counted, or someone had told me to count. Twenty-two men. Yes, that was it, twenty-two men crammed on this tiny, oval-shaped tin tube, clinging to each other, sometimes squabbling, sometimes dying. I had watched so many die or just swim away.

Now the three of us lay slumped in the raft, chest deep in water, exhausted, waiting for night to fall. We did not expect to see morning.

My eyes closed again. Take me away from here, please. The sounds of the sea receded and a radio buzzed in the background, a chair was in the corner of a cluttered room, a sideboard against the wall, a woman with a teacup, a man with the newspaper – talk of bombs and gas and air raids.

I held out my cup and my mother filled it with fresh tea. She was talking.

'I don't see why you have to go off fighting this war when there are plenty of other things for you to do here in London, and I don't see why you should put me and your father through all the anguish. We want you here, where you can be safe. Why are you doing this to us?'

'I'm not doing it to you, I'm doing it because I have to. Dad fought in the last war and he was under-age. It's right that I should go. And anyway, it's done, I can't change my mind now.'

It had been one more argument, one more painful explanation. Poor Mum. So caring, so wonderful, but I could do or say nothing to ease her pain. Her eldest boy was going off to war.

I sipped my tea and glanced at my father, who looked up from the newspaper. His face said nothing and everything. His eyes told me that I was right, but also that Mother would feel it worst of all. I heard the clink of cutlery and plates in the kitchen as my mother cleared away. Our flat was small, cramped even. The five of us lived in two bedrooms and a living room. My two brothers had one of the bedrooms, so I had to sleep in the living room on a bed-settee. I could never go to bed until everyone else had gone and if ever we had visitors I had to wait for them to leave. And I could never stay long in bed in the mornings, especially if anyone came to the door. We had no bathroom, just a tin tub in the kitchen, one end poking out from behind an inadequate wooden flap fitted by the Crown Property Agents.

My small suitcase with my meagre belongings was propped up against the wall in the corner of the living room, ready for the following day when I would *leave. I did not want to leave my family, but I could not wait for the morning.*

On my raft, the sounds of the sea took hold again and the first early-evening breeze signalled the coming night once more. The sun weakened still further. My heavy eyes closed.

More images and sounds spilled into my head. I was walking across the courtyard of our block of flats. A group of small boys were kicking a soft leather football, its inner-tube bladder poking through the slit in the leather where the lace should have been. Two grey pullovers lay crumpled on the ground a few feet apart as a makeshift goal. The sounds of the boys' shoes scuffing over the tarmac echoed round the courtyard, the ball skidding off the imaginary pitch and out of play.

I ducked into the stairwell behind the goal and ran up the dimly lit concrete stairs two at a time until I got to the third floor. Walking along the balcony, I looked over the stone wall down to the boys playing football, their shouts echoing against the identical blocks of flats all around us. I knocked on the door of number 17 and heard my mother call to my father to let me in.

It was 1938, when war had seemed so close. All I wanted was to join up. But I was barely seventeen and needed the permission of my parents, which neither was prepared to give me. Chamberlain was doing his level best to avert war, 'Peace in our time' and all that, but in between the optimism and the hopes of peace everyone knew war with the Germans was only a matter of time.

If the truth were told, I was rather looking forward to it. I had left school at fourteen because my father could not afford to keep me there and I lived with my parents in our Crown Property flat in north London – 17 Swinley House, Redhill Street. I can't say I disliked living in the flat – after all, it was my home – but it wasn't my idea of adventure. And I hated my job, an apprentice upholsterer in a furniture factory. It never seemed to take me beyond sweeping the floor and making the tea.

My father had done his bit in the First World War and told me some of his stories and experiences, enough at least for me to feel the excitement. I was young enough to overlook the horror of the trenches and see only the glory and the adventure. I wanted my piece too.

When, in 1939, war looked increasingly inevitable, I was still living at home and still sweeping the floor at the furniture factory. But all the time I dreamed of joining the Royal Marines. I looked forward to my eighteenth birthday in May, when I could volunteer without my parents' permission. Of course, I would rather have signed up with their full consent. I realise now that my mother must have seen this coming for at least two years. Not only in anticipation of another war but mostly in fear of losing her family and watching me go off to fight.

My father continued to try to persuade me not to sign up, but nothing he said could change my mind. I was determined to go and not even the tales of trench warfare from the First World War were enough to put me off.

I spent the last week of August on holiday with my Aunt Lucy in Stokenchurch and returned home on Saturday 2 September. Waiting for me in the flat was a letter from the furniture factory telling me that business was bad in view of the impending war and there would be no more work for me. So now I was out of a job, but another letter said that, as a Boy Scout, I should report to the nearest Air Raid Precaution (ARP) station for civil defence duties in the event of war.

On the morning of the day war was declared, Sunday 3 September, I was at my girlfriend's house in Tufnell Park. I sat in their kitchen listening to Neville Chamberlain tell us that, as of 11 a.m., we were at war with Germany. We listened, spellbound, to Chamberlain's laboured delivery of his sombre message.

We had all been expecting this for so long but it still came as a shock to hear the Prime Minister speak this way. My enthusiasm for war was dented, at least momentarily, as the four of us sat together silently after the broadcast, trying to take in what we had heard.

Back at home the mood was quiet and none of us was sure what to say as we ate lunch. My mother and father had heard Chamberlain's message and wondered whether the bombing and gassing would start as soon as people had been suggesting. For me, this meant I would have to go down to the ARP station and report to my Scout troop for ARP duties. I was very excited but not sure of what I would have to do.

Without waiting to finish my lunch, I left quickly, closing the front door behind me. I rushed along the balcony to the stairs. Running down the concrete stairs three at a time, I was oblivious of what I must have left behind me. I could barely contain my excitement at the prospect of a war of my own, while my parents, who had already been through one war and didn't want another, now watched their eldest son prepare to go off to fight.

I ran across the courtyard and on towards my designated ARP station. From that very first minute we had expected, just as Dad had said over lunch, to be bombed and gassed. To me, it wasn't a phoney war at all. This was it. This was what we had been waiting for.

I relished the chance to work at the ARP station. I wouldn't be fighting the Germans but I would be doing important war work, defending our country from the ravaging invaders. These were proud moments for me. After months of waiting for the inevitable, I could finally do something exciting.

When I reached the ARP station in Albany Street, I was not the only one who had reported for duty. A number of other Scouts had turned up and three or four officially designated ARP wardens were distributing ARP kit. After announcing my arrival, I was told, ''ere, put this lot on, sit over there and wait for your instructions.'

I duly complied and within a few minutes was equipped and ready to defend my country. Having been expecting war for so many months everyone thought it would start in London the moment it had been declared, so there was much running around and panic in those early hours. The major fear was that the Germans would start dropping poisonous gas.

I walked out into the street in a very thick oilskin coat, wellington boots, a sou'wester, gloves and a gas mask. Armed with a football rattle and covered in patches whose colour would change if they came in contact with poisonous gas, I set out to save my countrymen.

The 3rd was a blisteringly hot day and here I was trussed up like a North Sea fisherman, wandering the streets, frightening children and desperately worried that my patches would change colour. But I would be all right – I had my rattle, my wellies and a sou'wester. Hitler would be arriving within the hour.

In fact, he didn't come that day, either in person or in bombs. And I wasn't asked to shuffle round the streets of London again. Instead I was moved from the Albany Street ARP station to ARP HQ in Camden High Street, where I answered the telephone and pushed paper around. The phoney war had begun.

In truth, for the next few weeks my life was rather boring. I had no job and no war to fight. It was all being played out in the newspapers, a long way from me and mostly at sea.

CHAPTER 2
Northern Patrol, Winter 1939

If the war at home was phoney, the war at sea was real from the very start. On the first evening, the passenger liner *Athenia* was sunk by a German U-boat, with the loss of 112 people, many of them American citizens. For the Royal Navy – and Winston Churchill, now back in charge at the Admiralty – the first job was to gather the fleet for the defence of Britain. Scapa Flow, in the Orkneys, was the ideal place to position the fleet in a war against Germany. From there the Navy could control the exits from the North Sea and enforce a blockade against ships trying to reach German ports.

Churchill paid an early visit to Scapa to see the fleet for himself. As he gazed upon the ships he could not help but observe that he had been there before, at the start of the last war. Later, he remembered:

> My thoughts went back a quarter of a century to that other September when I had last visited Sir John Jellicoe and his captains in this very bay, and had found them with their long lines of battleships and cruisers drawn out at anchor, a prey to the same uncertainties as now afflicted us. Most of the captains and admirals of those days were dead, or had long passed into retirement. The responsible senior officers who were now presented to me as I visited the various ships had been young lieutenants or even midshipmen in those far-off days. But an entirely different generation filled the uniforms and the posts. Only the ships had most of them been laid down in my tenure. None of them was new.

Among the lines of 'battleships and cruisers' was a twenty-year-old light cruiser in the 12th Cruiser Squadron, HMS *Dunedin*. She had been readying herself for war for several weeks. On 21 August, after ten days of exercises in the North Sea, she had returned to Portsmouth. The next day she received orders to sail by noon on Friday 25 August, but first she had to change her ship's company from one of mostly boys to a war complement. Two-thirds of the boys were sent ashore and for the next three days and nights new members of the crew arrived by the lorry-load, on foot and even on double-decker buses in a rapid mobilisation effort.

Dunedin's captain was Charles Lambe. Descended from Rear-Admiral Sir Thomas Lows, who fought at the Nile, Lambe had served on the battleship *Emperor of India* in the First World War. By 1933 he had risen to the rank of commander before becoming equerry first to Edward VIII and then to George VI. He carried on his meteoric rise through the ranks and was made captain in December 1937. He became captain of *Dunedin* in January 1939.

By Sunday 27 August, at around 2 p.m., Lambe had taken *Dunedin* to Scapa Flow. There he found most of the Home Fleet and *Dunedin* formed part of 12th Cruiser Squadron for service on the Northern Patrol. After three days in Scapa, she weighed anchor and conducted a number of firing tests, but before too long new orders were received which sent *Dunedin* out to sea with the fleet. By Friday 1 September, rumours were rife on board that war was about to break out and that *Dunedin* would be on the lookout for the German passenger ship *Bremen*. The 6 p.m. BBC news heard on the ship's radio confirmed that Germany had invaded Poland.

On Saturday 2 September, *Dunedin* received official orders from the Commander-in-Chief Home Fleet that she should prepare for war, and the next twenty-four hours were spent ammunitioning and embarking stores. News from the BBC said that Britain had given an ultimatum to Germany to leave Poland.

Next day, as Chamberlain delivered his sombre speech on the radio telling the nation that Britain was at war with Germany, the ship's company of *Dunedin* could hear the message over a speaker on deck near the torpedo tubes. The bosun's mate also piped the news, but since it was nearly lunch time as well he piped two messages at once, all in one breath: 'War-has-been-declared-against-Germany-afternoon-watchmen-to-dinner.' From 9 a.m. until seven p.m., *Dunedin* remained at action stations, poised just like the rest of the country, on the knife edge of war, ready for Hitler to arrive.

But just as in London, the war did not reach *Dunedin* on that first day. Instead, the ship returned to cruising stations after the crew had listened to the King's speech.

In the Atlantic on 4 September, *Dunedin* patrolled the foggy waters, but after a couple of scares, when ships appeared through the mist only to be recognized as friendly vessels, she returned to Scapa for provisions and oil.

Dunedin sailed with three ships of the 12th Cruiser Squadron to take over the Northern Patrol after another brief spell in Scapa. Vigilance was the name of the game in those early days. Nobody knew quite what would happen or how the Germans would conduct the war, but *Dunedin*'s role was to stop and challenge any ship which might be attempting to reach German ports. Captain Lambe understood very well the need for everyone on board to be alert to other ships. He even started a sighting fund, under which 2/6d for every day's patrol would be awarded to the first lookout reporting a ship which turned out to be a suspicious neutral or enemy and resulted in its capture.

As the weather began to worsen, *Dunedin* challenged three vessels in the space of a few hours. First, on September 8, a Belgian trawler, from which the boarding party brought back a welcome haul of fish for supper, and then, early next morning, a Dutch oiler, which *Dunedin* had shadowed all through the night. Finally, mid-morning on Saturday 9 September, a Norwegian liner was sent on her way.

By Sunday the 10th, the weather had deteriorated still further. The sea roughened and *Dunedin* was battered by cold crashing waves. When the night sky dimmed and darkness began to set in, the sea continued its unrelenting attack on the ship. She rolled and pitched and heaved up and down the waves. Torrents of water smashed against the sides and all across her decks. Life, in short, became very unpleasant. And then tragically, around 8 p.m., *Dunedin* suffered her first wartime casualty. Boy 1st-class Richard Muckersie was washed overboard. The guardrails had been cleared away to allow the torpedo tubes to be brought to the ready and he must have slipped through the gap. Leading Seaman Raymond Harris, who had joined *Dunedin* in June and would serve until April 1941, heard the lifeboat being called away and dashed out to the upper deck. He and a group of others hung on to the rails, trying to see in the gloom, peering desperately through the sea spray for any sign of Muckersie. Captain Lambe, shocked to hear of the boy's accident, turned the ship around to retrace her own wake, but in the darkness and such heavy seas no sign was found. Wearing heavy leather boots and an oilskin when he went over, Muckersie would have stood very little chance in the atrocious sea. The following evening, Monday 11 September, barely a week into the war, Captain Lambe conducted *Dunedin*'s first funeral service. The sound of three rifle volleys and the Last Post marked Muckersie's passing.

The following day, *Dunedin* encountered and boarded an Italian tanker flying the Norwegian flag, *Alfred Olsen*, which had left Italy the day before war broke out, bound for Hamburg with 12,500 tons of oil. As *Dunedin* anchored in Scapa on Wednesday 13 September with her prize, Captain Lambe could reflect on a successful outing, but now he would have the sorry duty of informing Muckersie's next of kin of the unfortunate accident.

In the next few days *Dunedin* came across two more merchant ships, one Russian and the other Swedish. The Russian was singularly uncooperative and forced *Dunedin* to fire three blanks from her three-pounder as a warning. She had no cargo and was homeward bound, so *Dunedin* took no further action. The Swedish ship, on the other hand, did not look as innocent, so a boarding crew from *Dunedin* took her into Scapa.

On the afternoon of Tuesday 19 September, the captain assembled much of the ship's company on the quarterdeck and explained *Dunedin*'s role in these early stages of the war. He told them that they should be constantly on the lookout for German U-boats, which were known to be operating in the area. He also made clear that *Dunedin*'s chief role was to help enforce a blockade against Germany by preventing as many ships as possible from returning there. It was *Dunedin*'s job to stop and search every ship and to take them over if there was any suggestion that they might be bringing merchandise to Germany.

On Sunday 24 September, *Dunedin* was patrolling in an area seventy-five miles off Archangel in reasonable seas when she received a signal telling her that a British warship was attacking a German merchant ship. *Dunedin* steamed at full speed to give assistance and found HMS *Calypso* engaging a ship with 'ENA' painted on her side and flying no ensign. *Calypso* sent a boarding party and found that the crew had already begun scuttling her and were abandoning ship in two boats. With the engine room flooded, she was impossible to save, so *Calypso* retrieved her boarding party and *Dunedin* and *Calypso* each picked up one of the boats containing the abandoned crew. *Dunedin* took on board the first officer, six Germans and about twenty-five Chinese crew members. The Germans were put in the gunroom, the Chinese in the recreation space.

In the meantime, the merchant ship, though sinking, refused to disappear completely. *Dunedin* and *Calypso* circled her for half an hour before opening fire to finish the job, *Calypso* with seven salvoes, *Dunedin* from her No. 2 six-inch gun with three rounds of high explosive, the third hitting right at the waterline.

The ship, by now identified as the *Minden,* finally sank and *Dunedin* and *Calypso* could reflect on a good job well done.

Captain Lambe wrote to his mother that:

I had a large party of prisoners, mostly Chinese, aboard for several days. Everyone was saved. It all felt very unreal having these men under guard on board – just like a badly made cinema film, but life is like that now.

Conditions on the Northern Patrol were about as bad as could be imagined. For the men on board, for officers and crew alike, the war had begun in a most unpleasant way. It was light for barely seven hours a day in winter and the sea seemed to find new ways to crash and rattle against the ship, tossing it this way and that and throwing anything untethered around cabins, messes and decks. It was miserable. In the coming weeks, *Dunedin* continued to patrol in filthy weather and to intercept several suspicious ships, many of them Norwegian or Swedish.

In London, by October, I was thoroughly fed up. My patriotism and energy were undimmed but I was not making the contribution I wanted. So I volunteered.

I was interested only in the Marines. No one in my family had been a Marine and I had no friends in the Marines, but something drove me on to join. Perhaps the Marines offered me better excitement than the other services, certainly the Army. Memories of the bitter trench struggles of the First World War were still in the front of people's minds, not least that of my father, who continued to press upon me his own bitter recollections of those terrible times. The Army represented foot slogging and attrition; the Marines offered much more – adventure, daring and heroism. I was young and idealistic. The Marines would suit me fine.

Without telling my parents, I went to the recruiting office at Whitehall one day in October and put my name down for the Marines. I was shocked to learn that I could only join for a twelve-year period. They were not taking recruits for the duration of the war alone, which is what I had intended to do. This gave me a very difficult dilemma. Either I joined for twelve years or I would not be able to join at all. I was so set on the Marines that I took a deep breath and signed. A few days later I returned for the medical, then waited to be called up.

Nothing changed much for the next several weeks. I carried on at the ARP HQ in Camden and, like thousands of other Londoners, waited for the war to touch us at home.

In Europe the German army was overrunning everything and everybody in its way. While awful atrocities were taking place in Poland, the war still barely touched us in Britain. But it was all around us in many ways and the newspapers were full of it. Shortages had begun to affect us slightly too, but the violent impact of the war had yet to occur in Britain. For Britain the war was in someone else's backyard or at sea.

The news of the sinking of the Athenia, *a British ocean liner bound for Canada with 1,103 passengers, on the very first day of the war had made the threat of Hitler seem real to us all, as did the loss of the battleship* Royal Oak *in mid-October. But in our everyday lives we were in a constant state of preparation for a war being fought somewhere else. At home, meat, butter and sugar were rationed, but we were far from the real deprivations that would affect us all later in the war.*

In the bleak waters on the Northern Patrol, on 8 November, a submarine was reported off *Dunedin*'s port bow just as she was leaving harbour. The captain, knowing that a U-boat had been reported in the area by aircraft the previous day, slewed the ship towards it and ordered four depth charges to be dropped. Nothing appeared on the surface to suggest that the submarine had been hit but it would at least have been shaken up. The memory of the audacious sinking of the *Royal Oak* by a U-boat the previous month was still very vivid. U-47, commanded by Günther Prien, had sunk *Royal Oak* from inside Scapa Flow in a breathtakingly daring mission. Nothing now could be taken for granted.

There seemed no respite from the lashing of the sea, as Raymond Harris wrote in his diary the following day:

> The weather is blowing up to its usual patrol weather for us now. I think that by the time we get on leave (whenever that may be) the roads will be too narrow for us to roll along.

And for the next few days the weather worsened still more. At night it was impossible to get a decent sleep as the wind howled incessantly and the ship rolled back and forth on violent seas. Anything loose slid along the deck all night. And when any ships were sighted it was almost impossible to board them. On 10 November, for example, *Dunedin* had to take a Swedish merchant ship into the lee of the Faeroe Isles before she could be searched. Any let-up in the weather was short-lived and then, as *Dunedin* was patrolling between Greenland and Iceland, she ran into a blizzard on 11 November. That night was one of the worst at sea experienced by everyone on board. It was bitterly cold and the sea was so rough that *Dunedin*'s motorboat was smashed.

Shortly before 7 a.m. on Tuesday 14 November, a large explosion – followed almost immediately by the sound of the alarm rattlers – awakened Raymond Harris and most of the ship's company. It was difficult to tell if it was meant to be action stations or collision stations but most people took it to be the former. Raymond's immediate reaction was to grab his lifebelt and clothes and make straight for the deck, but he had just enough time to dress properly in sea boots, oilskin, balaclava and sou'wester.

He made his way to the deck through a crush of men doing the same and a queue built up between the mess deck and the gun deck screen door. Then the lights went out on the mess deck and men began to get impatient for movement. Fortunately, despite the lights going out, there was little panic as men began to realise that the explosion had not been followed by others and that *Dunedin* appeared not to have been damaged. She was neither listing nor shuddering. In fact, she was moving without problems and, although the darkness on the mess deck did not help, there was an uneasy confidence that the danger had passed.

It took Raymond Harris fifteen minutes to get on deck. If *Dunedin* had been hit, most of these men would not have made it to safety in time. As Raymond reached his action stations, word had already been passed round that the cause of the alarm was a rogue depth charge falling over the side. Fortunately, it had been set for deep detonation.

As the weather continued its attack on *Dunedin* and as she carried on patrol after patrol, the men became weary of the constant presence at sea. The cold, the wind, the rolling and pitching had all taken their toll. But finally, on 16 November, the captain announced that ten days' leave would probably start on 27 or 28 November. For Raymond Harris this could not come soon enough. He wrote in his diary on 20 November:

> Thinking of leave makes the time drag. Have thought about it two or three times today and was surprised that it was still Monday.

Two days later the news improved and the crew was told to expect to be in Glasgow at 7 a.m. on Friday 24 November for a refit. Raymond spent Thursday morning cleaning and fixing *Dunedin*'s aft torpedoes. His mind wandered to Dilys, his fiancée, and their impending wedding. The banns had been read on 15 October and all Raymond could think about was getting home and to start the wedding plans.

Raymond finished his torpedo work at around 2.30 that afternoon and cleaned up ready for his last few hours on board. By early evening the atmosphere was nothing short of excited. Like children on Christmas Eve, the crew could talk of nothing else but what they would be doing the next day. Father Christmas would arrive early this year in the shape of ten days' leave. The war had been going for only a few weeks, but these had proved to be long, arduous and frustrating weeks away from family and loved ones, an affliction which would dog *Dunedin*'s crew throughout her war.

However, the captain was preparing to give the crew some bad news. A signal had arrived at 6.30 ordering *Dunedin* to return to the Northern Patrol immediately. Within minutes, she was steaming due north at twenty knots, away from Glasgow, away from leave.

Raymond expressed everyone's exasperation when he wrote in his diary:

> What a slap in the face for us. Another twelve hours and we would have been in the Clyde. Everyone is as miserable as hell, who wouldn't be? All the Captain has told us is that German surface ships have been reported at sea and *Dunedin* has orders to return to Northern Patrol.

At 9.30, he was back working on the aft torpedoes.

For the next few days *Dunedin* scoured the northern waters for the 'pocket' battleship *Deutschland*, which had been in the North Sea and North Atlantic since late August. She had reportedly sunk the *Rawalpindi*, an armed merchant cruiser, with great loss of life (it later turned out that the *Scharnhorst* had sunk the *Rawalpindi*).

The weather worsened as the search continued and *Dunedin*'s only respite came from her oiling needs in Sullom Voe. At one point around sixty-six ships, including French ones, were looking for the *Deutschland*. The whole crew was kept on alert to keep watch as vigilantly as possible. In the heaving seas and blowing wind, crewmen strained to get a glimpse of any vessel.

In the early hours of 25 November, *Dunedin* challenged a darkened ship with a private signal on a box lamp and later on an Aldis. When no reply came, Captain Lambe was ready to blow it out of the water, but *Dunedin*'s signalman of the watch, who lived in Kirkwall, amazingly recognised it as a local vessel. Lambe called her up again and she identified herself as the *St Clair*. Lambe later admitted that without any identification or recognition signals, she should have been blasted. Fortunately, he had waited just long enough.

Later the same day, two other darkened ships appeared and *Dunedin* once more made challenges with guns ready. Again, both were friendly, the *Caledon* and the *Ceres*. By midnight on the 25th, the wind had freshened to gale force and visibility was reduced to half a mile in driving rain.

A little before midnight on Monday the 27th, action stations sounded around *Dunedin* as the lookouts spotted yet another darkened ship. Captain Lambe altered course in pursuit in pouring rain. Guns were loaded and the men stood ready to engage. In the darkness it was difficult to make out what the vessel was. It looked about the size of a cruiser and, when the waves rose to set her outline against the night sky, a vague silhouette revealed the jagged shape of gun turrets and funnels.

Deutschland was more a cruiser than a battleship. Built between the wars, she was smaller than a battleship, to meet the conditions of the Versailles Treaty, but she was a formidable fighting machine, more than twice the tonnage of *Dunedin*, with six eleven-inch guns. Against *Dunedin's* six six-inch guns, it would not be an even contest.

Tension mounted around *Dunedin* as the darkened cruiser was challenged to identify herself. The gun crews were ready and nerves were taut. The ship was barely visible in driving rain and it was difficult to make out her course. *Dunedin* gave chase at fifteen knots but soon lost her. Shortly after midnight, *Dunedin* spotted the darkened ship again and trained her guns in the right direction. Lambe challenged the ship and was relieved to learn that it was *Delhi*, one of *Dunedin's* sister light cruisers. Relief spread throughout *Dunedin* and everyone was stood down.

The search for *Deutschland* continued after a brief stop in Sullom Voe for oiling. By now the mood among the ship's company was not good. The promise of leave had come and gone and now *Dunedin* was again on the seemingly never-ending trail into the rough and cold of the Northern Patrol, as far as the Arctic Circle. By the evening of Wednesday the 29th she was steaming at twenty-five knots north-eastwards towards the Norwegian coast with orders to keep searching until 8 the following morning, by which time she would be a mile within the Arctic Circle. If she had sighted nothing by then, she was to return to harbour.

The quest proved fruitless and so, on the morning of Thursday 30 November, *Dunedin* turned back, still searching for *Deutschland*, but en route to port and – everyone hoped – long-awaited leave. Finally, on 4 December, *Dunedin* came alongside at Govan. After such a long time at sea, leave came as blessed relief to all her crew, who fell in on the jetty at around 3.30 p.m. Kitbags in hand, three weeks' pay in their pockets, the men marched through the gates to the strains of the band and dispersed in their separate directions.

For Raymond Harris it was a leave that he would never forget. He travelled through the night from Glasgow to London and then on to Bognor Regis, arriving there just before 9 a.m. on Tuesday, tired from his long journey but thankful to be back home.

The first thing he did at Bognor Regis station was to phone Dilys who told him that the wedding plans were going well and they would be married the next day – a far cry from the privations and unreal world of the Northern Patrol.

For the next ten days, Raymond lived on cloud nine. Ten idyllic days of honeymoon and seeing friends, of living life again, and putting the cold, harsh realities of the Northern Patrol firmly behind him. He even managed a forty-eight-hour extension to his leave. For the people of Bognor, the war was a reality mostly in the newspapers and on the radio – just like it was for Londoners. For Raymond Harris, life in Bognor was as far removed from the war as it was possible to be.

When finally his leave was over he sat on the 7.05 a.m. train from Bognor on 16 December and contemplated life on the Northern Patrol again. He recalled how everyone had confidently predicted in September that the war would be over by Christmas. But with Christmas approaching, it was clear that this was just an illusion. Even though to most people the war was phoney, for Raymond it was very real and had been from the first day. He had already experienced the tension and anxiety of being in combat. While *Dunedin* had not yet fired a shot in anger – *Alfred Olsen* did not really count – all her crew knew the perils and the dangers.

As all the many hundred other Raymonds set about their journeys back to *Dunedin* from all parts of the country, none expected an easy life. No one relished his return to the swells and gales, the rolling and the pitching, the biting cold, the wind and the sea spray in their faces. And yet they all returned with a purpose and all knew they had a job to do. They all left families and friends, all had people they wanted to defend, but none knew when they would see them again.

If the crew expected *Dunedin* to be a home from home when they got back, most of them were disappointed. Raymond found it looking like a rubbish dump, with wires, wet paint and equipment all over the place. She was cold and unwelcoming, frosty and distant.

In London, meanwhile, the phoney war continued. The first German plane did not appear over the city until 20 November and even this amounted to nothing when it turned back at the first scent of anti-aircraft fire.

From the South Atlantic, good news reached us about the scuttling of the Graf Spee *following the Battle of the River Plate on 13 December, just about the time my call-up papers arrived. Returning to the flat from the ARP station I saw the letter on the sideboard and opened it in a hurry. I was to report to the recruiting office in Whitehall on Wednesday 20 December. By now my mother was resigned to my going but she could hardly welcome it and could not believe it had happened so soon.*

My father tried to be more positive, telling her that the war would be over early in the new year and we could all get on with our lives again. I failed to mention that I had signed on for twelve years.

I couldn't wait to get back to the ARP station the next day and tell them all that I was off to join the Marines and for a week I could barely contain my excitement. On Tuesday night, the 19th, I packed a small suitcase with a few clothes, a toothbrush and not much else. I barely slept that night. I'd been away from home before, at Scout camp and at Aunt Lucy's, but this was different, this was a new life spreading out before me. Where would they send me? Where would I find my adventure? I was on my way to beat the Germans and save the country.

The next morning I said goodbye to my father before he went to work. We exchanged few words and shook hands. As much as he had tried to dissuade me, he must also have understood my motivations. I hoped that he was proud of me. After all, he had done it himself for the First World War and he had been under-age.

My mother, on the other hand, was overwrought. She cried and cried and could barely let go, telling me that I should not be doing this to the family. I tried to explain that I was not doing anything deliberately to harm the family, but that it was my duty. Dad had done the same thing in the First World War and thousands of others were doing so now. I would not be away long. Nothing

I could say could ease her pain and nothing I could do would stop her crying.

When finally I left, she was still crying. In the courtyard down below, I turned to look up and saw her standing there, leaning against the balcony wall, a handkerchief against her face. Her hand moved in a barely perceptible wave and then I was gone from her view.

I walked through Cumberland Court outside Windsor House, the adjacent block of flats, and down Edward Street. I was breathing deeply and nervously, catching my own emotions, triggered by my mother's tears. But I was undeterred and, by the time I reached the bus stop in Hampstead Road, I was fully in control and on my way to war.

Sitting on the bus, I watched the faces of the other passengers and wanted to tell them what I was about to do. I felt an immense sense of responsibility and wanted to tell them that I wasn't on my way to work or to the shops, I was on my way to war and that I would be their hero. I barely noticed the conductor ask for my fare.

In a little while the bus had reached the southern end of Charing Cross Road and was turning into Trafalgar Square. A couple of minutes later I was standing on the pavement at the bottom of Whitehall, outside the recruiting office.

It was about 9 in the morning and the streets were thronged with people arriving for work. Some shop fronts had Christmas decorations but there was hardly a spirit of celebration in the air. Whitehall is drab at the best of times. All those government offices lend the whole street a stern and serious demeanour, now emphasised by the taped-up windows and piles of sandbags outside every entrance.

The recruiting office was small, probably a converted shop. 'Your Country Needs You', said a soldier staring at me from a poster in the window. Well, here I am, I thought, and I hope I'm not too late.

I don't know what I expected when I walked in. A red carpet and a welcoming committee perhaps. After all, I had come at the suggestion of His Majesty. I was here to do my bit. I was going to be a hero. In fact, I thought I already was one.

I announced myself to the recruiting officer and soon I was filling out forms and completing the formalities.

Several other recruits were similarly scribbling away at their forms. When we had all finished and been 'welcomed' by the recruiting officer, we were given a health check. We went into an adjoining room and were told to undress. Looking around, I could see no screens and no side rooms, just open floor space and a desk. As one of the other recruits began to take off his clothes, the thought dawned on me that I would have to stand naked in front of strangers for the first time in my life. In the cold of a December morning, I nervously stripped and held my clothes in a crumpled ball in front of me to hide the worst of my nakedness. All around me, the others were sheepishly doing the same. The doctor impatiently told us to put down our clothes and soon we were standing in a line, silent, eyes fixed somewhere in the distance.

We shuffled past the doctor, who poked, prodded and muttered. We said 'aahh', he ticked his papers. We dressed. It was over.

After we had dressed, the talking began again, and as the warmth returned to our bodies we set about our task. Next we were given rail passes to Deal, in Kent, and the 'king's shilling', literally a shilling coin symbolising our official marriage to the armed forces. We were in. Or almost. I had one last choice to make. As we went out, there were two exit doors, one marked 'Marines', the other 'Fleet Air Arm'. The recruiting sergeant told me to go through the one I wanted and said that I would soon be on my way. This was a bit of a surprise. I had been under the impression that I was signing on for the Marines and the Marines alone. Now I was being given a choice. It didn't make sense. While the others hesitated, I made straight for the Marines door and, after one or two more fomalities, was soon on my way up the street to Charing Cross station.

I was not alone walking to the station. A small band of us were on our way to Deal. We were all strangers to each other, Len Cox, Charlie Bell, Ted Maskell, 'Bunny' Bundock, Fred Tinknell and a few others.

Charing Cross station was awash with travellers that day, the epitome of England on the move. All different service uniforms were on show as servicemen and civilians jostled and shoved their way across the concourses to and from the trains. We tried to keep together as a group as we fought the human tide and made for what we thought was our train. The whole place seemed in utter confusion but we finally found the Deal train and sat down in an empty compartment.

Outside, the muffled sounds of announcements informed the scurrying *passengers where to find their trains. Breath hung heavy in the cold December air. Steam from the engines rose to the high ceiling and hung densely over the platforms and passengers.*

We needn't have hurried ourselves. The train didn't leave for at least another half-hour.

Our little group nervously engaged in conversation, but we were all very apprehensive, both of each other and of what lay before us. As the train sat motionless in the station, the conversation ranged from where we lived to which football teams we supported.

When the train eventually shuddered into movement amid whistles and choking of steam, our excitement heightened and we became freer to talk about our impending adventure.

One said, 'Right, 'ere we go then and about time too. If this show is goin' to be all over in the new year, we'd better get a move on'.

'Yeah, we don't want Hitler buggering off before we've had a pop at him'.

Laughter now took over from nerves as the train pulled out across Hungerford Bridge, stopping briefly at Waterloo and London Bridge. Soon we were rattling through London's suburbs and into the Kent countryside.

By the time we reached Deal it was dark and very cold. Laughter and apprehension had turned into fatigue and a will to get to wherever we were going.

On arriving, we were shown to our barracks and were met by a marine who told us to get undressed and have a shower. I protested that I had had a bath that morning and surely did not need to shower. The marine looked at me with a mixture of disdain and annoyance and made abundantly clear that he could not care less whether I had had ten baths that day, I was showering now.

So I showered, having learned my first lesson about doing as I was told.

Later we were taken to eat. The 'dining room' had a particular smell – something between a hospital and a potting shed – with white-painted brick walls. We sat in our small group, adrift in a sea of bare trestle tables, awaiting our meal.

Soon a cook wheeled in a dustbin. 'You got stew tonight.' Wielding a ladle, he slopped dollops of oxtail soup on to our plates and we ate our way through the thin and tasteless liquid, our first 'military' meal. When it was over, we went to the receiving room for more formalities.

We were told to make our own mattresses. We were shown into a room in which it looked as if someone had carried in a complete haystack and then turned on a huge electric fan. Straw was everywhere.

'Right, you lot' – why did everyone in the services always start an order with 'Right, you lot'? – 'gather up as much straw as you can, stick it in them canvas mattress covers over there and tonight you'll be able to go bye-byes like babies. And I don't want see any straw left in this room when you're done.'

With that, he left and we stuffed as much straw into the covers as possible. After about half an hour of wrestling, we had each produced not beds but lumpy sacks of solid straw, about as comfortable that first night as sleeping on a bed of coal sacks. No 'bye-byes' for us.

After a few nights of sleeping on lumps, the sacks settled down and we had genuinely comfortable beds.

Training began immediately after we were kitted out with uniform. Even though we were at war, the Marines at Deal were given peacetime training, which consisted of daily bouts of parade bashing and drill with occasional periods of recreation and lectures. It wasn't quite what I had expected. Wasn't I supposed to be trained to fight the Germans? It seemed that I had joined up merely to be marched systematically around a large square and shouted at.

In the cold waters off Scotland, *Dunedin* prepared for her first wartime Christmas. She sailed on Christmas Eve and was back on patrol by Christmas Day. At the Christmas morning church service, the captain wished all the ship's company a happy Christmas and hoped that they would have a better one next year. Each man was issued with a bottle of beer and a Christmas card from the King and Queen and then it was back to patrol.

Within a few days the ship was awash with 'buzzes', or rumours, such as that *Dunedin* would soon be 'going foreign'. The captain did little to dispel the thought that *Dunedin*'s time on the Northern Patrol would soon be over. Indeed, orders had arrived on 10 December transferring her to the Americas and West Indies Station to relieve HMS *Perth* once *Dunedin* herself had been relieved and her refit had been completed. For the moment life returned to the 'normality' of the Northern Patrol, but by and large January was a quieter time for *Dunedin*, with few sightings of suspicious ships.

Finally, the rumours of a release from the Northern Patrol came true and *Dunedin* left Scapa Flow on 27 January 1940 for Portsmouth in a gale and very rough seas. From Portsmouth she sailed on 6 February for Bermuda to join the Americas and West Indies Station. Her duties would be to keep German merchant ships from returning to Germany. Not a great deal different from being on the Northern Patrol, but with the huge advantage of doing it in the clear blue waters of the Caribbean.

The winter of 1939–40 was one of the coldest on record in Kent and we had to endure bitter cold and snowy weather for weeks on end. For me, Christmas Day 1939 was miserable. I had hoped to be at home, but leave was cancelled and I spent a dreary day in the barrack room, trying hard to muster some Christmas spirit. For a while I sat in the canteen with some of the other lads and we had a drink or two, but it was a Christmas I wanted to forget.

At times, during the early days of squad bashing and fitness training, I questioned what I had done by signing for twelve years. I sat on the end of my bed one day, cleaning my equipment and asked myself how I could have been so stupid. It had all seemed so clear to me before. My place would be at war, in the front line, defending my country. Instead, I was here, shining my boots. I paused for a moment and hung my head in my hands, dazed and bewildered at what I had done. I seemed to be getting the worst of all worlds. I was freezing to death and we were losing the war somewhere else.

We were still several months from the real threat of invasion, but as the weeks wore on my doubts slowly receded and I got into the swing of the Royal Marines as our training shifted to more interesting things, such as actually firing guns. I began to enjoy life a little more and started to look upon my twelve-year status with a more positive attitude. I decided to make a success of my time. I also learned much about the history of the Royal Marines and why they existed. I was given a booklet called 'The Story of the Royal Marines' and in its opening paragraphs I read the passages which would become my guiding principles:

The Corps of Royal Marines is a body of soldiers especially organised and trained for service in the Fleet as well as on shore. It is raised and paid by the Admiralty, and constitutes an important part of the Naval forces of the Country. In other words the marine is a soldier, and trained as such at the Depôt, but this is only a commencement. He is intended for the purposes of the Navy; and so, after he leaves the Depôt he commences the second part of his training; in gunnery and general preparation for embarkation as part of the Fleet. After the recruit has been thus instructed, he goes to a sea-going ship, serves most of his time in a ship, and becomes an essential part of the Navy: yet always remains the 'specialist' in Military work on board, just as other members of the ship's company are 'specialists' in seamanship, engineering, etc., etc.

Remember then these two points: –

I. You are a 'soldier' specially trained for the Fleet.

II. Although a 'specialist' in Military work, you are trained for the general work of the ship, and to bring about the perfect efficiency of the British Navy, and that is the main reason for the existence of the Corps.

Above all, we were taught about the Royal Marines' esprit de corps *and the historical tradition of the Marines whose origins stretched back to the time of Charles II. We would be soldiers at sea, with clear naval functions, but with an added loyalty to our corps. At times it would set us apart from the sailors and we would endure the usual inter-service rivalries. To the sailors we were the 'Leather Necks' and we would endure the age-old phrase 'Tell that to the Marines', as if we would believe anything.*

I came to understand what I had joined and relished the comradeship and sense of purpose. I came to understand the esprit de corps.

In England, although invasion was not yet a threat uppermost in people's minds, everywhere we went outside the barracks we saw evidence of the preparation of our defences. Barricades in the streets, piles of sandbags everywhere, troop movements and a general feeling of alarm. We spent much of our time erecting the barricades or digging trenches.

As the cold weather eased off and spring approached, news of the fighting worsened as Hitler's troops poured into Holland and Belgium in early May. By now I was nearing the end of my training at Deal and it was less and less clear what I would be doing in the coming weeks. Would I be in the front line of defence against the invasion or would I be sent somewhere completely different?

Churchill's arrival as Prime Minister on 10 May brought a huge change in attitude among everybody. In the face of continual German victories, a fresh government with a new leader was essential.

This was a time of paradox. On the one hand we were almost ecstatic with joy that Churchill was now at the helm, but on the other, the next few weeks could have seen the invasion and the overthrow of our country. We were all a little scared, but we were also resolute. None of us knew how we could possibly win; we just knew we would.

The war gradually came closer to me as our troops on the continent began to suffer and retreat towards the Channel ports. On 26 May a Spitfire piloted by Flying Officer Michael Lyne crash-landed on Walmer beach at Deal. Lyne had been hit over Calais by a German fighter and with great skill – his engine dead – had glided back across the Channel and landed on the beach. I was part of the duty squad at the time and was dispatched to guard the crashed aeroplane. We had been patrolling the cliff tops at Deal, armed with grenades, our Lee Enfield rifles and fifty rounds of .303 ammunition, our standard weaponry when we were 'ashore'. With fixed bayonets, we did our best to keep inquisitive boys away from the aeroplane and supervised the rescue of the pilot. I saw where the bullets had hit the Spitfire and also that Lyne had been hit in the knee, and I watched as the ambulance took him off to the Royal Marine infirmary.

I looked on in awe at the pilot, in my eyes a much older and mature man, but in reality he was probably no older than me. His war had merely started before mine. I watched as he was carried from the Spitfire, its green and grey camouflage pockmarked with the evidence of battle. It was a moment in which I felt I had touched the war and yet, in truth, I was still a spectator.

The full horror of Dunkirk was beginning to unfold. Ignominious defeat was turned into heroic triumph as little by little 'our boys' staggered back across the Channel in a 'Kiss Me Quick' armada of pleasure steamers and fishing boats. For several days the men straggled back through the Kent ports. While we young recruits prepared ourselves for war, these men had already had their fair share. My barrack room overlooked the railway line and I could see, for several days, the returning soldiers passing through. They looked a sorry sight. Some managed to poke weak smiles through the grime and tiredness, but mostly they just slumped in their seats or on the floor, weary and dirty, just glad to be out. And yet in those faces was born the fabled Dunkirk spirit, the incredible illusion that this horrific defeat had been a victory.

Soon, however, the strange euphoria of Dunkirk descended into darkness with the realisation that we no longer had a foothold on the Continent, that the Germans could literally see us from Calais and that nobody would help us but ourselves. This was no phoney war. I did not know when or if I would ever see my family again.

By mid-June, my Deal training was over and I was transferred to Eastney barracks at Portsmouth. I travelled to Eastney by train, via London, and as my train pulled into Charing Cross I could not help remembering my journey in the opposite direction six months earlier when, as an anxious volunteer, I had sat with new-found friends in the carriage, nervously chatting about this and that, not knowing what lay before me. Then I had been just another civilian on his way to who knew what. Now, as the hiss of the brakes and the whistling of the guards beckoned us to a new destination, I had thrown off the childish anticipation of an adventure and was dressed instead in the garb of a stature beyond my age. I was in the King's Squad, allowed to wear our blue uniforms, chin straps down.

We were led that day by Sergeant Howe, who, as the train heaved itself to a halt, told us to 'Look smart now and remember what I told you this morning, you're on show. You're not wearing the best Royal Marine uniform for nothing. We have to walk from here to the main station, so let's not allow these Londoners to think they're being defended by a ramshackle bunch of layabouts. So, I want to see the finest example of marching this city has ever seen.'

We rose from our seats, grabbed our bags from the overhead netted racks and shuffled to the door. Once on the platform we formed up in a group and Sergeant Howe fell us in. Passengers poured from the carriages and scurried past us, eager to get home or to work. We stood to attention on the platform, ramrod stiff, in an exact straight line. Sergeant Howe walked up and down in front of us, not saying a word, but giving us each a stony stare.

When he had finished his little parade in front of us, he stepped back and stood motionless, his hands firmly behind his back, surveying us with a slow sweep of his head. I was getting hot, sweating in the early summer sun under my thick uniform. How much longer? The platform was emptying now and still we stood, waiting.

Quietly, slowly, like a gardener muttering about his prize roses, Sergeant Howe finally spoke: 'Very nice, lads, very nice.' A faint but definite smile softened across his face. 'Now then, let's make 'em proud of us.'

Sergeant Howe had been tough but fair and for six months he had been our father, mother, teacher and friend, as well as a marvellous drill instructor. He had never sworn at us and had never insulted us, but somehow he had cajoled us and remodelled us. I like to think he turned us from raw civilians into trained soldiers.

A few seconds later we were marching up the wooden steps to the walkway leading out of the main station to get to Waterloo station. We passed more passengers scurrying to catch their trains or to get to work. When we reached the entrance to Waterloo station Sergeant Howe bade us halt and we stood, motionless, awaiting further orders. The vast cathedral of the station lay before us and a mass of Londoners hurried this way and that, passing behind us and in front of us. Sergeant Howe said, 'Right, stay here, boys, while I go and sort out which platform we need. Stand to attention. Let's keep the show going for London.'

London had not changed, even though we had been at war for nine months. Londoners seemed no less busy, no less animated. I tried to see into the faces of passing people as I stood to attention. Some caught my eye, most just sauntered past. A young girl, no more than six years old, her gas mask box strung around her neck, turned her head to keep looking at us as she stretched her arm up to her mother's hand. Three boys in grey shorts and scruffy dark jerseys stopped beside us and stood to mock attention, one of them issuing orders to his friends. A group of soldiers walked past, throwing us a curious glance.

Sergeant Howe returned a few moments later and gave the order to move. We turned to our right to march across the concourse and I noticed out of the corner of my eye a man moving backwards in time with us. He had to keep dodging other people and I could not quite make out at first what he was up to, especially since I had to keep my eyes to the front. The more we marched the more I could sense him trying to stay in touch with us, his coat flapping about his legs as he ducked and weaved in and out of the crowd. I could not get a good look at him until we were at least half-way across, when he moved in front of us, still moving backwards and clearly trying to watch our progress.

I glanced at the sergeant ahead of us, then fixed my eyes on the man doing his backwards dance. A smile crept over my face and the man realised I had seen him. But he knew that I could not wave or do anything other than keep marching, eyes front, in step and in perfect rhythm. The man stopped, in position for my eyes to be able to lock on to his without turning my head and without breaking my step. He wore a grin fit to split his face and he slowly nodded his head as first I approached and then went past. As our group of thirty marching marines thundered along in ten rows of three, hob-nailed boots grinding into the floor, I allowed myself a barely perceptible nod and a tight-lipped smile. The man, my father, touched his hat and waved me gently on.

Later, at Fratton station in Portsmouth, we were greeted by the Royal Marine band, which marched with us all the way to Eastney barracks. This young man, in his smart blue uniform, felt very tall.

After the relative tedium of Deal, with its parade bashing and teaching routine, the move to Eastney gave us all some sense of anticipation that we might soon be asked to make a real contribution to the war effort.

The whole country was now geared to the impending threat of invasion and as I made my move from Deal to Portsmouth I graduated from peacetime training in the rear to a frontline waiting position, spending most of my time doing small arms and sea service training.

In July, when France fell, Churchill was confronted with the dilemma of what to do with the French fleet. To him, the decision to seize it was a necessary but hateful one, 'the most unnatural and painful in which I have ever been concerned', he wrote in his memoirs.

Some of the French navy was in Dakar in West Africa, some of it was in the Caribbean and some of it was scattered in ports around Britain, including Portsmouth. Churchill could not let any of these ships get into the hands of the Germans and he could not allow the French to keep them. The only option was to take them for ourselves. Two battleships, four light cruisers, some submarines, eight destroyers, and about 200 smaller mine-sweeping and anti-submarine craft lay for the most part in Portsmouth and Plymouth.

In the early morning of 3 July all the French vessels at Portsmouth and Plymouth were taken into British control. For me, this meant my first piece of action.

At 3 a.m., I stood on Portsmouth harbour with a group of other marines waiting to board a French warship. Fighting the French was not quite what I had expected when I had joined up but it was action of a sort.

I had my Lee Enfield rifle in hand, fifty rounds of ammunition at the ready, poised to become part of a little piece of history – one of the last Englishmen ever to fight the French. Agincourt, Crécy, Trafalgar, Waterloo, and now Portsmouth docks! I stood at the end of a long line of glorious English victors.

I waited with seven or eight other marines, most of us barely out of training, most of us – if the truth were told – rather nervous of what was about to happen. It was hot enough that night without the added tension of an impending fight. The summer of 1940 was unseasonably warm and we stood with guns ready, sweating, our throats drying up with nerves. French or not, this was our first 'action'.

Whistles blasted out across the docks to signal our move. As quietly as it is possible for a group of armed men to rush across a wooden gangplank on to a metal ship, we boarded the French warship. As briefed, we made straight for the sleeping quarters. Behind us another group made for the wireless room. Within seconds we were at the door of the sleeping quarters, pushing it open and surging inside. About a dozen French sailors were in their hammocks. By now, two or three had heard us and were startled. While one of us stood guard at the door, the rest prodded and shoved the sailors awake.

It was soon obvious that that there would be no fight, no unpleasantness, but a lot of shoving and pushing as the dozing French sailors came to realise that the British had arrived. We poked them awake with our rifles and directed them up on deck. The ordinary seamen and officers were separated and the officers were taken to HMS Victory. They looked surprised and not a little dazed.

Later that day I wondered how they must have felt. Defeat by the Germans was bad enough, but to be unceremoniously rounded up at rifle point by the British must have hurt. The final irony of their situation was their incarceration on the flagship of the Battle of Trafalgar.

CHAPTER 3

Caribbean and Atlantic, January 1940–March 1941

After leaving Scapa Flow and the harshness of the Northern Patrol on 27 January, *Dunedin* made for Portsmouth in another appalling sea. She stayed in Portsmouth for a week, before departing for the warmer climate of Bermuda and the Caribbean. She left around 10.30 a.m. in fog and on yet another rough sea, as if the Northern Patrol were still tugging at her.

Later that night *Dunedin* met up with HMS *Diomede*, with whom she would be sailing to Bermuda. Unrelenting seas battered the two ships all the way across. Late in the afternoon of Monday 12 February, *Dunedin* came to a complete stop after salt water had entered her oil tanks and caused a loss of steam. All the lights went out and it took the crew an uneasy hour to change tanks. Still the gales and lashing seas refused to give *Dunedin* any peace and three days later she lost one of her boats, ripped from her grip and tossed into the sea.

When *Dunedin* finally arrived in Bermuda on 17 February, the sun shone and the harsh conditions of the Northern Patrol and the Atlantic crossing were well behind her. The crew would count these days in Bermuda and the Caribbean as among their happiest of the war. The weather was good, the sailing was safe, the captain was well-loved and only the French were hostile.

With Bermuda as the main base, *Dunedin* visited almost every Caribbean island during her tour, principally on the lookout for German blockade runners, merchant ships trying to break out into the Atlantic.

Dunedin did not have to wait long to find two German merchants.

The first of these was the *Heidelberg*, which had broken out of Aruba in an attempt to make it into the Atlantic and home. *Dunedin* spotted her at 7.30 a.m. on Saturday 2 March, after leaving Jamaica the day before, and fired three 6-inch sub-calibre across her bows as she did seem to be stopping. The German crew had begun scuttling her before a boarding party could be put on board, setting fire to their ship, then taking to the lifeboats. *Dunedin* picked up around twenty-five of them (mostly boys) and then fired some full 6-inch shells into her. *Heidelberg* burned for hours, finally sinking around 5 p.m.

The second was the *Hannover*, a 5,600-ton merchant ship out of Curaçao which was caught by *Dunedin* off San Domingo on 8 March. She was on her way to Germany, attempting to break the blockade, with a cargo of grain and cotton, when she spotted *Dunedin* in the distance. With no chance of escape the crew fired a charge in the propeller shaft and started several fires in an attempt to scuttle her. Having seen the *Heidelberg* slip from his grasp, Captain Lambe was hoping for a better result this time. He immediately sent over a boarding party, led by Lt Leslie Philpott, as *Hannover* began to list to starboard. The boarding party arrived alongside just as the crew were getting into the last lifeboat, but if the ship was to be saved the boarding party would need the assistance – reluctant or otherwise – of the German engineers. *Dunedin*'s own Sub Lt (E) Hughes could see that some of the crew bundling themselves into the lifeboat were probably engineers, so he and others in the boarding party drove them back onto the ship.

Down in the engine room, Hughes found water rushing in and fires burning as the ship listed further to starboard. He had no way of telling whether the Germans had placed explosives down there, but he was at least comforted that the German chief engineer was content to come below. He gave no help, but his presence alone was enough to convince Hughes that he need not worry about scuttling charges. The emergency lights were on, but the situation was critical. Hughes and his party waded in ever-deepening water as they set about trying to stem the tide. In atrocious conditions they tackled the relevant valves one by one, sometimes having to replace valve covers and bolts against the terrific pressure of the incoming water. Some of the valve spindles had been bent out of shape by the Germans in their scuttling attempt. For Hughes and his men it was a desperate race against the clock as the water level continued to rise, pushing the ship perilously further over to starboard and forcing them repeatedly to dive into the water in courageous attempts to stop the water coming in.

This gargantuan effort finally paid off when all the valves were closed off and the water stopped coming in. And there was another piece of good news – the water level was so high that it had put out the fires in the generators. The German chief engineer now started to give some assistance and pointed out the bilge pump and the bilge valves, which were also below the water line. Hughes had the ship's electrician come down to connect the emergency switchboard direct to the bilge pump and he began to pump out the water. At the same time he found a junior German engineer and posted him in the emergency dynamo room under armed guard and severe threat as to what would happen to him if he let the engine stop.

Meanwhile, fires still burned in the holds so *Dunedin* was called alongside with her fire hoses rigged. She pumped water into *Hannover* until the fires were under control, but not without increasing the starboard list to about 14 degrees. With the ship ready to be moved on, a line was attached and *Dunedin* began to tow *Hannover* in the direction of Kingston, Jamaica, the White Ensign now flying above *Hannover*'s swastika. The fires remained a constant threat throughout the voyage and it was not until *Dunedin* and *Hannover* reached Kingston that they could really be described as under control. It had taken an extraordinary effort by Hughes and his men to prevent *Hannover* from sinking in the first place and then to keep her upright and in a state to be towed to safety. Somehow the emergency dynamo was kept running day and night, despite the assurance of the Germans that it would seize up in three hours. Every night and morning it was necessary to cool decks and hatches with water to keep down the heat from the fires smouldering below. With a cargo of cotton and oilcakes it was impossible to subdue the fires completely.

With the assistance of the Canadian destroyer *Assinnboine*, *Dunedin* tugged the smouldering and smoking *Hannover* all the way to Kingston, arriving on 13 March, one week after the capture. Below decks, Hughes and his men worked around the clock in impossible conditions to keep her upright and her engines going. As the little convoy limped into Kingston, *Dunedin* had delivered a broken but basically seaworthy vessel. Only the damage to the electrical installation had prevented the ship being sailed under her own steam. The winches, capstan, steering gear, main and auxiliary engines were essentially in good condition. It was a marvellous catch and one that the Navy would come to prize. Captain Lambe was mentioned in dispatches and several of the men received decorations, including Hughes, who was awarded the DSC. Initially re-named *Sinbad*, but later named *Audacity*, *Hannover* was converted into the Royal Navy's first escort carrier, and used to great effect in the Battle of the Atlantic.

A few weeks before my father had found himself standing on Portsmouth docks, waiting to capture a French ship, *Dunedin* was trying to tie up a number of other French vessels in the Caribbean. Three Vichy ships were in *Dunedin*'s area: the cruiser *Jeanne d'Arc* at Guadeloupe, and the cruiser *Emile Bertin* and aircraft carrier *Bearn* at Martinique. Captain Lambe, in cooperation with the captain of HMS *Fiji,* and later with the assistance of the governor of Trinidad, attempted to negotiate the handover of the three ships, but without success. However, they remained in the West Indies and were thus denied to the Germans. *Emile Bertin* was a special prize because she was carrying gold bullion, which the Admiralty wanted to keep from falling into enemy hands.

On another occasion, *Dunedin* was in Guadeloupe for stores and oiling when the local Vichy French put up a boom across the harbour to keep *Dunedin* in. Captain Lambe tried to negotiate himself out, but after three or four days it was clear that the French would not give him free passage. So he decided to break out under the cover of darkness. He assembled his officers and explained what he wanted them to do. He told the engineers to get up steam and with the engines at full ahead, *Dunedin* made a dash for the harbour entrance and burst through the boom. Despite French fire from the shore, she managed to break out.

In June, *Dunedin* suffered only her second war casualty with the loss of Colour Sergeant Fisher, who died in hospital in Martinique. For other crew members, the chief preoccupation was communicating with home and getting used to not being able to tell their loved ones where they were. Some devised private codes to let their families know what was happening to them. This was reasonably harmless, because even if the correspondence were to fall into enemy hands, each family had a different set of codes. Chief Petty Officer Telegraphist Alick Grant wrote one such coded letter to his mother on 18 June 1940:

> It's much too hot to write anything like a letter but there is a possibility of a mail going today some time and I'm not going to be left out of it. More important still (to me anyway) is the fact that we will probably get some mail today, we have not had any for nearly a month now and with things happening at home as they are it's not too nice to go a long time without any mail.

> Still I suppose it's our own fault in some ways we go dashing all over the ocean to all sorts of queer places but that is all in the job so we mustn't grumble. Have only been able to write once in the last fortnight so you will no doubt be wondering as well what's gone wrong with the mails.

> Have been rather busy lately but I did manage to write the majority of the relations, sent Harry and Charley a short note each and when I finish this I'm going to write Hubert and then the whole crowd of them can go to —— If you write any of them please give them the hint I've got a lot more to do than write aunts and uncles. It's a good job we send letters free or they would never get any.

> Things don't look at all good at home these days, haven't seen a paper for a long time and we only get the main items of news on the radio but that's far from being good, still it's going to work out alright in the end so we must not get down-hearted over it. Heard an appeal on the radio for shotguns the other day, have you sent mine? Reckon they should send me home and then I could use it myself!

> Nothing more to write about now, will be writing again tonight if time permits and then I may have something to write about. Hope this finds you well and not worrying too much leaving me in the very best, your loving son, Alick.

This seemingly anodyne letter home gave Alick's family a tiny inkling of what was happening. 'Hot' and 'busy' were code words for close action with the enemy; 'Harry' was British Guiana; 'Charley' was Panama; and 'I'm going to write to Hubert' meant the ship was going to Jamaica.

In August, the Duke and Duchess of Windsor were in Bermuda, on their way to Nassau in the Bahamas, where the Duke would be governor. They came to tea with Captain Lambe aboard *Dunedin*, an event well remembered by Boy Harry Cross, who was assigned to assist the Duchess as her 'call boy'. Or, as he put it, 'one of my jobs was to shove the chair under her when she sat down'.

In Bermuda at about this time, Harold Broadway joined *Dunedin* at short notice with what is known in the service as a 'pier head jump'. A general practitioner in peacetime, Broadway had joined HMS *Pembroke* at the Royal Naval barracks at Chatham on 26 March 1940 for some basic naval training. He stayed at Chatham until 16 May, when he was appointed to HMS *Malabar*, the naval dockyard in Bermuda.

Harold was married to Mary and had two children, Christopher and Shelagh, all of whom he left behind in England. But by August he had made plans for them to come and join him in Bermuda.

The fortunes of war, however, had no respect for domestic plans. Harold would not remain on a shore-based facility for long. As plans for his family's move to Bermuda crystallized, he was presented with the prospect of joining HMS *Dundee*. This would be a disaster, because she was due to sail before Mary and the children arrived. In the event, a second opportunity arose, which he was able to take. Captain Lambe needed a new junior doctor in *Dunedin,* having dispensed with the previous one, so Harold was appointed to *Dunedin* as Second Medical Officer. Since *Dunedin* was Bermuda-based, he would be able to see the family reasonably frequently. What could be better?

Mary and the children had set sail in the *Orduna*, one of many ships in an outbound convoy from Liverpool (possibly the same ship that carried Lambe's future wife, Peta). She was due in Bermuda some time before the end of August, with luck before *Dunedin* sailed. The voyage was not without its dangers and it must have been a very nervous time for Harold as he waited for the *Orduna*'s arrival. Indeed, the convoy was attacked by U-boats and six ships were lost. For five-year-old Christopher, the tragedy of the losses was hidden beneath the excitement of the action.

As men abandoned their sinking ships, desperate to get into the water, Christopher thought he could see 'ants' crawling down the sides and falling into the sea.

Orduna herself was untouched by the U-boats and she duly made it to Bermuda on 24 August, just in time for the family to see Harold before he joined *Dunedin* three days later.

Dunedin sailed almost as soon as Harold joined her. Captain Lambe put *Dunedin* through her full power and gun functioning trials after her period in the dockyard. She rattled and groaned at the speeds she was asked to make.

Harold fell hopelessly seasick almost immediately. The oppressive heat below decks gave no respite, but he continued his medical duties. Only the deck breeze gave any relief and it was not until Captain Lambe was able to ease down that Harold started to feel human again.

Harold had no idea that his life was about to change even further - dramatically and ironically. *Dunedin* called into Bermuda again very briefly on 13 September but was gone the next day, before he could take any leave. Worse still, she had been ordered back to the Clyde for deperming (this reduced the magnetic signature of the ship permanently, to protect her against magnetic mines) and rearming, temporarily withdrawn from the America and West Indies Station for anti-invasion duties in the UK. Harold had spent just three days with his family in Bermuda and now he would soon be back in home waters. He contemplated life's ironies and the things he would miss, the things he had already missed, like Mary's birthday and their anniversary.

News reached him at this time of the loss of *Dundee*, the very ship he had avoided in order to spend a few days with the family.

Dunedin's voyage home passed largely uneventfully and she docked in the Clyde in the early hours of Monday 23 September, where she stayed until 11 October.

Harold tried to make the most of his change of fortune. He took advantage of *Dunedin*'s time in harbour to see something of the surrounding countryside and also to try to get in touch with his parents in England. He was struck by the awful realisation that he would not only not see his wife and children for a long time but also go many weeks without even hearing from them. The isolation born of the lack of mail began to make itself felt. He wrote on 3 October:

> I'm a wee bit worried. I haven't had a letter from anyone since my arrival in Great Britain and we've been here nearly a fortnight now and I wrote to my people and your people on arrival. I've tried to phone them, but couldn't get through and I know that Bournemouth and Bristol have both had it hot the last week or so. But perhaps they didn't know my address as I couldn't give the name of the ship then and they mightn't have got my letters of a month ago. We've had two air raids here in the last few nights. I regret to say that I slept soundly through them and only heard about them next morning. Seeing as I was supposed to go to Action Stations this was pretty poor. The people up here aren't taking the war badly at all – all amusements are in full swing, but London has had a frightful doing I believe. But I think the tide has definitely turned in this war and we are now on top.
>
> Well, love, I hope you are beginning to like Bermuda and not to feel so lonely and that the children are happy. Although I long to have you all with me I'm terribly thankful that you are in a place of safety.

At about the time Harold was writing this letter, twenty-year-old Leslie Russell from Battersea also joined the ship. He had been called up in July 1940 and joined the Navy as a probationary supply assistant, assigned to HMS *Royal Arthur* in Skegness. He then spent August at HMS *Glendower* before transferring to the Royal Naval barracks in Portsmouth. Leslie was an intelligent and sensitive young man whose life – like that of thousand of others – was abruptly interrupted by the outbreak of war. As the politicians and generals plotted history's grand course in 1938 and 1939, Leslie was planning his future. He had passed the clerical officer's Civil Service examination and had worked in the Tithe Redemption Commission in London since 1936. He enjoyed his job and looked forward to a long and steady career.

He also looked ahead to marrying his fiancée, Jean, who worked with him at the Commission. They planned a life together and, like many others, suffered the frustrations of doing so amidst the continuing gloom of the war. Leslie had stayed at the Commission when the war had started, but by the summer of 1940 he had been conscripted into the Navy, a naive but thoughtful recruit who could not quite understand why people's lives should be so easily torn apart at their most formative and hopeful times.

Two days before Leslie moved to the naval barracks in Portsmouth in September 1940, he wondered what lay before him and how he should cope with it. He wrote to Jean:

> After I had phoned you, I sat in a shelter on the promenade and read for a while – then I sat meditating. It was a lovely evening, although slightly cold. The sea was calm and the sun shone on the hills around the bay and the banks of cumulus cloud. It was a beautiful and peaceful sight, but it made me rather sad. It seemed so tragic that there should be a war raging and I wondered if this beautiful countryside was worth fighting for and, if necessary, dying for. I could not make up my mind, but I think that if a person is dying he must suffer terribly in his last moments, thinking of all the sweet pleasant things he has to part with. Then I thought that it is only now that we truly appreciate them. I then wondered who had the right attitude to the war and to life. There was I in this beautiful place, in a state of melancholy and there, in the town, were sailors, soldiers, and airmen having a good time, eating, drinking and making merry, I suppose the right course is somewhere in between.

On 4 October Leslie had his first taste of what he could expect when he made the journey to Glasgow to join *Dunedin*. In a grey, damp mist the following morning, a lorry took him and a group of others to the ship. That night, on 5 October, he wrote again to Jean:

> We arrived in Glasgow at 9.30 last night and [were] taken by lorry to the ship this morning. The *Dunedin* is a D Class Cruiser – it is very crowded and living space is cramped – in fact everyone gets in everyone's way. Under these conditions, I fear there will be no privacy at all and I am told that, when we are at sea, there will be little to do except read, write and listen to the wireless. I do not know when we will be leaving the port and, when I do, I won't be able to tell you where we are going. I'm sorry to sound so mysterious but we have all the usual precautions about giving away information to the enemy, so you will be careful about this too won't you?

Leslie set about the job of getting used to his new surroundings and finding his way around the ship. In his letter to Jean of 6 October, he wrote:

I'm gradually settling down. I have a locker where I can keep all my gear and have a place to sleep. One of the chaps in our mess also has 'World Books' – he has any number of them including 'The Seven Pillars of Wisdom' and he says he has had plenty of opportunity to read – I'm hoping for the same luck!

I have already been given a definite job to do in the stores – mainly to do with nuts and bolts! As far as I can see, I shall be in the stores most of the time and probably one of the sailors who never sees the sea. I shall feel its effects however – at least everyone seems certain of that.

There are only fourteen in our mess – suppliers and writers so it means less washing up to do when I'm on cook duty. I'm gradually getting some idea where everything is on board, although I haven't so far strayed from the few decks and gangways where I know I'm safe. The chaps already on board seem to have had quite a good time and have shown me snaps of all the places they have visited.

For the next several days the ship was full of buzzes about where they might go next. There was much talk of the harshness of the Northern Patrol and the twelve-year blokes delighted in scaring the new recruits with stories of freezing waters and mountainous seas.

Harold Broadway too could sense something was about to happen. Officers were coming and going and new members of the crew kept appearing. He wrote on 9 October that it was quite likely that things would be 'getting a little more exciting soon'. By now, he had heard a little more about the sinking of *Dundee* and knew that all of her officers had been killed, including the surgeon-lieutenant.

Dunedin was about to undergo a major change in her activities. In Scotland, Harold could believe that the war was taking place somewhere else. There was little evidence of bomb damage and he was able to spend much time ashore, readjusting to 'normal' life after his months in Bermuda. He had taken a bus into the country and walked to the top of a mountain in cold, crisp, fine and frosty weather. In town he had found it strange to see buses, trains and trams once again. The war seemed a long way away. The biggest change to *Dunedin* came at the top, with the departure of the much-loved Captain Lambe, recalled by the Admiralty and appointed Assistant Director of Plans in the War Cabinet offices. Captain R.S. Lovatt, from HMS *Rodney*, replaced him and joined the ship on 11 October for the short voyage to Portsmouth.

In the south of England, things were different. Portsmouth, Bristol and Bournemouth were all being hit by bombing raids and invasion was still a major threat. *Dunedin* would now join the anti-invasion defences.

Harold wrote home on 15 October that things were rather different now and that *Dunedin* was 'properly mixed up in this 'ere war'. He reported at least three air raid warnings a day and that much 'stuff falls around from out of the sky'. His days of mountain walks and trams were over.

October and November saw *Dunedin* continuing her anti-invasion duties either in Portsmouth itself or in the Channel. On board, Leslie Russell kept up a stream of letters to Jean:

On 13 October:

When on board all letters from me will be censored and no telephone or telegrams can be sent from outside. Although yours aren't censored, I do keep them all so be careful what you write.

Try to hold on to the rest of your leave. It is just possible that I'll get some leave before Christmas. Everything is so uncertain and we never know definitely what our programme is until the last minute. Rush jobs, changes of instructions are always liable to upset any plans so just 'expect me when you see me' – but not just yet.

I'm afraid I've let the side down – I was seasick whilst still in sight of land. Never did I think I'd not be able to sit down to a meal. I look forward to the day when I shall think nothing of a rough sea.

On 17 October:

The place where I sleep has just been painted and my No 3's are again going 'through it'. By the time I have finished here I expect my blanket, pyjamas, suit and camp bed will also be smothered, try as I might to avoid it.

I forgot to tell you that I'm not using my hammock – all the spaces are full at the moment. It's a pity because they are more comfortable than camp beds although not so easy to put away in the morning.

The Captain addressed the crew yesterday and said he could not promise any leave. But we have been lucky so far haven't we? – we were together just two weeks ago and there are some on board who haven't been home for nine months.

On 20 October:

This morning we had 'divisions'. We were inspected by the Captain and had a short service afterwards. Naturally we had to be smart and tidy. The rest of the day was our own and I'm afraid I slept most of the afternoon. I get up each morning at 6.30 and go to bed at 10.00 ish – sometimes a bit later. On weekdays work starts at 8 o'clock, dinner at 12 o'clock and finish at 3.30 – so I have plenty of time to read your letters and reply to them – at least at the moment.

On 23 October:

One of the greatest things to pass away time on board is buzz-telling. A buzz is a rumour and there are any number of buzzes every day – usually about leave or movements. Someone gets some inside information and a buzz is started. The smart people, of course, make up their own rumours. Somebody might say, as a joke, that the ship is going to Scapa and soon everyone is trying to find out if it is true. It's difficult to ignore all this, yet we all know that if we are off somewhere we're not told officially until the last moment.

On 24 October, Harold Broadway heard from his wife for the first time since he had left Bermuda in August:

Your letter dated 29.9.40 arrived this morning, the first word I have had from you since I last saw you, and as it sounded a happy letter it cheered me up no end.

Well, I'm glad you're where you are with the children. Sherborne had a frightful attack about a fortnight ago – 240 quarter-ton bombs were dropped on the town and £250,000 worth of damage. Only 16 people were killed, but half the town is more or less homeless I believe. Daddy is much more concerned with the death of Jack (their dog) than any of these things. It's a good job I'm fairly close at hand to see to some of the business affairs of the practice etc. If Thubron leaves, there's a slight chance I might become PMO

[Principal Medical Officer] and get an extra half stripe and what is more important, the pay to go with it, but I think that is unlikely. It's much warmer here than in Glasgow. I had a glorious week there which you may have heard by now. But it's warmer here in more senses than one – Jerry is over about three times a day, we get practically no time ashore at all. In spite of having had a good number of pastings, you still have to look for damage in the town, and of damage to military or strategic importance there is none. The civil population takes the air raids with the greatest unconcern – their attitude towards Hitler's barbarism is one of contempt more than anything else. We're all of us hoping to get a weeks leave some time – I could do with it now so that I could attend to the interviewing of the new locum and that sort of thing, but I'm afraid there's none coming for about another month. What happens after that remains to be seen.

I'm still liking the life in this ship and like the other officers in the wardroom. If it wasn't for the separation from my little family I would much prefer this to a shore job.

On 25 October, Leslie wrote:

We were paid this morning. I drew my usual 26/-. Soon it will be a little more as I've almost finished my first three months.

Letters are collected on board at 8 am daily so this letter won't leave until tomorrow. I have felt very tired lately as I sleep in a room with a noisy fan going all night. I must consider buying some ear plugs.

On 26 October:

The Royal Marines band has just begun playing in the passageway outside, presumably for the benefit of the officers at dinner (supper to us!). The office is situated near their quarters. It's a nice change to hear some music – they're playing one of the tunes from one of the Italian operas we've seen, but I can't remember which one.

Our meals vary – sometimes very good, at others the potatoes are barely cooked and the cabbage all mushy. But I can't grumble as there is plenty to eat. We are allowed a certain amount of choice too. Our mess chose to have a light breakfast of only bread, butter, marmalade and jam and tea. Then a good dinner of meat pie or pudding or roast meat, potatoes, roasted or boiled and cabbage or peas with an occasional sweet. Tea consists of bread, butter, jam and tea and supper is a fairly heavy meat too – sausages, mash or egg and chips or liver and bacon and tea. I did suggest that we have coffee sometimes but nobody seems interested.

During stand-easy in the morning we can get hot water to make cocoa at our own expense.

In the town, the bombing carried on, but Harold shared the contempt expressed by the population:

As I said last Sunday, I can't say what we're doing but we're still doing it. We had two air-raids yesterday, each with between 30–50 German planes overhead, and there was a nice display of fireworks but surprisingly little damage done. I think they'd be more likely to hit their targets if they just didn't bother to aim at them at all. They attacked a village near Dorchester in great form and killed one pig, two hens and 5 ducks. The once or twice they got close to this ship I think were mistakes.

Leslie wrote on 31 October:

A letter too from home telling me that two bombs fell close to them a few days ago. It is very worrying and I feel so helpless – I hope all is well in Streatham.

My biscuit tin is getting very heavy and full of your letters and I reckon you have a lot of mine for a bonfire as well – but somehow I think we'll both keep them all.

On 4 November:

I heard today that London had a raid-less night last night so I am hoping you were able to sleep well although I realise that you're all expecting the sirens to go at any moment.

In the skies above southern England, the Battle of Britain was raging. On a walk in the country, Harold got a grandstand view. He wrote on 7 November:

We drove out into the country and started a walk along the hilltops. The sirens had gone before we left the town, and suddenly the sky overhead was just alive with twisting aeroplanes – it literally appeared full of them, and we could hear the machine gun fire and bursts of flame right overhead. It was one of the most thrilling sights I have ever seen. Suddenly an aeroplane crashed in flames and hit the ground only about 300 yards from where we were standing (it gave us a fright all right) so we dashed across the fields to see if we could help the pilot if he was still alive, but he was just a charred remains by the time we got there – one of ours unfortunately, although four jerries also crashed further away.

Unknown to Harold, the Commander-in-Chief America and West Indies had requested *Dunedin*'s return as soon as possible. Leslie, meanwhile, went home for a long period of leave, returning to the ship on 17 November. Having spent much time with his fiancée, Jean, his reunion with *Dunedin* was not a happy one.

On 17 November:

When I opened my case to unpack I felt so low. I took out my books and thought I had been too optimistic last week and am not in the mood at all to settle down to hard work. But I must try because so much depends on it, but I'm not too sure of myself.

Please let me know how low you are feeling. They do say that pleasures have to be paid for but I'll consult the Daily Express Astrologer and let you know how many years it will be before I get more leave.

Thank your mother for letting me stay – conditions are difficult enough without having extra burdens. I hope the gas and water are now back to normal.

On 18 November:

When I came back on board there were a lot of buzzes. It was quite a contrast to the week before I had leave when everything had been quiet and no rumours at all.

Harold, too, had been on leave, returning the same day as Leslie after visiting his parents. He wrote on 19 November:

Mummy and Daddy are both well, but I find myself out of sympathy with the outlook and way of living of the old folk, and to be quite honest was quite glad to get back to the ship. But I must say I take my hat off to them for their pluck and courage. My last night with them there was an air-raid overhead, lasting for nine hours without ceasing; bombs were dropping all the time and the house shook like a leaf; a land mine exploded only two fields away from them and three bombs fell in Ferndown; it was really quite terrifying, but they laughed and joked all the time and showed no sign of panic. I felt very proud of them. Yes, the old generation have their faults, but we must hand it to them for courage. And again, to be quite honest I was glad to be back in the ship because of its comparative safety. I feel rather worried about the old folks.

I've written about enough to go by airmail. So bye bye love. I'll be seeing you some day.

Leslie, meanwhile, was still thinking of the leave he had just finished. He wrote on 20 November:

Let me tell you some more about leaving you on Monday. The journey wasn't too bad but I feel now that I have died a little and won't live again until next time. But I am going to try and study and save and keep fit, but on Monday evening nothing seemed worthwhile. I am thinking, apart from everything we did, of the small things which I appreciated even more now. Saucers, tablecloths, lovely meals, decent clothes, clean towels, baths etc. It makes me realise more than ever that I am a civilian in sailor's clothing and won't easily change my outlook. I also felt so angry when I arrived back – revolutionary too. I felt like throwing myself in the sea.

I don't want to scare you but the buzzes are very strong. I maybe telling you long before it is necessary but sometimes we go off before there is time to let anyone know. If you do not hear from me for about four days you will know something has happened.

I have an awful dull ache – I am not the person I was last week. I hope you are safe and well.

On 22 November:

I am beginning to settle down again and things are not too bad. I have been cook of the mess today and have spent a lot of time washing up, peeling potatoes and brussel sprouts. We were also paid today, which made a pleasant change in the usual routine. We are given the money without an envelope so I always hang tightly onto mine in case the notes, or rather note, gets blown into the sea.

On 23 November:

When I say you may not hear from me for a few days please do not get 'jumpy' or a feeling of uncertainty – we would probably not be out for more than a week and by the time you begin to worry it would be all over and I'll be back writing normally again.

Leslie had written this last letter knowing by the activity around him that *Dunedin* was preparing to go to sea. Indeed, at around 7 that evening, she left Portsmouth at about eight knots, accompanied by the destroyers HMS *Witch* and HMS *Berkeley* in search of an enemy E-boat or destroyer. A convoy was at risk.

Captain Lovatt's intention was to sweep to the westward at sixteen knots to the limit of the Portsmouth Command (3 degrees west) and then turn south towards Guernsey to try to keep between the enemy destroyers and their bases.

Dunedin kept up her search, but nothing happened until just after 1 a.m., when two flares were seen descending between five and ten miles away. A few moments later more flares were seen descending on about the same bearing and then, with visibility under one mile, a large aircraft came at *Dunedin* out of the darkness, directly towards her port beam. The aircraft was shining a brilliant light at her and, as it got nearer, began to make signals with its Aldis lamp, but these were unreadable.

Then the aircraft circled *Dunedin* before flying over her from astern. By this point, Captain Lovatt had concluded that this was an enemy aircraft and gave the order to open fire. But just as the guns were ready to shoot, the aircraft's signals were read as SOS, so Lovatt rescinded his orders immediately. The aircraft flew alongside *Dunedin*'s starboard at about 400 feet, signalling the correct coloured lights, then turned away when it reached *Dunedin*'s bows to disappear on a westerly course.

As the sound of the aircraft's engines faded in the distance, the taut nerves on board *Dunedin* began to loosen. Half an hour later, Lovatt received a signal with the intelligence that the Germans might be laying mines to *Dunedin's* north. Lovatt sailed north in the hope of intercepting the minelayers on their way to Cherbourg. In the event, nothing was found and *Dunedin* headed for home in worsening visibility.

As she approached Portsmouth once again, at around 7.30, Lovatt signalled his report of the encounter with the aeroplane:

> At 0107 in position 050 degs 12.5' north 002degs 40' west an unknown aircraft circled round *Dunedin* making SOS by lights and then flew off in a westerly direction. No action was taken by my force. Have nothing else to report.

Later, Lovatt was to learn that he had been within a few seconds of shooting down a Wellington bomber.

For Leslie Russell's fiancée, Jean, life was about to change further still, with her own 'evacuation' to Bournemouth. Her office, like so many in London at this time, was being moved out of the city as the Blitz intensified. For Leslie, this was good news. He wrote on 25 November:

> So you're off to Bournemouth at last! You said the train left at 11.20 am. I hope you get a nice 'billet' with someone you work with in the office. When you settle in it could be quite pleasant – certainly some far worse places to live.

For Leslie and Jean, the move to Bournemouth should have meant they would be closer together and could have more opportunities to see each other, but life still seemed so uncertain. Leslie continued his letter, contemplating the future but not knowing what it would bring him:

> I enjoyed my leave so much but now I feel desperate when I think that is all the leave I am going to get perhaps for six or more months. You seem to be bewildered by the unreasonableness of the situation like I am. You will probably disagree, but in some ways it would be better if I did go off to some far off place. I think we might accept and grow reconciled to the situation more. At the moment, hanging on here, not knowing what the next move is and being so near and yet so far makes life very tantalising.

The availability of leave became no better in the coming days – just six hours one day in three, not enough for Leslie even to get to Bournemouth. For Jean this was not acceptable, so she resolved to go to Portsmouth to see Leslie, if only for a few hours. Together they planned to meet on Sunday 8 December, but there was plenty of time for it to go wrong. Leslie wrote on 29 November:

> On Sunday 8th December, if I'm still on the same job I should get leave from 12.30 to 6 pm. I wish I could get to Bournemouth and back in that time but it's not possible and in any way, we are restricted to the precincts of the port so it rests with you whether you really feel you can come to see me for a few hours. But, you must be prepared for disappointment – not an idle warning I'm afraid. Yesterday the Liberty men were all ready to go ashore and their leave was cancelled. This could easily happen to me and the snag is I could not warn you in any way. If this does happen can you be at the station at 4.30 in case I am free later? You see it is a very risky adventure but, if things go well and you are really willing, I will give you the final OK as near as possible on Thursday.

Life on board went on as normal and Leslie tried hard to get through the days before he would see Jean again. The air raids on southern England continued, with Bournemouth and Southampton being hit. *Dunedin* herself was not hit, but there were frequent alarms and many air raid warnings, with the occasional bomb falling close by. On Sunday 1 December the air raid sirens interrupted Divisions just as the Captain was reading the prayers.

If Jean were to see Leslie, she would have to change trains in Southampton so Leslie could not be sure their plan for the following Sunday would work. The fragility of leave showed its face too, with a scare on Monday 2 December that all leave was about to be cancelled.

Leslie got on with his duties and also managed to go ashore with a couple of friends for a few hours before the weekend, only to emerge from the theatre one evening in the midst of another air raid on Portsmouth. Rather than hang around, they returned to the relative safety of *Dunedin*.

The bombing of Portsmouth continued, but still *Dunedin* was unharmed, despite much damage even in the harbour itself. On the evening of 5 December fires broke out all over the harbour, lighting up

HMS *Vernon* and *Dunedin*. Fortunately, an overcast sky brought the raid to an early end.

Leslie's leave remained in doubt until the last moment, but on Sunday he managed to go ashore as he and Jean had planned. For a few hours they were able to put the war to one side, enjoy each other's company and pretend that the disruption and the parting would soon be at an end. Later that evening, in *Dunedin*, Leslie wrote:

> I have just waved goodbye to you. Thank you for a lovely day – I was able to forget the Navy for a while and enjoy the countryside and the pictures in our special way. So we'll be tough won't we and hope that I'll still be here in three weeks time…

Britain became nothing more than a target for the Germans through the autumn and winter of 1940. London was smashed nightly for weeks during the Blitz and many other towns could not escape the same fate, Portsmouth included. I thought of Mum and Dad, and my brothers, Eric and Jack, in London, and wondered how they were coping with the nightly terror of bombs and fire, and the sheer sleeplessness of it all. As a strategic military port, Portsmouth could not expect to remain unscathed and we frequently suffered the full brunt of German bomb attacks.

One night I was on air raid duty with one other guard and a corporal, when bombs and incendiary devices hit Eastney barracks. Noise and fire and explosions were all around us as we rushed across a bridge to take cover, when the corporal shouted, 'Down!' We hit the ground as a bomb flew over us and smashed into the ground beyond us. Face down, pressed against the dirt, my hands around the back of my head, I braced for the impact, but nothing happened. The bomb didn't go off.

Next morning, in the quiet light of day, I went back to the bridge and saw what had happened. The bomb had landed in a nearly dry moat just beyond the bridge where we had been walking. By now the bomb disposal boys were at work, but it was quite clear to me that the bomb must have come in at about body height and that if we hadn't hit the ground it would have smashed into us. Someone up there loved me that night.

Civilian casualties were high in the Portsmouth area, especially as a result of incendiary bombs. Portsmouth had more than its fair share of firebombs and tragedy. Nowhere was safe. Hospitals were hit as well as civilian homes. One night, incendiary bombs hit the nurses' home at the Royal Portsmouth Hospital and patients from the hospital had to be evacuated.

I was on duty again the night the naval barracks were bombed on 10 January 1941. In a horrendous air raid, enormous damage was done to Portsmouth and the Marines were called out to help with the fire-fighting. I took charge of a mobile trailer pump, which could be connected to hydrants and moved around relatively easily. The barracks burnt furiously and another marine and I did our best to help the fire-fighting efforts. With the fire raging ever more violently and with the sound of German machine-guns in the air, we could not have been more vulnerable, but we each held a hose pipe and tried to put out the fire. The sergeant in charge of us, meanwhile, simply told us that if we wanted him, he would be in the shelter some yards away – and with that he disappeared into its safety, leaving us to cope with the fire. We later learned that he had been awarded a medal for his night's work!

When, finally, the fire was under control, we went inside to search for bodies. The building was still alight and we had to pick our way through very carefully to avoid the smoke and falling beams. We found very little and by morning the barracks had been gutted. Walking back through the streets, exhausted and drained, I saw water running all over the streets and hose pipes strewn everywhere. Many people were walking the streets, bewildered, some pushing pram-loads of possessions, some just wandering aimlessly, refugees in their own homeland.

Every night of the bombing the local services and people of Portsmouth acted out their unsung heroic dramas. The fire brigade worked tirelessly night after night as the firebombs rained down seemingly incessantly. The fires spread fiercely throughout the night until they could finally be brought under control, but new fires seemed always to break out until dawn.

Events like these were repeated throughout the country, and the grim task of burying the dead would become a recurring feature of everyday life. The Royal Marines, myself included, frequently assisted at funerals in the city, marching alongside the slow, sombre procession of hearses from the city centre to Kingston cemetery as the city bade farewell to its latest civilian victims.

The threat of invasion continued to be a major concern and every precaution was taken. In *Dunedin* on 12 December the crew went to second degree of readiness – instead of the usual third degree – because for the next few days the river would have a spring tide, ideal for invading vessels.

Throughout December, everyone aboard *Dunedin* began to think of Christmas, a New Year, and the promise of better things to come. Harold Broadway wrote openly to Mary about their 'reunion in the New Year', more in hope than with any sense of certainty. At least he could look forward to slightly better conditions on board. He had been made up to Principal Medical Officer and been given a bigger and better cabin, twice as big as his previous one. It was better ventilated and being more amidships, suffered less from the vibrations he had suffered in his cabin near the propellers.

As the second Christmas of the war approached, word spread in *Dunedin* that she might soon be on the move. The captain even gave the ship's company some indication that they would soon be leaving port. For several days the rumours intensified and Leslie took the opportunity to see Jean again for an 'early' Christmas. Returning from their rushed time together, he wrote on 21 December:

> got back safely – I hope you enjoyed our 'Christmas Eve' short though it was. It is so possible that we won't see each other for a while that is why I came to see you – and, if this is so, we now have the satisfaction of being happy for a short while. If I do go soon I suppose we must look upon it as another chapter in our book of trials.
>
> We must remember that we are no worse off than lots of other people – we really are two of the lucky ones – I missed Dunkirk, London bombing and Libya.
>
> Have just heard we are leaving. I have your Christmas parcel and won't open it until Christmas day.
>
> I must stop writing – they are collecting the mail – have so much more I want to say.

Dunedin was indeed preparing to leave. At dusk on 21 December she sailed down the Channel en route to rendezvous in the Atlantic with convoy WS 5A. In worsening weather, she made her way towards the convoy, practising depth charge attack as she went. The captain also announced that long-range enemy bombers were thought to be heading towards the convoy.

In horrendous weather and huge seas, *Dunedin* sighted the convoy at 12.30 p.m. on the 23rd, bound for North Africa. The convoy was made up of twenty-one merchantmen and nine escorts – four corvettes, *Cyclamen*, *Jonquil*, *Geranium* and *Clematis*; two carriers, *Furious* and *Argus*; and three cruisers, *Berwick*, *Bonaventure* and *Niaid*. *Dunedin* took station on the starboard side of the convoy to begin with but shifted to the port side later. Her job was to take five of the merchantmen to Gibraltar.

HMS *Furious* could be seen pitching violently and her stern sometimes appeared to be completely out of the water. Many of the crew were horribly seasick, but by Christmas Eve they were somehow resigned to it.

Christmas Day dawned and the weather was as foul as it had been the day before. The convoy was now some 700 miles west of Cape Finisterre. At 7.35 a.m. dawn action stations were sounded and, to everyone's great surprise, an alarm starboard was given as soon as *Dunedin* closed up on the convoy. Fortunately, the 'target' was *Berwick*, but ten minutes later, through the spray and mist of the gloomy morning light, gun flashes were seen about five miles away on the starboard side. It was the German 8-inch cruiser *Admiral Hipper* firing at – and hitting – *Berwick*.

The convoy scattered and the cruisers *Berwick* and *Bonaventure*, stationed respectively three miles ahead and on the starboard side of the convoy, turned towards *Hipper* and opened fire. One of the escorting corvettes also opened fire. *Dunedin* steered across the front of the transports in the convoy and made smoke to screen them from the enemy. *Furious* did her level best to fly off her aircraft, but this proved impossible in the appalling weather.

Hipper was hit at least once in the encounter and the British warships – *Dunedin* in tow – gave chase. In poor visibility, she disappeared from *Dunedin*'s view, but only after a magnificent effort to catch up in the dreadful conditions. As the newer warships sped ahead in pursuit of *Hipper*, *Dunedin* raced behind at twenty-eight knots, desperately trying to get into the firing line with the other cruisers, but she could not keep up.

By now the convoy had dispersed and a number of ships had lost contact with the main group. *Dunedin* searched for and somehow found *City of Canterbury*.

For *Dunedin*, this had been nothing more than a close encounter. She had not managed to fire a shot in anger and *Hipper* had got away. She had also lost contact with the convoy.

As *Dunedin* continued on to Gibraltar, the ship's navigator was heard to say to Captain Lovatt that he had not been able to fix the ship's position to within fifty miles. The sky had been obscured for days and the constant alterations during the *Hipper* incident had not helped. Gradually, however, conditions improved and by the 28th the sea had subsided for *Dunedin*'s approach to Gibraltar. Leslie Russell, who had been one of the many men to suffer terrible seasickness, was now getting back to normal and was thankful for the calmer seas. He noted with considerable understatement in a letter to Jean that *Dunedin* had been 'rather busy' and that his Christmas dinner had consisted of a slice of bread and a lump of corned beef.

Harold Broadway, too, contemplated the previous few days. He wrote on 29 December:

> Well, I'm afraid we left before the arrival of the Christmas mail, and God knows when it will catch up with us now. But thanks so much for your cable – I was amazed to receive it miles out at sea, miles from anywhere, even if it was two days late – just when I was feeling particularly homesick for my wife and family.
>
> We'll remember Christmas 1940 for many a day. I felt pretty ill on my second day out, when it was pretty rough. But a plate of oysters (one of the chap's birthday party) the night before leaving may have been contributory to that. But Christmas Day was far worse – my Chief P.O. says the worst day bar none in all his 17 years of service, and Christmas dinner consisted of a slice of corned beef between two layers of sour bread, the galleys being a bit waterlogged and everyone being kind of busy anyway. But now the sea has calmed down and the weather become balmy and the sun is shining and it's quite like a holiday cruise once more and I'm not averse to this kind of seafaring.

I don't know when we'll get into port nor when nor where we'll go from there, but I know where I'd like to go.

I'm afraid I haven't much news that I can tell you here on paper, so I'll end this little note with love (of course) to yourself and the children and may the New Year see our reunion and peace in the world

Dunedin arrived at Gibraltar early that day but left within hours, after refuelling, to rejoin convoy WS 5A on its southerly passage.

On 2 January she encountered a darkened merchant ship, which was boarded and found to be SS *Amtelkerk*, bound for Freetown, in Sierra Leone, from Liverpool, and with Admiral Burke, the commodore of the main convoy, on board.

The following day, *Dunedin* rejoined the convoy in the late afternoon with escorts *Formidable* (the flagship), *Norfolk*, *Dorsetshire*, *Furious*, *Isis*, *Encounter*, *Broadwater* and *Calundine*. On the 4th, *Dunedin* broke off in search of a missing aircraft – a Fulmar – from *Formidable*, but sadly no trace was found. The next day, *Dunedin* arrived at Freetown, entering the harbour ahead of WS 5A. She stayed until the 10th.

For the crew of *Dunedin* this was their first time in Freetown. After the horrendous seas and terrible weather of Christmas, conditions would have seemed somewhat brighter, even though the chances of going home must have appeared bleaker than ever. In the comparative calm of the post-*Hipper* period, Harold Broadway summed up the mood in his letter of 5 January:

I do hope you and the children are all well and happy. I'm terribly disappointed that the prospect of seeing you again for a long time has become so remote. But at any rate, now that I'm thousands of miles from England as well there's certainly no point in your returning, as I can assure you that life in Bermuda is very much pleasanter than life in England these days. Goodness knows when I'll get mail again, either from you or from England. We seem absolutely isolated.

I should like to have spent a little longer than we did at our last port of call. It was a very pleasant spot. This second sea trip has been very different from the Christmas one – we have had nothing but blue skies, calm seas and warmth for the last week and at night it is just lovely, listening to the swish of the wake and seeing the phosphorescence in the water and the stars above.

January had brought a huge change for the men of *Dunedin*. After the weeks of anti-invasion duties and then the horrendous seas at the time of the *Hipper* incident, her voyage south gave the crew new things to do and think about, and new conditions in which to work. The temperatures rose and they had time to explore their new port of call. For Leslie, it meant a series of novel experiences, ranging from sleeping on deck at night to strolling around native villages where topless women did their washing in a stream, and listening to music on the newly installed loudspeaker on the upper deck. Life was suddenly very good, but the lack of mail since leaving Portsmouth just before Christmas reminded the men on board of the realities of their existence. Leslie wrote from Freetown:

> Ashore again today and went swimming – thoroughly enjoyed it – temperature just right. I have been longing for a swim and it was great soaking myself. The trunks are a very good fit too but I must stop eating so much and get more exercise. The bathing beach is a couple of miles from where the ship is docked so we went by lorry and so able to see something of the countryside.
>
> Today I was thinking that I should be glad to be somewhere where air-raid sirens are not constantly sounding and shelters are not known, but somehow I think most of us would rather be at home. We are all worried not knowing how the folk at home are faring. We have had no mail on board but that is quite understandable – I expect you now have to wait for overseas mail service. I think the mail boats have to wait for convoys and they are not regular.

Among the young midshipmen on board was Keith Mantell, who had joined *Dunedin* on 20 October 1940 after a spell in HMS *Rodney*. Life for Keith took a turn for the better with an invitation from the Commander-in-Chief South Atlantic, Vice-Admiral Raikes. He and five colleagues were taken by car to the vice-admiral's summer house, about four miles out of Freetown, where they enjoyed tea and tennis. *Dunedin* herself underwent a change too: she was painted light grey to match the tropical climate.

Harold Broadway was also making the best of things in Freetown. He wrote on 9 January:

Here I am, reclining in a deck chair on the quarter deck in the shade of one of the guns, writing to you. It seems that we are not allowed to send air mail from here, but I think I've prepared you for a long wait.

We've been here almost a week now, to my surprise anyway. I've had two afternoons ashore; the first time I just looked around the town (the native bazaars are rather interesting) and then went for a long walk in the intense heat into the country beyond, which I at any rate enjoyed, never having seen such a variety of birds and butterflies. On the other occasion I went with MacKay; we hired a car and had a drive through the countryside and then on to a bathing beach, where we surf-bathed. We had the proper surf boards and it's one of the most thrilling sports I know. I now appreciate the expression 'riding the crest of a wave'. So I'm making the best of what is generally regarded as a pretty bleak spot. It's certainly hotter than I've ever known it before, including last July and August and it's not a health resort. As usual I haven't the vaguest idea when or where we go next.

At sea, late in the evening of the 14th, three white lights were spotted on the horizon and *Dunedin* went to investigate. She found two French merchant ships and a French destroyer, the *François Gazelle*. *Dunedin* shadowed them until dawn before being called off the chase by the Admiralty. In another 'scare', *Dunedin* headed for the spot where an enemy vessel had been sighted, but she found nothing. Returning to Freetown on the 16th, she encountered a darkened ship, but since she was low on oil she could not get close enough.

Harold Broadway, meanwhile, continued to see the brighter side of life and began to enjoy the scenes around him. He wrote on 16 January:

Here we are, returning from another week at sea in this floating oven. I've never been so hot before – I believe it gets quite cold in Bermuda this time of year – but although we sweat and grumble, life is really rather pleasant, and personally I seem to keep in the best of health in the tropics. There has been a full moon all this week and the nights have been wonderful – just a gentle warm breeze and the swish of the waves as the ship glides gracefully through. We've seen a few sharks, flying fish and porpoises, but on the whole there is not much to look at except the sea. The dawn is often very lovely, the sunsets rather disappointing. We do our work early in the morning and late in the evening and sleep during the hottest part of the day, or at any rate try to. The canvas baths have been rigged in the starboard waist, so we can bathe. We've also started deck chairs and deck quoits again and the sea has been calm all the time.

The chief trouble is that I'm not getting any nearer to you and I guess it will take about 3 months for your mail to reach me and we cannot send any air mail or cables from here.

I haven't by any means given up hope of seeing you all one day – it'll be a little time yet though, I'm afraid.

Give the children a big kiss and hug from me. Tell them I catch their kisses from the moon. And do keep me well informed as to how they're getting on and send me a few snapshots.

The war seems to be swinging over a bit in our favour now doesn't it! I wonder when all this senseless destruction will end and we can all be reunited.

Dunedin made a brief visit to Bathurst (now Banjul), in Gambia, where she landed fifty soldiers and airmen. She also dropped a depth charge on a suspected submarine on the way in. Harold managed to get ashore at Bathurst and found it a pleasant change from Freetown. He wrote from Freetown on 21 January:

We're back from yet another sea trip to one of the out-of-the-way places in the Empire. I had a day ashore there; I liked it better than this place, the climate being drier, less steaming than it is here. I met the RAMC Captain when I went ashore. We first visited his hospital, which was exceedingly interesting. He had cases of every variety of tropical disease that I've ever heard of and was very interested in his work and it was all exceedingly instructive – dysentery, leprosy, everything. Then we drove out about ten miles in his car through some remarkable country when we saw the most remarkable birds too, to a glorious bathing beach where we did surf-bathing again. Then we came back and had tea with his No 2 who was ill in bed with malaria. Then we had another drive around, visited the officers' mess and so back to the ship and thence, in due course, to this steaming place again; but the little break in a healthier climate did us all good.

The next day, *Dunedin* left Freetown and turned north to Gibraltar, escorting two shiploads of Royal Marines, arriving there on 5 February. She stayed for nine days, during which time there was much speculation on board about where she might go next, with buzzes rife among the crew. It seemed as if every conversation began with 'What's the latest? What have you heard?' It got so bad that an order was issued telling the crew to be more careful.

Dunedin left Gibraltar on 14 February, escorting two ships, *Kenya* and the Polish *Sobieski*, accompanied – for the first twenty-four hours – by the destroyers *Wishart*, *Fortune*, *Vidette* and *Foresight*. Once more the weather was appalling and fierce gales blew, reducing *Dunedin's* speed to a paltry five knots. Three days into the trip, the weather finally let up and she could increase her speed to seventeen knots. She was homeward bound again.

On the 18th, *Dunedin* and the convoy moved to within range of German aircraft, but it was the danger from U-boats that caused some concern the following day. Captain Lovatt received a signal telling him that a U-boat was shadowing the convoy, so it altered course and, it seems, shook the U-boat off. No attacks were made.

On 22 February, having been away from the UK since 21 December, *Dunedin* came in sight of the west of Scotland. Green fields stretched down to the coast against the dramatic backdrop of the snow-capped mountains in the distance. By 9 p.m., she had anchored in the Clyde, some three miles from Greenock.

Two days later, 150 bags of mail arrived and a Christmas spirit filled the ship. Leslie received twenty-five letters and two parcels from Jean and lots of Christmas cards from his family. Harold too was able to catch up on his family news with forty-two letters in two days.

A few days later, on Sunday 2 March, *Dunedin* left Greenock for Devonport.

By this time I had completed my training and was waiting patiently to be drafted to a ship. Every day I checked the notice-boards for my name and for weeks on end I would come away disappointed as more and more of my comrades' names appeared.

It took so long for my name to appear that I was sent on even more training. So I did advanced sea training as a gun layer. By the end of the training I was paid an extra threepence a day and must have been the most experienced and well-trained gun layer who had never fired a gun in anger and who had never been to sea. As time wore on, I became more and more impatient and resented the daily trudge to the notice-board just to be humiliated. What was the point of all the training and all the preparation if I wasn't going anywhere? Was I destined to stay at Portsmouth for the rest of the war?

Finally, on 16 March, as spring was poking through the winter gloom, I stood at the notice-board with one of my mates, incomprehensibly gazing at my name on a list. I said nothing, just stood motionless, staring. For so many weeks I had been coming down here and had come to accept that my name would never appear, and yet, here it was at last: 'Marine Gill, HMS Dunedin'.

I had never heard of her, but I soon found out that she was a light cruiser, currently in Devonport in dry dock for an overhaul.

By the following day the military bureaucratic machine had churned out my 'chit' and my movement orders. I went to the company office to get a rail warrant and left Portsmouth to go to Devonport on 18 March.

I came upon Dunedin just after 6 that evening. She looked small, but sleek and very cluttered. The gangways were narrow and every space had been filled with equipment and machinery. Maintenance men and sailors were all over her, welding, banging, cleaning, and mending. The air was filled with the sounds of men at work, metal on metal, as they went about the task of refitting a ship that could already boast a war record.

Before I stepped on board I took a long look at what was to become my home for the foreseeable future. I remembered the day I had left Swinley House, my mother's face and her fraught tears. I remembered how I had skipped down the staircase, my suitcase in hand and my hopes in my head. I remembered my burning desire. I remembered the months of training. And here I was. This was it.

CHAPTER 4
South Atlantic, April–May 1941

I spent my first night in Dunedin *trying – and failing – to sleep. After months of anticipation, the reality of life on board one of His Majesty's ships was not quite how I had imagined it. As far as I could see, there were too many people for the space available. I had barely enough room to sling my hammock and, as a new boy, had to take whatever space was left over. The best I could do was find a spot under a bulkhead light infested with cockroaches. I lay there, eyes wide open, listening to the continuing banging and activity around the ship and trying to ignore the scratching of the cockroaches scurrying around the light a few inches above my head.*

Next day I was given ten days' embarkation leave.

I went home to see my mum and dad and my brothers. Many of my friends had joined the services by now, so there were few people for me to see. I had a bit more money than I had been used to before I joined the Marines, so I was able to get to the pub and to the cinema to pass the time. I took the opportunity also to visit my Aunt Lucy in Stokenchurch. To get there I had to get up early in the morning, walk across Regent's Park to Marylebone station, catch the workmen's train to High Wycombe and then a bus to Stokenchurch, all for about two shillings.

Mum, of course, was pleased to see me, but her feelings were not really any different to when I had left for Deal in December 1939. She was still distraught at the idea of my going to sea and must have thought that I would not come back. As each day of my leave passed, she must have dreaded the time when she would have to say goodbye. She also did something I will never forget. She had promised me, Eric and Jack that she would buy each of us a gold signet ring on our twenty-first birthdays. I had thought no more about this until, before I left for Plymouth, she handed me a gold signet ring, which I wear to this day. I was only nineteen and she was convinced she would never see me again.

Come the time to leave for the ship it is hard to imagine how my parents must have felt. Parents, wives, sisters, brothers all over the country said their goodbyes to their loved ones, not knowing if they would ever see them again, not knowing what the future would bring. My father put on a brave face, but my mother was inconsolable. The tears flowed more even than when I had joined up.

I cannot say that I was not upset, especially seeing my mother in such an emotional state for the second time. But I was different myself now. It is a cliché to say that my training had made a man of me, but I was now confident, fit and self-assured. The pull of the emotional heartstrings was very strong, but I felt able to cope with anything and now had a purpose, a mission.

When I returned to Dunedin on the 28th March, she was still in dry dock, but it was clear that the ship was not far from being ready. There was still much rushing about and frantic activity, but there were fewer civilian maintenance men on board and a noticeable increase in the number of officers and other men returning to the ship. My watch was back on board now and I began to get to know the other marines and some of the sailors. There was not a great deal for me to do in the first few days except to try to get to know the ship and how it functioned.

HMS Dunedin was a light cruiser, conceived during the First World War and delivered in peacetime. In 1916 she was just an idea in the minds of the Admiralty, a theory in the battle against the German navy. Word had reached the Admiralty that the Germans were producing a new type of cruiser, with five 6-inch guns and which would outclass and outgun the British C-class cruisers. The new D-class cruisers would be longer than the C class and would have an additional 6-inch gun. While the D class lay on the drawing board, yet further modifications were made to the design as a result of lessons learned at the Battle of Jutland: better protection for the magazine, a third torpedo tube and depth-charge rails.

Dunedin was not the first of the D-class litter. Danae, Dauntless and

Dragon were ordered in September 1916, although none was completed for anything other than brief war service. *Dunedin* was in the second batch, ordered in July 1917. Her birthplace was Armstrongs Yard at Newcastle-upon-Tyne.

As the war for which *Dunedin* was planned came near to its end she was still under construction in the yard. Eight days after Armistice Day, on 19 November 1918, she slipped down the launch ramp into the Tyne. The war for which she had been conceived had passed her by.

She was finally completed a year later and joined the 1st Cruiser Squadron, Atlantic. In 1923 she was one of the ships of the Special Service Squadron which left for a world cruise, the so-called 'Booze Cruise', which was designed to demonstrate to the world that Britannia still ruled the waves. She sailed from Devonport in the company of HMS *Hood*, HMS *Repulse* and four of her sister cruisers, *Dragon, Delhi, Danae* and *Dauntless*.

The cruise arrived in New Zealand in April 1924, after an epic voyage taking in Freetown, Cape Town, Durban, Zanzibar, Trincomalee, Kuala Lumpur, Singapore and Australia. *Dunedin* was transferred to the New Zealand Division in place of HMS *Chatham*, while the rest of the cruise carried on its voyage.

Dunedin's New Zealand days were a rich adolescence of sun, clear waters and ceremony. Her job – to show the British flag in the Pacific and Australasia – was done with pomp, panache and efficiency, although she gave some valuable practical assistance when she came to the rescue of New Zealanders in February 1931 after an earthquake had struck Napier. In conjunction with HMS *Diomede*, she arrived in Napier on 3 February from Auckland with food, tents, medical supplies, doctors and nurses, and stayed until 11 February. *Dunedin* twice left the New Zealand station for refits in the UK, once in 1927 and later in 1931, when she was away for seventeen months.

On her returns to the New Zealand station she resumed her normal duties. Plying between ports and hopping from island to island, *Dunedin* showed her colours. No doubt there were hard times and everyone on board would have regretted the long days at sea and the time spent away from their loved ones. But today, anybody reading some of the captain's reports of *Dunedin*'s duties and activities could be forgiven for thinking that life was just one big party. The captain and officers spent much of their time paying official calls on the local mayors, governors, consuls and sundry public officials wherever they went. In many places, particularly on the remote islands, the arrival of a warship was a major event and an excuse for dancing and celebration. One entry in Rear-Admiral Bruges Watson's report of 15 October 1934 gives a typical flavour:

> *HMS Dunedin* arrived at Papeete at 0830 on Friday, 13th July. I exchanged calls with the British Consul and the Governor of French Oceania. Consuls of other nations called in the afternoon and were given the usual guns salutes. M. Alain Gerbault was at Papeete with his yacht, in the course of one his cruises around the world, and we were able to afford him some help in carrying out minor repairs to his craft. The week commencing Saturday, 14th July, was the occasion of the annual fête at Papeete. On Saturday the ship was dressed overall and a salute of 21 guns fired at noon. In the forenoon I attended a service at the war Memorial, the Royal Marine detachment also being landed for the ceremony. Later I and some of my officers went to a 'Vin d'honneur' for the returned soldiers, and in the afternoon went to the local race meeting. In the evening the Governor gave an official ball at Government House and the ship was illuminated. On Sunday I had lunch with the Captain of the *Zelee* which had arrived from Bora Bora. On Monday 16th July, I attended a ceremony of unveiling a memorial to Pierre Loti. On Tuesday 17th July, I gave a dinner party on board and afterwards I and my officers gave a dance on the quarterdeck. During our stay a considerable amount of private entertaining was done. Association football and rifle shooting matches were held by the ship's company, who also enjoyed the dancing booths and sideshows which lined the waterfront.
>
> After a most enjoyable visit to Papeete, HMS *Dunedin* sailed for Moorea at 1100 on Friday, 20th July, and arrived at 1315.

Later, in December 1935, *Dunedin* had one of her encounters with royalty when the Duke of Gloucester arrived in HMS *Sussex*. He went first to Australia and then to New Zealand for a state visit. *Dunedin* joined in the full pomp and ceremony accorded to British royals – with the Duke aboard HMS *Australia*, *Dunedin* and *Diomede* formed an escort with *Leith* and *Laburnum* astern. The escort proceeded up Wellington harbour, passing anchored New Zealand ships and cheering crowds. A royal salute was fired and a royal guard of seamen formed up on the jetty when the Duke landed.

The visit lasted several days and took in Wellington and Auckland. *Dunedin*'s last royal duty was to escort HMS *Sussex,* carrying the Duke, out of New Zealand waters.

This was not the end of *Dunedin*'s southern hemisphere existence. In 1936 she went to Port Pegasus on Stewart Island in search of a copy of the Treaty of Waitingi, which was believed to have been buried on an island there. The treaty had been signed in 1840 by the British and the Maoris when Britain had claimed New Zealand as its own. In a bizarre hunt, *Dunedin* sailors were dispatched to dig for the map. Perhaps not surprisingly, nothing was found.

For her swan song on the New Zealand station, *Dunedin* visited Hawaii. On what must have been a thoroughly enjoyable cruise, she went to the American island via Raratonga and Tahiti, returning via Fiji.

T.D. Herrick, DSC, RN, who served in *Dunedin* from 1934 to 1937, described her as a happy ship with a cheerful wardroom and a good ship's company. Her New Zealand days would prove to be among her happiest and when, in February 1937, she left for England, she would have done so with a heavy heart.

Dunedin's voyage home took her through calm seas to Tahiti, the Panama Canal and on to Jamaica before making the Atlantic crossing.

The Britain to which she returned was very different from the one she had first left in 1923. Then the country was still a post-war victor, wounded but triumphant, ready to resume her role as imperial ruler. In 1937, all that had changed. The vanquished had risen and Hitler had been Chancellor of Germany for four years. New war clouds were forming over Europe. And there was a new king, George VI, brother of Edward VIII, who had abdicated for the love of Mrs Simpson.

Amidst the uncertainty and fear of another war, the country nevertheless looked forward to celebrations as the King prepared for his coronation on 18 May 1937. It was a day of great national rejoicing, a day on which to forget anxieties, a day to relish. And *Dunedin* would play her part. She had become the flagship of the 9th Cruiser Squadron and the King himself came aboard on 19 May to inspect her.

From November 1937 until being commissioned for war duties, *Dunedin* became a training ship for Boys and – perhaps ignominiously – she was employed as a torpedo bomber target vessel.

And now, in 1941, as men joined and rejoined *Dunedin*, they made their own inspection of the ship, their own assessment of what was to be their home for the coming months. Above all else, it was very cramped with a full war complement, some 480 people cramming into the cluttered and narrow spaces.

Dunedin had an operational range of around 4,000 miles, with a maximum speed of twenty-nine knots. She had six hand-loaded 6-inch guns placed along the centre line of the ship in single, manually operated mountings. She also had three hand-loaded 4-inch anti-aircraft guns in single, manually operated mountings and a number of small-calibre weapons. To complete the armament she carried twelve torpedoes in four triple-tube mountings on the upper deck.

An IFF (Identification Friend/Foe) radar set (RDF) was fitted in 1940, but this was of very limited use. She had no other radar equipment and, apart from some antiquated hydrophone detector equipment, no ASDIC or submarine detector apparatus was fitted. In fact, despite the depth charges on the quarterdeck, this was a ship with almost no anti-submarine potential. This was no accident or oversight. When she had been built, in 1919, the threat was far less from submarines than from surface ships.

Now, in April 1941, as the new arrivals familiarised themselves with *Dunedin*, she was readying herself for her next challenge. More and more of her personnel were arriving, as it became clear that she would soon be leaving Devonport. The ship became increasingly crowded as ever more new faces appeared on board. Joining at this time was thirty-six-year-old Edward Unwin, *Dunedin*'s newly appointed commander. The most senior officer in the wardroom mess and the ship's executive officer, he was second in command after the captain. It was his job to see that the ship functioned smoothly and that it operated successfully, but, like everyone else, Unwin had little time to get used to his surroundings. The future was uncertain and levels of apprehension were high, made worse by the loss of one of the telegraphists, Frederick Howard, who had gone missing

– presumed killed – in a recent heavy air raid on Plymouth. He had been buried in the rubble of the Royal Hotel on 20 March.

Leslie Russell had been on leave and had managed to spend time with Jean in Bournemouth for a few days. Returning to *Dunedin* was not a happy experience for him. He found the ship depressing, cheerless and in a mess. With his future once more locked into the uncertain destiny of *Dunedin*, his thoughts stayed with Jean. He wrote on 20 March:

> There are guns going tonight. At times like these I feel how terrible it would be to be killed suddenly without an opportunity to reassure you and say goodbye. If we were together I should not mind, but the thought of you hearing news of my death without any last message from me, causes me more pain than anything.
>
> It is not a cheerful subject so I'll not say more – but I just think, like everyone else, that the sooner this war is over the better, though I find it hard to be optimistic about it.

During the following days, Leslie began to sense that the buzz of activity on board must mean that *Dunedin* was readying herself for another voyage and that time was running out to see Jean again before they sailed. He wrote on 29 March:

> We are now back to normal cramped conditions in the mess as everyone is back from their leave. I feel so frustrated and depressed. I have leave tomorrow (Sunday) from 11.00 am to probably 7 am on Monday morning – 20 hours of liberty. I have been right through the rail timetables and the Sunday services are hopeless – I just can't get to Bournemouth and back in time. It can't even be arranged by you coming to meet me in Salisbury or Exeter. If it had been possible I would have dashed ashore and wired you but I am on duty and have to be on board – we were only told of this leave today. It has practically sent me crazy trying to think of ways and means.

The following day, Leslie was still feeling the frustrations of not being able to take his leave:

> The others arrived back as expected so I have had to vacate my comfortable billet in the office and slung my hammock in my usual place outside the store

– rather cheerless surroundings! We tried to cheer up the others as they came back but the buzzes are beginning again.

I have come to the conclusion that any peace of mind or contentment we achieve at the moment is only a fragile thing. It only needs the slightest thing to go wrong and we fall to pieces. The war is such a lousy thing – everything is on such a weak foundation while it lasts. For instance, I felt so low today – the twenty-four hours leave I have had to abandon – the thought that we might leave here any day – I just don't seem to have the strength of character to face up to these feelings – although as I write I'm talking to you and it does help to put things into perspective and I try to remember how lucky we have been so far.

On the morning of 3 April, Dunedin *began to move. I felt the peculiar sensation of the ship being floated out of dry dock. After the rigidity of the previous few days, my legs learned new lessons in balance and walking. My head and stomach wondered what the hell was going on.* Dunedin *had finished her refitting now and was ready to go back to sea. Much work had been done on her in a month of solid effort. Within hours of arriving at Devonport she had been deammunitioned in preparation for dry dock and to have sixteen defective fuel tanks repaired. Her bottom was cleaned of weeds, her rudder and starboard propeller shaft were put back in place after overhaul and no end of maintenance and repair work was carried out.*

As Dunedin *reintroduced herself to the water, she was reammunitioned – a lengthy and difficult operation that took the best part of twenty-four hours to complete. After basin trials to test the engines, we slipped No. 7 wharf on 6 April and moved out to Plymouth Sound to buoy.*

A large number of new hands were still arriving, including thirty-five boys from HM Ships Ganges, Impregnable *and* St George. *For these boys, training had been considerably shortened and now they were heading for the real thing. One of the youngest boys, Boy McCall, had barely turned sixteen. The Commander-in-Chief Plymouth, Sir Martin Dunbar-Nasmith, VC, paid us a visit and addressed the ship's company, telling us that we would be in Plymouth for a few more days and would then go to sea.*

I did not know where Dunedin *would take me, but as we sat in Plymouth Sound I felt sure that what followed would change my life.*

Little did I realise that I would get an early taste of 'action'. On the night before we left, I was resting on my bunk when the air raid sirens sounded. Within seconds action stations were piped and I leapt up to take my position on the High Angle 4-inch gun. As gun layer, it was my job to fire the gun.

Sitting at the gun, all I could see were searchlights criss-crossing the sky, desperately feeling for German bombers. We could hear them rumbling overhead and soon we could hear the thump of explosions on the mainland. I gripped hard and looked skyward through the gun-sight into the darkness.

And then, suddenly, two searchlights trapped a bomber and she was in my sights.

'Enemy plane in sight!' I shouted. 'I've got him, I've got him'.

This was it. Bloody hell, I'd been in Dunedin only a few days and here it was, my first chance to shoot at the enemy. I waited for the shout confirming that the breach was closed and that I could fire. My eyes stayed glued to the German plane. The searchlights were rock-solidly on him. Somewhere on the mainland were two searchlight operators who knew they had caught something and were waiting for someone to fire.

So was I. Me. Give me the word, just give me the word! Where was that bloody call? What was happening? More seconds passed and I screwed my eyes to keep sight of the plane as it wriggled free of the lights. Come on, come on! But there was something wrong with the gun mechanism and the breach could not be closed.

And then the plane had gone. My first 'action' hadn't even started.

The next day, 8 April 1941, I was instructed what to do at abandon ship stations. It would be my job to release two Carley floats from behind the bridge in front of the forward funnel. To do that I had to climb up on to the top of the blacksmith's shop and unclip the catches holding them in place. One float was on top of the other and, when the catch was released, I had to push them down to the deck, then slide them over the side – and I had to do it as quickly as possible. The floats were made of an oval ring of copper tubing, about ten feet long and eight feet wide. The tubing was covered in canvas and was wide enough to support a man sitting astride the perimeter. Inside the perimeter was a rope mesh attached to a wooden grating which allowed people to stand on the inside of the rafts waist deep in the sea.

As I heaved them back on to the platform after the exercise, I silently hoped that I would not have to do it for real.

At around 8 that evening, we sailed en route to Gibraltar. By 10 we were hammering along at top speed and I got my first experience of Dunedin's capacity to shake and rattle as the propeller shafts strained and sent vibrations coursing through the superstructure. I was aft lookout, but all I could see was the ship's wake and the receding shoreline. My thoughts turned to what I had left behind and I wondered when I would see England again. For me and the other newcomers to Dunedin, this was nevertheless a time of excitement and anticipation, sailing to war into the unknown. It was different for the 'old hands' – Leslie included – who had been denied one last spot of leave. Nobody knew when or if Dunedin would return. The buzzes said November or December.

On our first full day at sea, 9 April, we closed on two Spanish trawlers and the following day dropped a depth charge in an exercise. Most of us aboard were not aware that this was to happen and the first thing we knew about it was when a huge plume of sea water rose up behind us and a loud explosion rumbled through the sea.

When England's shoreline was far behind us, my excitement turned quickly to disbelief when the nauseous curse of seasickness befell me. On Friday and all through the weekend, the weather worsened and the sea threw Dunedin and everyone in her all over the place. I was horribly seasick. I could not work, I could not stand up, I could not lie down, I was useless. The captain himself could have personally ordered me to work and I would not have been able to respond.

I heaved up on deck, I heaved up in the mess, I heaved up over the side. On one occasion I struggled to the side of the ship to throw up only to find another bloke doing the same. The trouble was, I was down wind of him, so I took his 'output' straight in my face.

I had never felt more sorry for myself than this. Someone told me to pull myself together and fall into work – it would be the best thing for me, they said. OK, I'll try anything, I said. And so I fell in on deck to be allocated a job. I stood there, clutching the safety line, as the ship swayed this way and that, its movement made more erratic by the zigzagging, and listened while a sergeant sent men this way and that. I had not eaten for days and my stomach was beginning its upward push towards my throat when my turn was about to come. But just as the sergeant reached my name, a huge wave crashed across the deck and knocked me over so hard that one of my shoes came off.

I collected myself and steadied against the railing. Stooping, wet, with one shoe, I scowled at the sergeant and then staggered away to lie down somewhere. I think the rest of them just stood and had a jolly good laugh. I felt miserable and spent most of my time huddled against two warm-air outlets, afraid to go below, feeling very sorry for myself.

The weather was so bad that Dunedin *was forced to reduce speed on the 11th. And later that day the forward davit of the motor cutter was ripped away by the sea, leaving the cutter suspended by its stern and crashing against the side of the ship. She was damaged so badly that she could not be saved, and before anyone could cut it loose, the after davit was torn off and the cutter fell away into the water.*

Mercifully, as Dunedin *approached the Mediterranean the sea became slightly calmer and my seasickness receded. By the time we reached Gibraltar and had tied up in the harbour, it had gone, never to return while I served aboard* Dunedin.

Leslie too seemed finally to have conquered his seasickness. He wrote on 12 April:

> I am not feeling so bad this trip although it was a bit rough on Friday. I have played draughts once or twice and read a little. Luckily my work has kept me fairly well occupied. We have been paid today – I'm going to keep saving for that house and we'll need a lot for our next holiday – we must have it all mapped out so that we won't waste a moment.
>
> At the moment there are very few buzzes as to our future movements. I think we are all resigned to the worst.

For Harold Broadway, *Dunedin*'s southerly path was confirmation that he would not be reunited with his family in the near future. Since returning to home waters from the Caribbean, he had hoped that *Dunedin* would go back so that he could see Mary and the children again. The Commander-in-Chief West Indies and Americas Station had again requested, in March, *Dunedin*'s return to the Caribbean, but this had been refused (with a promise that the request would be 'borne in mind'). As *Dunedin* approached Gibraltar, Harold contemplated what might have been and began to plan what he would do after the war even though he had no idea what the war would bring for him. He wrote to Mary in Bermuda on 13 April:

> …they've sent us in the wrong direction once more…I was so damn certain that I should be seeing you very soon in the course of our voyaging. I still think, as I said before, that sooner or later I'll be with you there again, but I'm afraid this trip postpones it for an indefinite period.
>
> …I think we would have had more chance of being happy together in Bermuda than at any place or time else in our lives. As it is we'll have to live again the old humdrum existence in General Practice although I'm seriously thinking of emigrating after the war; it's going to be damned hard to earn a decent living in England and our children will be paying for this war when they're our age. I've thought of the USA and Australia. Ah well, time will tell. The main thing at present is for us all to get through this war alive. There's one thing, we're no worse off at present than anyone else in a foreign-serving ship in the Navy and a damn sight better off than the army in the Middle East, for instance. One can't go to war without these separations. But I certainly shan't stay on in the Navy after the war is over. I've looked at all the ocean I want to for a long time to come. I take rather the same view of the Navy as Mr Fred Astaire.
>
> Well, dear, this trip has been the first one on which, although the weather has been rough, I haven't been seasick, but I don't mean from that that I felt particularly happy; in point of fact I didn't, and it has been bloody uncomfortable. Let's hope we sail next on smoother seas. I've no idea now as to where we'll eventually end up on this trip.

Dunedin entered Gibraltar harbour early in the morning of Monday 14 April. Before nightfall she had left again, having had time only to oil and gather a few provisions. Nobody was given shore leave but some, including Leslie Russell, made it ashore on duty a couple of times, mostly to help provision the ship.

While Harold Broadway was correct to wonder where *Dunedin* would end up, preparations on board pointed to a hot summer. In short, after the ship left the Strait of Gibraltar, Captain Lovatt took her south, bound for Freetown. The temperature rose steadily each day and the men were now wearing less and less, just white shirts and shorts. And if there was any doubt that *Dunedin* was headed for a tropical climate, the crew was issued with sun helmets.

What's more, on 17 April Harold gave his 'well-known talk', as he called it – the dreaded VD lecture. This was as clear a sign as any that *Dunedin* was heading for a foreign port with native women. At least he held the talk on the quarterdeck, where the men could get some welcome breeze in the steadily rising temperatures.

Harold described in graphic detail what would happen to the men – and their private parts, in particular – if they fraternised with the 'lady' natives. A short message to say keep away from the women should have been enough, but this was lost on plenty of blokes; it wouldn't have mattered how many times you told them, they would still have set off like rats up a drainpipe the minute they hit the shore. The unlucky ones would come back with the dreaded 'tear' (because of the tear-shaped drop of gunge oozing from the tip of their dicks).

En route to Freetown, *Dunedin* escorted *Queen Elizabeth* and encountered two Spanish trawlers, a Spanish navy ship and a Vichy French vessel. Captain Lovatt sent out boarding parties to the navy ship and to the fishing vessel, but neither proved troublesome.

Dunedin arrived in Freetown on the afternoon of Sunday 20 April and stayed for a week. In the coming weeks and months, much time was spent in Freetown and the crew came to know it quite well. Harold Broadway, Leslie Russell and many others in the ship's company had been here before and knew exactly what to expect. On this visit, Harold was in no hurry to go ashore, preferring instead to sit on the quarterdeck writing letters home.

The main trouble with Freetown was its smell. The welcoming sight of its rolling green countryside and dry land was quickly relegated to the back of the senses by the atrocious stench. And usually the men would be watching the approaching landfall with arms aching from a collection of jabs to ward off the expected virulent diseases, such as blackwater fever.

Freetown might not have been a pleasant place, but beautiful spots could be found if you looked hard enough and if you came ashore with a wider objective than just sitting in bars. Harold Broadway usually found time to get to the beach and to take note of the exotic animals running wild.

After a couple of visits to Freetown I and some other blokes, my best friend Nobby Hall included, would jump straight into a taxi the minute we went ashore and go to a beach away from the town. Here we found exotic white sandy beaches and clear blue water by a village of mud huts, where topless native women washed their clothes on the rocks and smoky wood fires marked the ground.

The sun would beat down on us and we would lay in the shade of a banana tree or swim in the crystal-clear waters. Children from the village would wait for us to end our swim then rinse our feet with bottles of sea water for a penny a time. They would scurry around us, smiling and jostling for our attention, then wait patiently for our next dip.

We even found one of those 'far corners which shall be forever England'. Two English ladies had set up shop several years earlier and now ran a teashop which we visiting servicemen would seek out. I don't think many men found this shop, but a group of us would seek it out most times we went ashore. And there, in a respite from war and thousands of miles from home, we were served tea and sponge cakes in the quiet of an English tearoom. I swear if we closed our eyes we could hear the thump of willow against leather from a village green outside.

Idyllic days and a million miles from the war.

Freetown was also home to the rougher side of service life. It was not all sandy beaches and clear water. After days and weeks at sea, a lot of the blokes would simply let rip. Women, drink, bars and – sometimes – violence as the drink became too much in the sultry tropical climate. We were told plenty of times at our lectures on board ship not to go near native women and native bars, but too many blokes ignored the advice.

Petty rivalries between crews would sometimes needlessly develop into fights, which the Military Police – or occasionally us Marines - would break up, and then the crews would lose their next shore leave.

With very few MPs about, the Marines were often called to do shore patrol, looking for trouble and hoping to stop it before it got out of hand. Most of the time during the day there was no trouble, but by the time we were waiting on the quayside for the liberty boat in the evening, some of the blokes were boozed up and ready for a fight.

Back on ship any trouble ashore was usually forgotten and we would all get on with our jobs and doing our duty. On deck at night, and especially on the nights before we departed again for the open sea, we could see a lone palm tree on the point of the harbour silhouetted against the sunset. The beauty of that moment would be lost in a trice the next day as Dunedin *headed for the open sea and the danger of war, but for a few moments we could bask in the natural glory of nature.*

We left Freetown on 26 April to join a convoy three days' sailing away. On the way, on the afternoon of the 28th, I had my first experience of the Crossing the Line ceremony as Dunedin *travelled south over the equator.*

The day's events were best described by Lt-Commander Sowdon, in a letter to his wife, Monica, a month later:

The event that I am now allowed to mention is that we did on a date that I cannot mention (some time ago) cross the line, crossing the equator that is. Of course I had done it before as I did it with you, but I had not seen the ceremony which is customary in HM Ships. I forget if you saw it at Navy Week. Anyhow it is a great occasion for dressing up.

King Neptune was done by Barrat our second doctor as he is a big chap and has crossed the line many times in merchant service. His queen was a leading seaman. His herald was Lt Beveridge and there was a guard of honour of pirates and the band in all sorts of rigs. The day was dull unfortunately and there was some rain but it was not cold of course.

The show started after lunch, the canvas baths having been rigged up during the forenoon. King Neptune and his retinue went down into the paintshop to which there is a hatch right forward on the forecastle and all the hands crowded by the No 1 gym. Then up came the herald and shouted to the bridge "ship ahoy". The Captain answered and was then requested to come down to receive King Neptune as the ship was entering his domain. Then a sort of proclamation was read, and King Neptune inspected the guard of honour of pirates followed by his queen in long flaxen plaits and a dress which to the best of my knowledge had been found amongst the rags that are sent on board for cleaning purposes. Then started the presentation of certain orders. The Captain got the order of the empty sardine tin. The Commander [Unwin] who had recently spoken to the men about throwing paper and stuff about got the order of the ash tray. These orders are all on a bit of string and were hung around our necks. Ben Bolt got the order of the gin bottle. I got the order of the scrubbing brush (being mess deck officer). The Pay [Lt-Cdr Skinner] got the order of the sour loaf (a bit of tin cut to the shape of a loaf and 'sour' written on it) because at one time the bread was not too good. Mr Lowey got the order of the dud electric lamps. Broadway got a bunch of herbs. And then finally the youngest boy in the ship received a bar of chocolate on a bit of string. He is what you would call a dear little boy and looks about 13, though he is 16, I suppose.

That part over every one went aft to the bath where the King watched and superintended the ceremony. Each man in turn caught by the pirates, was made to sit on a seat and the barber (dressed in chef's hat etc) splashed his face with lather using a large paint brush (lather was water and dough); his assistant stood by with an enormous wooden razor. Then the chap was tipped into the bath and ducked. I having crossed the line before was exempt but to make sure I took the precaution of putting on old socks and gym shoes and emptied my pockets of keys and money. Just tropical shorts and shirt of course. I had a good view of it all and towards the end went nearer to get a closer look when I was seized on and tipped in, much to the amusement of the sailors who thought I was quite unprepared for the whole thing. I hope to be able to send you some photographs of it later on; not taken by myself as you can see me looking on but that is all. Finally Neptune and his queen were both tipped in and the ceremony came to an end.

For me, barely three weeks out of Plymouth and still only nineteen, this was more than a symbolic nautical ceremony. As a member of King Neptune's guard of honour of pirates, I was thrust with a number of my Marine comrades to the centre of attention of the whole ship and made to feel as if I had finally arrived, that I really was part of a bigger thing. And it was fun too.

The following day, with the equatorial frolics behind her, *Dunedin* saw HMS *Devonshire*'s Walrus aircraft and later made contact with *Devonshire* and HMS *Illustrious*, who were escorting SS *Empress of Japan* and SS *Monarch of Bermuda*, both packed with troops and bound for the Middle East.

Illustrious and *Devonshire* left about 11 a.m. and *Dunedin* turned north with the convoy. The weather was still very hot and the sea turned rough.

Apart from a quick stop in Freetown, *Dunedin* took the convoy all the way to Gibraltar, with escorts *Highlander* and *Boreas* and later *Velox* and *Wrestler*. Before reaching Gibraltar, some of her boiler tubes burst, causing steam to escape from the foremast funnel and taking out one boiler. This was to dog *Dunedin* for the coming months, keeping her maximum speed to twenty-four knots.

She arrived at Gibraltar, leading the convoy into the harbour, and stayed there for two and a half weeks, undergoing a short refit in No. 1 dock. *Dunedin*'s defective boiler would take too long to be fixed, so it was shut down, leaving her with only five boilers.

Nothing of great significance happened in Gibraltar. For the ship's company, it was a chance to see more of the Rock and to witness the comings and goings of the fleet, including such names as *Renown*, *Repulse*, *Argus*, *Ark Royal* and *Sheffield*. The sad news arrived of the sinking of the *Hood* by the *Bismarck*, with huge loss of life. News reached *Dunedin* too of the astonishing episode with Rudolf Hess, who had flown a Messerschmidt to Scotland, apparently to speak to his old friend the Duke of Hamilton on a peace mission. No one quite knew what to make of it.

Dunedin passed out of Gibraltar harbour on 25 May, in company with Force H (*Renown* and *Ark Royal*). Once clear of the Rock area, she parted company as *Ark Royal* and *Renown* headed north in pursuit of *Bismarck*. As Gibraltar receded, the ship's company was left with the empty feeling of not having received any mail. This did nothing to help morale and left a shadow of depression over the ship, for nothing had reached *Dunedin* since she had left Devonport nearly two months earlier.

Leslie Russell had written on 23 May:

The big grouse at the moment is the mail question. Since we have been here two ships have arrived from home waters with mail. They each had quite a number of bags but nothing for us and we feel that something should have come by now – we have been here for over two weeks.

As *Dunedin* sailed south once more, Leslie kept writing to Jean and storing his letters ready to be sent at the next opportunity. In each, he lamented the lack of mail and, in so doing, captured the feeling that pervaded the ship.

In the coming days *Dunedin* saw little excitement, except for a number of Spanish and Portuguese ships, each of which was challenged. Every time *Dunedin* came across a ship like this, she stopped her and trained her guns on her while a ten-oared cutter was sent across with an officer to board the suspicious vessel. Midshipman Thomas Handley was often in charge of the cutter and accompanied the officer on board the merchantman, both armed with .45-calibre revolvers. Once on board, they went to the bridge and examined the ship's manifest and, if they had suspicions, demanded that a hatch or two be opened for inspection. Despite being taken in hand by a British ship, the crews of these ships were usually friendly and helpful.

For *Dunedin* this was neither the height of war nor the pinnacle of excitement. She was doing her job, of course, but she was a stagehand to the leading actors.

Harold Broadway summed up the feelings on the ship in his letter of 29 May:

It hasn't been too bad a trip so far; no major scares or excitements, but one gets a bit bored with just the sea to look at and the same old faces in the Wardroom…The news hasn't been too cheerful this week – the loss of the *Hood, Fiji, Gloucester* and *York* and several destroyers only partially set off by the sinking of the *Bismarck*. If we lose many more cruisers they'll be putting this old tub onto some rather more exciting work.

However, events elsewhere – in the Atlantic and in an old country house in Bletchley Park – were contriving to change the course of their lives for ever.

CHAPTER 5
Bletchley Park and Enigma

Fifty miles north-west of London, in the quiet rural countryside of Buckinghamshire, the railway town of Bletchley was home to a disparate collection of men and women whose sole purpose was to break the Germans' military codes. Their achievements are as famous now as any exploit of the war and yet the work carried on there was so secret that it was not officially acknowledged until the 1970s.

In the spring of 1941, the operation was well established and the Bletchley Park estate was a strange mixture of the manor house, with its mock-Tudor and Gothic styles, some cottages and a motley collection of Nissen huts. For the men of *Dunedin,* it was no more part of the war than the man in the moon.

Since the early days of the war, Bletchley Park had performed miracles in tackling the Germans' Enigma code, the seemingly impenetrable and totally secure system of transmitting messages to and from German fighting units. The Germans had been using it since the 1920s and had such confidence in its security that the thought rarely crossed their minds that it could be broken.

The Enigma machine was about the same size as a typewriter and looked like one. It had a typewriter keyboard, but when a key was tapped a letter would light up on a different letter board. A complicated system of electrical currents and rotors that moved every time a letter was pressed ensured that no letter was ciphered into the same letter twice. Thus, in the same message, A could be reproduced as C the first time, X the second,

W the third and so on. The number of possible permutations for a single message was enormous – some 159 million million million different possibilities. The person sending the message would type in the wording in plain language, take down the resultant letters that lit up on the letter board, then send these by Morse code to the recipients in the U-boats. The radio operators in the U-boats would take down the Morse code message and then tap them into their Enigma machine to get the plain-language message.

The Enigma system worked only if the sending and receiving machines were calibrated in exactly the same way. The daily settings for the machines were made in advance on a monthly basis and were laid down in documents carried in the U-boats. For the U-boats in the north and central Atlantic, these were the so-called Home Waters keys.

For the men and women of Bletchley Park there were – in very broad terms – two ways to break the code. First, through cryptanalysis, a painstaking examination of all the intercepted messages in a search for patterns. This involved extraordinary effort on the part of the brilliant minds that were brought to Bletchley Park and a number of imaginative methods were developed to do this. Cryptanalysis alone, however, could only go so far in breaking the codes, so a second means was needed to help unlock Enigma – capture of Enigma material itself from enemy vessels.

Success in combating the Germans' naval Enigma through cryptanalysis in March, April and May 1941 was impressive but also patchy. The decrypts were too few and too late. Within the Admiralty, the Operational Intelligence Centre (OIC) was responsible for assessing all the available intelligence, no matter its source, ranging from direction finding of signals to reports of agents on the ground, sightings by photo reconnaissance aircraft and whatever Bletchley Park could provide. On this basis the OIC would send intelligence material to the relevant commanders-in-chief. Sometimes it would be a straight repeat of an intercepted message, sometimes a broader piece of advice to add comments or to disguise the fact that it had originated from Enigma material. Intelligence based on cryptanalysis needed a very high security classification and became known as Ultra.

In April and May, the OIC could not rely on the virtually non-existent Enigma intelligence, but was forced to use the traditional and more familiar direction finding and chance sightings by aircraft. These were far from accurate and, in the face of mounting losses and an increase in U-boat production, the situation was nothing short of bleak. It was against this backdrop of an intelligence trickle that *Dunedin* had sailed south in April.

At Bletchley Park, the inability to provide timely intelligence was acutely felt. Something would have to be done. Harry Hinsley, the leading naval intelligence analyst there, had been reaching astounding conclusions about German naval movements purely though analysis of German signals traffic, but he realised that Bletchley Park could no longer rely on this alone. It needed new means to do its job. The only sure way of being able to read the Germans' messages was to get hold of the keys to their signals – the code books themselves, with up-to-date information on how the Germans were decoding their own messages. It needed – in Bletchley parlance – a 'pinch'. Hinsley had begun to work out that isolated and unprotected German weather ships stationed permanently in the north, around Iceland and Greenland, must have had Enigma machines and codebooks aboard. They did not use the Enigma machine when sending their weather reports, but they needed them to receive messages. Why not try to capture one of these weather ships?

Hinsley's idea was taken up and an operation was mounted against the weather ship *München* in early May. Three cruisers and four destroyers were dispatched from the Home Fleet on 5 May with Captain Haines, assistant director of the OIC in the Admiralty for radio intelligence, aboard the cruiser *Edinburgh*.

München was duly surprised on 7 May near Iceland and, despite the quick action of the Germans in throwing the Enigma machine itself overboard, Haines knew exactly what else to look for. On Saturday 10 May, he was back in Bletchley Park with the short weather cipher and the inner and outer Enigma settings for the Home Waters keys for June. It was a brilliant, decisive achievement.

While Haines had been on his way back to Bletchley, events elsewhere in the Atlantic were to give Bletchley Park an even bigger haul of Enigma material. Captain Julius Lemp, in U-110, had come across a North Atlantic convoy, also near Iceland, on 8 May. Lemp attacked the following day but the convoy was well escorted by a number of ships, including the destroyer HMS *Bulldog*, commanded by Joe Baker-Cresswell.

HMS *Bulldog*, along with HMS *Broadway* and HMS *Aubrietia*, pursued U-110 and brought it to the surface after *Aubrietia* dropped several depth charges. *Bulldog* and *Broadway*, seizing their opportunity, approached U-110 at ramming speed, but Baker-Cresswell realised at the last moment that he could capture the U-boat intact and brought *Bulldog* to a shuddering stop. *Broadway* too came to a standstill.

Broadway dropped two shallow-set depth charges and the Germans began abandoning their submarine in great haste. In their panic to get off, they had not left open the vents and the radio operator committed the cardinal sin of failing to destroy the Enigma material. In their belief that the U-boat was sinking, the Germans had, unbelievably, gifted it, and its precious intelligence material, to the Royal Navy. As its crew swam to save themselves, the U-boat bobbed about in the water. It seemed ready to sink, but in fact it stayed afloat.

Baker-Cresswell sent over a boarding party, led by Sub-Lieutenant David Balme. On entering the U-boat, they could not believe their good fortune when they found an empty, intact submarine. But this was not the biggest prize. Below decks, they found a treasure trove of intelligence material, including an Enigma machine, amazingly still plugged in and ready to operate. The Germans had done nothing to protect it.

Baker-Cresswell tried his best to tow the U-boat to Scapa Flow via Iceland, but the damage done by the depth charges was too great and before he could reach Iceland the U-boat sank stern first, its bow pointing straight up before sliding into the sea.

In Scapa, two men from Bletchley Park arrived with a single briefcase to take back the captured material. They were astonished to find two packing cases full, including code books, signal logs, pay books, the grid map of the north and central Atlantic and general correspondence. And, of course, a fully functional Enigma machine. The value of the haul was incalculable. Bletchley Park put it to good use immediately and, from the beginning of June, they would read German naval signals almost as quickly as their intended recipients and were sending translations to the OIC very rapidly.

As *Dunedin* sailed south from Gibraltar in late May, the seizure of Enigma material was about to change the lives of everyone on board. They didn't know it, of course. As far as most of them were concerned, they were simply on another patrol. But this was not all. Far to the north, in another Atlantic arena, the German battleship *Bismarck* had broken out into the Atlantic with the cruiser *Prinz Eugen*.

Bismarck and *Prinz Eugen* had left the Baltic on 19 May and sailed, via Norway, north of the British Isles to Iceland and Greenland on their way to the Atlantic. HMS *Suffolk* and HMS *Norfolk* were able to shadow her before HMS *Hood* and HMS *Prince of Wales* engaged her in the early morning of 24 May. This was to be a tragic encounter, with *Hood* sinking in minutes after being hit in her magazine by *Bismarck*. Only three of her 1,419 crew survived. In the confusion of battle, *Prinz Eugen* slipped away and made for Brest (arriving on 1 June), but *Prince of Wales* had managed to hit *Bismarck*, damaging her fuel tanks.

Bismarck sped from the scene still shadowed by HMS *Suffolk*, but by the early hours of 25 May, she had shaken off *Suffolk* and disappeared.

Dunedin had been in Gibraltar all this time and she was to play no part in the continuing pursuit of *Bismarck*. On the 25th, as *Dunedin* sailed south, the Admiralty tried desperately to find *Bismarck*. The haul from the *München* and U-110 affected the June Enigma settings, so Bletchley Park could not yet read Enigma messages in time and could offer no decrypt assistance. The best available intelligence came from D/F (direction-finding) fixes, but throughout the day, these were either incorrect or misinterpreted. At one time, the Admiralty concluded that *Bismarck* was heading back to the Iceland–Faeroes passage, when her intended destination was in fact Brest in western France.

Late on 25 May, the Admiralty concluded that *Bismarck* was heading for Brest, but they could not tell for sure. The real fear was that she had slipped free and would soon be within range of German air defences, but on the following morning a Coastal Command Catalina sighted her 690 miles west of Brest. Now the Admiralty could close in. The pursuit began again in earnest, with several Navy vessels involved, including *Ark Royal*, one of whose Swordfish aircraft crippled *Bismarck*'s propellers and steering with a torpedo. *Bismarck* now had no chance. *King George V*, *Rodney*, *Devonshire* and *Norfolk* attacked on the morning of 27 May and at 10.40 a.m. *Bismarck* sank.

With *Bismarck* sunk and *Prinz Eugen* back in port, the Navy had secured a major victory. But more was to come, and this time *Dunedin* would play her part.

As *Bismarck* came to her grief and as *Prinz Eugen* disappeared from the scene, a German supply fleet of six tankers and one supply ship was left on the high seas of the Atlantic. At Bletchley Park the captured material from the weather ships and U-110 came into its own and a flood of decrypts emerged, pouring into the OIC. June would see a bonanza of intelligence from Bletchley Park following the patchy service in May. At some points in May, the average elapsed time from interception was eleven days, severely undermining the value of the information. As May drew to a close, no intercepts were decrypted at all, but on 1 June all this changed and the OIC received translated decrypts within hours of their being intercepted. Decrypts came in thick and fast. In one eight-hour period on 16–17 June, for example, 100 decrypts landed in the OIC. For the German supply fleet, this level and speed of intelligence spelt disaster.

The tankers *Belchen*, *Esso Hamburg*, *Egerland*, *Gedania*, *Friedrich Breme* and *Lothringen* and the supply ship *Gonzenheim* would now feature in the everyday reading material supplied to the OIC by Bletchley Park. To the men of *Dunedin*, however, none of this meant a thing. The sinking of *Bismarck* had happened to the north without them and as May came to its close *Dunedin* was sailing south, unaware of the excitement in the manor house and huts at Bletchley and the part she would play in the denouement of the *Bismarck* drama.

CHAPTER 6
Capture of *Lothringen*, June 1941

When *Dunedin* neared port on the morning of 29 May, her crew looked forward to the long-awaited mail delivery and the chance of a rest ashore. As the green and lush coastline of West Africa came into view again, it soon became clear, however, that this was not Freetown. Instead, *Dunedin* was approaching Bathurst in Gambia and just to refuel. By mid-afternoon she had oiled and was ready to go – only one or two people had been ashore – and now they were off again, with no mail.

On Friday 30 May and into the following morning, *Dunedin* sailed west, away from the coast and out to the open sea. At around 9.30, south west of the Cape Verde Islands, she sighted the carrier HMS *Eagle*, its unique – and to some of the crew – unfamiliar shape standing out against the morning sky. Soon *Dunedin* had fallen in on her starboard beam and could see clearly the contours of this old but proud ship, the smooth lines of her flat flight deck disturbed by the crowded collection of masts, funnels and jagged metal amidships.

HMS *Eagle* had had a strange metamorphosis. In 1924 she had been converted from the hull of the battleship *Almirante Cochrane*, which had originally been laid down for the Chilean navy in 1913. She carried two squadrons of Fairey Swordfish biplanes, some eighteen aircraft and well over her nominal complement of 750 men. Since the start of the war, *Eagle* had served in the Mediterranean, the Far East and South America.

She was a fine-looking ship and on many a day in the coming weeks on the vast Atlantic Ocean the crew of *Dunedin* could look with great comfort and respect at her imposing profile.

And now, after weeks of boredom, perhaps something was going to happen. *Dunedin* and *Eagle* were to form Force F to patrol parts of the South Atlantic in search of enemy surface raiders and their supply ships. Specific intelligence had indicated that an enemy fast oiler would be within thirty miles of 28 degrees north, 34 degrees 40' west, some 900 miles west of the Canary Islands, from the afternoon of 2 June onwards, ready to refuel *Prinz Eugen*. *Eagle* and *Dunedin* were required to carry out an air search of the area.

Dunedin sailed north-east for about 300 miles before turning north-west for another 300 miles. Nothing was found on 2 June and on 5 June she made a rendezvous with the RFA *Bishopdale* and underwent the nerve-racking experience of refuelling at sea far into the middle of the ocean, 750 miles north-west of the Cape Verde Islands. *Eagle* went first and, as she sat tethered to *Bishopdale*, *Dunedin* patrolled in a wide circle around the two ships to watch for U-boats. At sea everyone on board was acutely aware of the need to keep a constant lookout for ships and U-boats, but the tense hours of a refuelling exercise were particularly uncomfortable.

While *Eagle* sat there like a sitting duck, anyone who ventured on to *Dunedin*'s decks looked nervously at *Eagle* and also at the surrounding water for periscopes. Refuelling usually took several hours while the ship stayed at action stations for the entire time. For some this meant being holed up in the hot and sweaty magazine for long stretches at a time, ready to help ensure that the shells got to the guns if they were needed. The cooling sea breeze could not dampen the tension surrounding the refuelling of *Eagle*. The Atlantic Ocean is a vast sea, but it becomes very small during a war when you sit there doing very little.

Eventually, *Bishopdale* completed her job and pulled away from *Eagle*, but by now it was too late for *Dunedin* to refuel, so she had to wait until the following day.

By now five of the German supply ships had either been sunk or captured elsewhere in the Atlantic. First hit was *Belchen* on 3 June, intercepted off Greenland by the cruisers *Aurora* and *Kenya*. *Belchen* had refuelled U-111 and U-557 a few days earlier and was in the process of refuelling U-93 when the British cruisers approached. Hurriedly disconnecting the fuel lines, *Belchen* scuttled.

The next day, June 4, *Gedania* was captured by the destroyer HMS *Marsdale* and further south later that evening, HMS *London* sank the *Esso Hamburg*. And this was not all that day. A third ship, the *Gonzenheim*, was forced to scuttle by aircraft from HMS *Victorious*, the battleship HMS *Nelson*, the cruiser *Neptune* and the armed merchant cruiser *Esperance Bay*. Ironically, the capture of *Gedania* was a mistake. The Admiralty had ordered her to be left alone for fear of compromising their intelligence, but HMS *Marsdale* had come across her by chance.

To complete an incredible three-day haul, the cruiser HMS *London* and the destroyer HMS *Brilliant* forced the 9,800-ton tanker *Egerland* to scuttle on 5 June, not far from where the *Esso Hamburg* had gone down the previous evening.

Dunedin seemed destined to miss all the action, but on 6 June *Eagle*'s aircraft came across a German blockade runner, *Elbe*, disguised as the Norwegian SS *Kristine Fjord*. She had been spotted sailing north at 7 a.m. by Swordfish on anti-submarine patrol thirty miles from *Eagle*. She had changed course and was attempting to flee at increased speed. This was an ideal opportunity for *Dunedin* to set off in pursuit, but by now she was oiling from RFA *Baxendale* and would not finish until noon. *Eagle*'s aircraft would have to go it alone.

Into the afternoon, *Eagle*'s Swordfish struggled to track down the *Elbe* as she continued to take evasive action. A solitary aircraft found her shortly before 3 p.m. and stayed with her until after 4 p.m. in the expectation that other Swordfish would arrive. When none did, the aircraft – piloted by Temporary Midshipman William Hughes – opened fire with machine-guns across *Elbe*'s bows. *Elbe* was finally brought to a halt when Hughes dropped two 500-pound bombs, both narrowly missing the ship. At this, *Elbe*'s captain decided that enough was enough and began scuttling the ship.

Hughes hung on until the last possible moment, shadowing *Elbe* and reporting her position. Not long after he had to pull out, a force of five Swordfish from *Eagle* arrived to finish the job. When the captain of *Elbe* ignored an order to steer south, the Swordfish dropped four more bombs, one making a direct hit in No. 3 hold. Already on fire from Hughes's efforts, *Elbe* was now engulfed in flame and listed to starboard. When the last aircraft left the ship at 6.25 p.m., she had righted herself but was settling by the stern and burning fiercely.

Eagle's aircraft reported seeing about eighty men escaping into boats as *Elbe* sank. *Dunedin* prepared herself to take the survivors on board and headed for the area where *Elbe* had gone down. *Eagle* passed through some wreckage but neither she nor *Dunedin* could find any trace of the lifeboats and the search was called off. *Dunedin* headed back to Freetown, but by Monday 9 June she had been ordered to stay at sea.

On the hot tropical seas the patrolling continued unabated in search of the remaining supply ships. In the intense heat of the sun, the open decks were always the most welcome part of the ship. Below decks the heat was stifling. With a wartime complement of nearly 500, the ship was a heaving mass of hot, sweaty, often irritable sailors and Marines, each trying to reserve his own space.

At night the most comfortable place to sleep was on deck, where there was the chance of a breeze. Very few people could stand sleeping below decks. Many slung their hammocks between gun supports on deck, or anywhere that would bring the welcome relief of a breeze. When not on duty, most people wore barely anything at all – underpants, soft shoes and a handkerchief around the neck. Soon the handkerchief would be soaked with sweat and would need to be dried out for later use.

On June 12 yet another of the supply ships, *Friedrich Breme*, was sunk by HMS *Sheffield* over 1,700 miles to *Dunedin*'s north. Of the original seven supply vessels, six had now been captured or sunk. *Dunedin* had reaped none of this harvest and even when the *Elbe* bonus had shown up, she had been stuck with the oiler.

With only one remaining supply ship, the Germans had to rethink their strategy. After the loss of *Bismarck* and the return to France of *Prinz Eugen*, the supply fleet had been redeployed to focus on keeping the U-boats at sea. With so many supply ships down, the main problem now for the Germans was how to replenish their U-boats in the south Atlantic. Many hundreds of miles from the French ports and running out of fuel, supplies and torpedoes, *Lothringen* was now their only source. But she was hundreds of miles to the north. The Germans had no choice but to send *Lothringen* south to meet four U-boats, U-103, U-107, U-69 and UA. Without fuel and supplies, they would have to be recalled.

Detailed instructions were issued to *Lothringen* on the evening of 12 June. She was to head south 'with all speed' to a point 10 degrees north, 35 degrees west-south-west of the Cape Verde Islands. There she would reprovision the southern U-boats. The loss of all the other supply ships had made the Germans very nervous and – no doubt – very suspicious about how the Royal Navy had been so successful. The instructions to *Lothringen* therefore included a special recommendation 'to keep a constant and sharp lookout'.

These instructions were decrypted and translated at Bletchley Park and were with the OIC by 1 a.m. on 13 June, just four hours after they had been intercepted by one of the listening stations in England. By daybreak on the 13th, *Dunedin* and *Eagle* had met up with RFA *Bishopdale* again for more oiling. This went on all day.

Eagle kept her Swordfish in the air for most of the day but nothing was found. Captain Lovatt could not know for sure where *Lothringen* would be, but if the intelligence was correct she would be steaming south somewhere to *Dunedin*'s west. Back in the OIC nothing related to *Lothringen* appeared after 4.30 that morning, when a decrypt had confirmed a U-boat rendezvous with *Lothringen* on the 17th.

Dunedin completed oiling late on 13 June and rejoined *Eagle*, now steaming south. It had been a long and frustrating day, both in the South Atlantic and for the OIC. *Dunedin* and *Eagle* had until the 17th to catch *Lothringen*, but by then she would be a honey-pot for U-boats.

At 1.20 a.m. on the 14th, the OIC received another decrypt from Bletchley Park confirming that U-69 and UA would be at the rendezvous on 18 June as planned. Despite the silence of the 13th, nothing had changed. But what about the rendezvous on the 17th? Was that still on? And then, forty-five minutes later, another decrypt arrived. U-103 and U-107 were to be in position with *Lothringen* on the 17th, UA and U-69 on the 18th. *Lothringen* was to provide supplies and eight torpedoes for each boat.

Could *Dunedin* and *Eagle* find *Lothringen* in time?

On Saturday the 14th, the two ships headed south into the ever-rising temperatures, *Eagle*'s aircraft scouring the sea as they went. But still there was no sign of the tanker. For Captain Lovatt and Captain Rushbrooke in *Eagle*, this must have been a trying and frustrating time. Either the Admiralty had got it wrong or *Lothringen* had gone somewhere else.

But the Admiralty had not got it wrong. In the OIC there was no doubt that *Lothringen* was on course to keep her appointment. At 4.16 that afternoon, Bletchley Park produced a decrypt of a message from U-boat Command to U-103 and U-107. It confirmed yet again that *Lothringen* would refuel the U-boats and gave a detailed description of her. And again it warned of possible enemy interest. 'Surprises are to be expected,' it said.

Lest there was any doubt remaining, yet another decrypt arrived at 9.58 p.m., this time of a message to *Lothringen* making clear that U-103 and U-107 would reach her on the 17th and U-69 and UA on the 18th.

Just before 1 p.m. on Sunday the 15th, as *Dunedin* and *Eagle* carried on their sweeps of the ocean, aircraft 5B, one of *Eagle*'s Swordfish, was closing in on a tanker at 18 degrees 37' north, 37 degrees 29' west, 1,800 miles north-west of Freetown. On board were pilot William Hughes, the observer, Philip Denington, and Norman Willis, air gunner, the same crew that had found *Elbe* nine days earlier. The aircraft signalled the tanker to stop and when no response came, Willis was given the order to open fire ahead of the ship. This fire was returned from the tanker and Hughes's aircraft was hit in the fuselage and main planes, fortunately causing no real damage.

The Swordfish then turned again towards the tanker and dive-bombed with two 250-pound bombs, scoring two direct hits and following up with machine-gun fire.

Within minutes the ship began to list and to circle, leaving a thick patch of oil on the surface of the sea, but Hughes could not stick around for much longer without running out of fuel. He signalled *Eagle* before departing, telling her what had happened and reporting the tanker's position.

In *Dunedin*, at 1.47 p.m., Captain Lovatt received orders from *Eagle* to pursue the tanker. He immediately changed course to 325 degrees and set off at maximum speed – only twenty-four knots now that one of the boilers was out of action. Leaving *Eagle* behind, those on board who did not know what *Dunedin* was involved in were now caught up in the excitement of the day. It was obvious that something was happening at last.

Meanwhile, another of *Eagle*'s aircraft, 5K – piloted by Charles Camidge - was racing to take over from Hughes. Arriving twenty minutes after Hughes had left, Camidge, with his Gunner Frank Dean and Observer William Lett, could see the tanker steaming erratically, damaged and leaking oil. Two white flags flew at the foremast and a white sheet was being waved from the bridge. At the same time some of the tanker's crew were trying to lower a motorboat, but Camidge saw what was happening and opened fire on it, causing the boat to drop into the sea with one man still in it.

Camidge did not want to allow anyone off the ship and so he then turned his fire on two other boats slung outboard on either side of the poop deck. From that moment on, no one tried to get off the ship.

Camidge still did not know the nationality of the ship and signalled repeatedly until he got an answer by lamp that she was German. Three other Swordfish from *Eagle* joined him around 3 p.m. and together they circled the stricken tanker for another hour until Camidge had to leave them to it and return to *Eagle*.

At 4.20 p.m., on his way back to *Eagle*, Camidge came upon *Dunedin* and reported on the situation. He told Captain Lovatt that the ship was thirty miles away, bearing 336 degrees and that the crew had not abandoned ship.

As the afternoon wore on, the activity on the ship and the general scurrying about told the crew that *Dunedin* was close to action. Anyone not busy was on deck searching the horizon. And then, around 5 p.m., a ship appeared in the distance.

Men began calling to each other: 'What is it?' 'Is it a German?' 'Can you see it?' 'Is it a warship?'

Captain Lovatt must have been very relieved to find the ship still afloat, having – unusually – not been scuttled by her crew. But he also knew that he could have been lured into a horrible trap. Why hadn't she been scuttled? Was *Dunedin* merely prey for a nearby U-boat? He made sure that the priority task of the circling Swordfish was to watch for U-boats.

Down on deck, the crew could see the tanker much more clearly as *Dunedin* approached. As the pipe to action stations was sounded, the captain hoisted the international signal, 'Stop. Do not lower boats. Do not use radio. Do not scuttle. If you disobey, I open fire.' The tanker was visible now in stark detail. The Germans could be seen throwing things over the side, presumably code books and other sensitive papers and machinery.

As Lovatt brought *Dunedin* in a loop astern of the tanker he dropped a depth charge, set to explode at 350 feet. A loud explosion shook the air and a huge plume of water flew up. If the tanker's crew were alarmed at this, then so were those on *Dunedin*. Depth charges meant one thing – U-boats. Either *Dunedin* was about to be attacked or Captain Lovatt was taking precautionary measures. It certainly made everyone on deck look more intently at the sea in search of periscopes. A few minutes later, Lovatt ordered a second depth charge to be dropped on the starboard side of the tanker. Then he swung *Dunedin* round in front of the tanker, slowing her speed as she went, and brought her to a stop on the tanker's port bow, not more than 200 yards away.

The tanker was lying stopped with a marked list to port, surrounded by a large patch of oil. The motorboat which Camidge had successfully prevented from getting away was now secured alongside, its sole occupant presumably back on board. The crew of the tanker knew the game was over as they began to form up on deck, some of them in German naval uniform.

Lieutenant-Commander Sowdon led the boarding party at around 6 p.m. As he approached the ship, he could not know what awaited him and his men. What looked like a routine boarding of a stricken ship could easily turn nasty. The German naval uniforms he had seen from *Dunedin* meant that there was a military presence on board. In the calm sea the cutter quickly reached its target, the oarsmen efficiently slicing through the water.

The tanker now loomed large in their view and men's faces could be seen peering down at them. A ladder had been lowered over the side. Sowdon thought immediately that the Germans had decided to play it sensibly, that there would be no fighting. He brought the cutter alongside and secured her just aft of the ship's motorboat. White flags flew at the foremast.

As Sowdon climbed on board, he found the crew gathered in two groups, one near the sea gangway and one on the fore and aft bridge. Nobody moved except one German sailor to give him a helping hand. While ERA Hicks and a marine sentry went aft to the engine room, Sowdon sent Sub-Lieutenant Hollinshead straight to the bridge. He placed guards on the bridge, in the officers' quarters, in the crew space and on the men assembled on deck. Sowdon then went himself to the bridge, where he found the captain, Max Friedrichsen, who was sixty-one years old, with a white beard and clearly in no mood for an argument.

On entering the bridge, Sowdon observed the captain briefly and told him that he had come to take his ship. Friedrichsen merely replied, 'All right. Then. She has been bombed.'

Friedrichsen and Sowdon moved off to see the holes in the tanks on both port and starboard and the rest of the damage to the ship. On the upper deck, bullets had hit two lifeboats and several men lay wounded nearby. The boats were full of gear in readiness for abandoning ship, one boat hung limply a few feet over the side.

Sowdon confirmed that the wounded men would be taken care of and looked around him at the rest of the scene. Three light AA guns, about one-pounders, each had a clip of cartridges in place with a full supply of ammunition to hand and one of them had about forty empty cases in the net. He remembered that one of the Swordfish had been hit, probably by these guns.

Meanwhile, below decks – in the presence of *Lothringen's* W/T operator – Percy Jackson, one of *Dunedin's* telegraphists, was sifting through the wreckage of a once functioning wireless office. All the machinery had been smashed and any papers that might have shed light on the ship's past or future movements had been destroyed or thrown overboard. It was a big disappointment, but Percy would not have been surprised. After all, he had been taught to do the same thing if *Dunedin* was hit. The best he could find were ciphered versions of W/T signals sent by *Lothringen* and a list of the confidential books held. The wireless operator said little except that he had destroyed all the secret papers. Percy reported that the Germans had been thorough in their actions and that he could find very few papers of any intelligence value.

Also in the boarding party was Lt-Commander Hughes, promoted since his heroics in *Hannover* more than a year earlier and once again leading an anti-scuttling operation. He had discovered from *Lothringen*'s chief officer that six scuttling charges were in position, although they were apparently quite safe. Sowdon was curious as to why the Germans had not scuttled the ship. It was not as if they had had insufficient time to do it before *Dunedin* arrived.

In *Dunedin*'s sick bay, Harold Broadway had been warned to be ready to see to German prisoners. The first 'ferry' ride brought the German doctor and four wounded men. Harold tended to them and quickly established that their wounds were not too bad, caused only by splinters from the bombing and strafing.

Throughout the rest of the evening, the *Lothringen*'s motorboat was used to ferry personnel, including German prisoners, to and from the two ships.

Around 7 p.m. shouted orders rang out to some marines to stand by to greet the motorboat in five minutes, with their rifles and fixed bayonets. Rapidly they scrambled to get their gear and were back on deck in three minutes.

By now the motorboat was on its way back, laden with about a dozen Germans in military uniform. Once they were aboard they were lined up on deck on the starboard side, while an officer questioned them, taking their names and a few personal details. The Germans shuffled about, looking confused and a touch scared.

When the officer had finished his questioning, the marines were ordered to take them down to the recreation space. Once they were settled in, guards were placed at the door. The crew could say goodbye to relaxing in there until the Germans were dropped at Freetown.

Back in *Lothringen*, Lieutenant-Commander Hughes and his team, now including Harold Lowey, the commissioned gunner, were tackling the scuttling charges and trying to bring the ship upright from its list to port. Hughes made an inspection of the oil and fresh-water tanks and concluded that the ship was not as badly damaged as the list would suggest and could be got under way fairly soon. But first he needed to bring her upright. With the aid of *Lothringen*'s chief engineer, Hughes ordered ERA Hicks to use the pumps to adjust the levels of two of the tanks and soon the ship was upright.

So far everything was going very smoothly. The Germans had effectively rolled over and given in. They had been nothing but cooperative and acquiescent, but still the danger was not over. The scuttling charges had to be disabled. Despite the captain's assurances, six live bombs had been found on the ship.

Hughes and Lowey contemplated the task ahead of them. They had gleaned from the chief engineer that six charges were spread around the ship but, as Sowdon had ascertained from the captain, none had been set to go off.

Harold Lowey moved quickly and found all six charges, two in the engine room and four more in the bilges. Working in a dark and sweaty atmosphere, he satisfied himself that none had been set to explode.

In *Dunedin*, Captain Lovatt had concluded that *Lothringen* should go unaccompanied to Bermuda, where there were docking facilities. She would also be less vulnerable to attack the nearer she got to the Caribbean.

Meanwhile, Percy Jackson returned to the wireless office without the German W/T operator to see if he had missed anything. He surveyed once again the shambles and wreckage caused by the wireless operator apparently taking a sledgehammer to all the equipment. Behind the demolished radio-gramophone he found the W/T cipher log in plain language. It had probably slipped down when the operator had put his sledgehammer to the radio. In it would be all the ship's movements, but, more importantly, it could be matched with the ciphered versions of the signals he had found earlier. This could be very useful. Percy, of course, knew nothing of Bletchley Park, nor of the weather ship 'pinches' and the Enigma haul from U-110, but his find would eventually be added to Bletchley Park's treasure trove.

In the dark of one of the bilges, Harold Lowey was having a little trouble with some of the charges. The fuses were set off by a friction device that caused a spark when pulled. On one of the charges, the device had been lashed up so that when Harold pulled it off its anchoring it lit. The fuse had a long lead time, at least seven minutes according to Lowey, but he took no chances and cut the burning fuse quickly.

Two other charges in the pumping compartment had extra devices on them that could have been clockwork fuses. Lowey could not be sure whether these were dangerous or not, or how long any fuse would take to ignite the charges. The simplest and safest thing to do was to throw them overboard, which is precisely what happened.

On deck, Sowdon was now nearly ready to get the *Lothringen* under way and to return to *Dunedin*. The prize crew was in place, the German prisoners were in *Dunedin*.

Captain Lovatt was anxious to get the job finished. *Dunedin* had been in the same position for close on three hours and the longer she stayed the more likely it was that she might be found by a U-boat. Shortly before 8 p.m., he received a message that *Eagle* had been sighted and was fast approaching *Dunedin's* position.

As she came into view, there was much mocking and jeering from the blokes on deck: 'About bloody time.' 'You're too late, we've done it all!'

But it was all in good fun. Without *Eagle's* Swordfish *Dunedin* would not have found *Lothringen* at all. The jeers turned to cheering and applause as a groundswell of self-congratulation swept through *Dunedin* at the capture of a major prize.

By 10 p.m. *Lothringen* was ready, with *Dunedin's* prize crew under the command of Lieutenant Beveridge. Of *Lothringen's* crew, four officers and nineteen ratings remained on board. Lovatt pondered his options. From the bridge he could see the imposing outline of *Eagle* silhouetted against the darkened tropical sky. He signalled to *Eagle's* Captain Rushbrooke his recommendation that *Lothringen* proceed to Bermuda, where there were docking facilities and there would be less chance of enemy attack on the way. He proposed also that *Dunedin* and *Eagle* should accompany her for the first three hours.

From *Eagle*, Rushbrooke had no hesitation in agreeing Lovatt's plan. It had been clear from the moment *Eagle* arrived on the scene that *Dunedin* had the situation well in hand.

After a few problems with hoisting *Lothringen's* motorboat back on board, the captured German prize was ready to go. Just before midnight, the three ships set off in the direction of Bermuda. Lovatt could feel rightly pleased with himself.

It took less than three hours for Beveridge, on board *Lothringen*, to report confidently that *Lothringen* could sail alone and, at around 1.30 a.m. on 16 June, *Dunedin* and *Eagle* turned and headed back towards Freetown.

As *Lothringen* and *Dunedin* sailed in opposite directions, the unseen hand of Bletchley Park continued to operate. Two more messages had been decrypted since the previous evening, both of which gave slightly amended orders to the four U-boats. The rendezvous with *Lothringen* had been altered to a point sixteen miles from the previously agreed location. Both these messages had been sent to the U-boats after *Lothringen* had been attacked and after she had herself sent two messages, the first reporting danger and the second that she was being bombed. More significantly, Bletchley Park observed that no messages had been intercepted by the evening of the 16th warning U-boats of any danger to *Lothringen* or any major change of plan.

From this, Bletchley Park concluded that *Lothringen*'s signals had not been received in Germany. As far as the U-boats were concerned, *Lothringen* would be at the rendezvous on the 17th and 18th. Unbelievably, she had been captured without anyone knowing.

Having thought this through, Bletchley Park – probably Harry Hinsley – sent a note to the OIC at 8.26 p.m. on the 16th outlining their observations and suggesting that *Lothringen* could go to the rendezvous as planned, with the prize crew, and meet the U-boats.

History does not record what the OIC thought of this and whether it was their idea in the first place or they asked Bletchley Park for their advice. But it was a daring plan that carried the prospect of ambushing four U-boats. Bletchley Park acknowledged that such an operation would risk compromising the source of the information, but they left it to the Admiralty to decide whether it was a practical proposition.

The risks would have been tremendously high and the logistics terribly complicated. Bletchley Park thought the element of surprise could be achieved because intercepted messages suggested that the U-boats had no means of recognising *Lothringen* other than by sighting. If the U-boats were not required (or allowed) to communicate by W/T or D/F signals, they would not know that *Lothringen* was manned by a prize crew.

Would it have been possible to surprise all four U-boats? Probably not, but one might have been a big enough prize. Having reaped the benefit of the capture of U-110 the previous month, it is understandable that Bletchley Park should have jumped at the chance to get another one – or even more. What part might *Dunedin* have played in such a complicated mission?

These and other questions must remain unanswered, because, as we know, despite the incredible potential of such a plan, *Lothringen* was sent on her way to Bermuda and *Dunedin* returned to Freetown.

It would be another five days before *Dunedin* arrived, another five days of heat and sweat, of zigzags and patrol, another five days with food supplies dwindling, at the end of the longest period at sea that she had ever spent. The euphoria of the capture of the *Lothringen* kept spirits up a little higher than they would otherwise have been, but even smelly, 'godforsaken' (as Harold Broadway was apt to call it), Freetown was beginning to sound good, especially as the prospect of mail loomed once more, the first since *Dunedin* had left England in April.

Twice on Tuesday 17 June the crew were reminded of the perils of their existence. Once in the morning and again later as it began to get dark, *Dunedin* passed empty life rafts. Who had been in them? Where did they come from? As they passed by, the rafts bobbed about on the ebb and flow, weightless with no one to steer them, no one to come home from the dangers of the deep, no one to be saved.

The German prisoners, of course, provided a novel topic of conversation and brought an unusual distraction. By and large they were no trouble. Much information was accumulated from them, either from casual or overheard conversations, or from examination of their documents and personal effects. By the time *Dunedin* had arrived back in Freetown, her officers had constructed a reasonable picture to report to the Admiralty.

The ship was indeed the German tanker *Lothringen*, formerly the Dutch *Papendrecht* which had been seized by the Germans when they had entered Holland in 1940. She was undoubtedly a supply ship and carried 1,000 tons of diesel oil for submarines and 11,000 tons of fuel oil for surface craft. She also carried thirty-two torpedoes, but her only armaments were her AA guns.

The crew appeared to be well fed, although some complained that they did not receive any of the special food (such as turkey and chocolate) which was being kept for U-boats and raiders.

The captain revealed that the reason the ship had not been scuttled and her guns were not demolished was that *Eagle*'s aircraft had machine-gunned the decks if anyone appeared. The chief engineer, he said, had refused to damage the engines and, in view of the fact that a tanker has no undercover communication fore and aft, he was the only one who could do anything. The naval ratings, however, appeared angry that the captain had not scuttled the ship. Some of them thought that he had panicked when the bombing and machine-gunning were happening and that he was worried he and the crew would be left to their fate if he scuttled the ship.

It seems that the naval crew members had tried to persuade him to fire the scuttling charges when *Dunedin* was sighted, but he had refused to do so, saying that they had something under their feet and it would be better to keep it there than take any risks. The chief engineer, Brammann, when asked why he had not damaged the engines, said that if he had done so, he would have been made to work night and day to repair them.

So, as *Dunedin* steamed towards the *Lothringen*, a furious row had been taking place between the naval ratings and the captain. Had the captain lost, *Dunedin* would have arrived on the scene only to find a sinking prize or no prize at all. Ultimately, the merchant crew did not have their heart in their job and were content to be captured, but, more significantly, the naval crew – although opposing the captain's intentions – placed naval discipline before initiative and ultimately obeyed his orders.

It was difficult to gain real information about the movements and intentions of the tanker, since all members of the crew were very cautious not to reveal anything about U-boats or raiders and were very much on their guard. It seemed quite clear, however, that the tanker had not supplied any ships, given that it still had all its fuel and oil on board. The prisoners' interrogators did find out, however, from Brammann and a couple of others that she was en route to a rendezvous with a U-boat two days after *Dunedin* had captured her – something Bletchley Park had known all along.

The naval party consisted of only a few experienced submarine ratings (one or two had Iron Crosses), the remainder being young and just out of training. They were probably not a complete substitute submarine crew, but they could have been part of a pool of spare submariners if necessary.

All the merchant navy and the older naval ratings appeared to be thankful to be out of the war and had no illusions as to the risks they were taking, the general opinion being that they had about a one in ten chance of returning safely. The younger naval ratings, however, appeared to believe they could sweep the seas of British ships with the maximum of glory and a minimum of danger. They were surprised to see British aircraft, as they had been told before leaving that Britain no longer had any aircraft carriers in service and that its most modern cruisers were no longer of any use, although they knew about the loss of the *Bismarck* less than a month earlier.

A little was found out too about their attitudes to the war and how they thought it was progressing. The general opinion of problems caused by British bombing raids was that damage at Brest and Hanover was particularly bad, and that Hamburg had been hit very hard in its dock area. The town itself did not appear to have been suffered to any extent.

They were somewhat bewildered at the Rudolf Hess affair, but none of them believed he was either mad or a traitor. Most of them tried to get out of their dilemma by suggesting that he was an idealist who wanted to stop the war. The captain did not think that Hess really knew any inner secrets but suggested he was simply seeking publicity.

As for the Italians, the Germans had a very low opinion of them and felt generally let down by them and by Mussolini in particular. The French would, they said, end up fighting against Britain.

For Captain Friedrichsen, this was to be his last trip. At sixty-one he had already had enough and he appeared content not to have to fight any longer. As a freemason he could not join the Nazi Party. He even had

British connections, having worked for several years with the Eagle Oil Company in Hampshire, and he had a sister-in-law living in London.

Overall, the Germans were a mixed bunch, ranging from the congenial and resigned Friedrichsen to Karl Becker, an ardent Nazi, unpopular with most of the others, who spoke no English but was clearly instrumental in ensuring that the crew said nothing about U-boats. He was an experienced U-boat wireless operator with an Iron Cross and a badge denoting that he had served in a U-boat which had been attacked with depth charges.

Dunedin arrived at Freetown on the afternoon of Friday 20 June in an appalling rainstorm and anchored in a bustling harbour full of merchant ships. As ever, it was a mixture of sheer beauty and unbridled stench. Approaching from the Atlantic, the deep green countryside behind the town and beyond it a huge mountain once more hove into view. After days and sometimes weeks at sea, the slow slide into the harbour provided welcome respite from the tension of mid-Atlantic patrols. On this occasion *Dunedin* held the prize of the German prisoners – who were taken to HMS *Shropshire* for passage to England – to keep the crew and her officers on something of a high.

Bletchley Park had been right to conclude that Germany knew nothing about the loss of the *Lothringen,* because each of the U-boats arrived at the rendezvous. U-103 and U-107 reported on the 21st and 22nd respectively that they were returning to Lorient. On the 22nd, since she had not met the U-boats, *Lothringen* was ordered to a new position.

After the loss of *Egerland* and *Gedania*, *Lothringen*'s disappearance was the straw that broke the camel's back for the four U-boats and each would be forced to return to France. The nearest tanker to these 'southern boats' was the *Corrientes*, moored in the Spanish Canaries, hundreds of miles to the north.

U-107, captained by Dönitz's son-in-law Günther Hessler, was back in France by 2 July, and he managed to sink two merchant ships on the way.

UA remained in the Freetown area for a while, but it would not be long before she was back in France for a major refit. She sank no ships at all in her seventy-six days at sea.

Jost Metzler, in U-69, also headed for home, and had the most eventful voyage of the four. Very low on fuel, he doubted whether he could make it to the *Corrientes* and limped along on one diesel. By chance he came across a northbound convoy on 26 June and, by night, attacked with his last four torpedoes, sinking two British freighters. Having reported the convoy's position and been chased by British escort vessels, Metzler carried on towards France. The U-boat made it to the *Corrientes* 'with her last drops of fuel' and then Metzler took her on to France, incredibly attacking and sinking a British freighter using only his deck guns on the way. He arrived in France on 8 July.

Two days later, U-103, commanded by Viktor Schütze, arrived back, having also refuelled from *Corrientes* on the way.

Without doubt, the mopping up of the German supply fleet was a major success for the Royal Navy. The *Lothringen* capture alone deprived the U-boats of thirty-two torpedoes and a vital fuel lifeline, causing four boats to return to France prematurely. UA was due a refit anyway and had enough fuel to stay in African waters a little longer, but she was the least successful of all the U-boats operating in African waters between March and June. The other three, despite some successes on their homeward voyages, were forced back early. Nevertheless, excluding UA, the U-boats that patrolled the South Atlantic at this time chalked up some of the best results of the war, causing immense damage to shipping, sinking seventy-two ships. With their fuel and provisions intact, who knows what further successes they might have had.

For the personnel of *Dunedin* and *Eagle*, the *Lothringen* success brought well-deserved recognition. Captain Lovatt was awarded the OBE. Lieutenant-Commander Sowdon and telegraphist Percy Jackson from *Dunedin* were mentioned in dispatches, as were Sub-Lieutenant Camidge and Temporary Sub-Lieutenant Denington from *Eagle*.

For the Admiralty and Bletchley Park, the story was not over. Yes, it had been a tremendous success, but had it been too successful? Would the Germans now realise that Enigma had been broken? The loss of the supply fleet, together with the earlier loss of the *Bismarck,* certainly gave them cause to question whether their codes had been compromised. But even after an extensive internal inquiry, their supreme confidence in their own system convinced them that Enigma was safe.

The Admiralty and Bletchley Park were not to know this for sure for some time, when it became apparent that the Germans had not made significant changes. Nevertheless, they remained nervous for some weeks, which probably explains why Bletchley Park's recommendation to use *Lothringen* as bait was not put into practice.

Such thoughts were far from the minds of the men of *Dunedin.* Arrival in port meant only one thing to most of them – mail. With none since *Dunedin* had sailed from England, the appearance of land on the horizon brought the prospect of news from home tantalisingly close. And yet, so often had the promise not been fulfilled, many on board were ready for another disappointment. This time, however, there was to be no let down. Fifty-one bags of mail were waiting.

Dunedin stayed in Freetown a week, enduring rainstorms seemingly every night and preparing herself for her next patrol.

CHAPTER 7
Atlantic Patrols, Summer and Autumn 1941

Two days out of Freetown, Harold Broadway was confronted with his biggest medical challenge since leaving Bermuda. A young marine had contracted appendicitis and needed an urgent operation. In his small and cramped sickbay, Harold had to conduct an operation he had never done before. He was a GP, not a surgeon.

His Sick Bay Assistant (SBA) had never conducted an operation either and knew nothing about anaesthetics. What's more, the ship was steaming at top speed and consequently vibrating very badly. Conditions could not have been worse. Nevertheless, Harold set about his task and even asked whether the captain could keep the ship steady for a while. History does not record Captain Lovatt's reaction, but Harold was somehow able to hold the knife steady. He also had to instruct his SBA how to administer ether from a bottle to anaesthetise the patient.

In what must have been very hot and humid conditions, Harold and his SBA did their best to deal with the patient, but the SBA was a little squeamish and fainted at the sight of blood, dropping and smashing the ether bottle on the floor. Harold struggled through to complete the operation and was barely in time before the escaped ether began to take its effect as he stood, scalpel in hand, trying to stay awake.

Somehow, with the SBA on the floor in a pile of broken glass and the doctor about to fall asleep, the marine survived and made a good recovery, albeit with a bigger scar than he might have expected.

For the most part, Harold's work was routine and did not involve such drama, but he was called upon to do a delicate eye operation and to treat people for the usual array of diseases, including malaria. Malaria was commonplace and treatable if caught early enough, but Harold was saddened to lose one patient with pernicious malaria in early July. He was a young signalman, Kenneth Cram, just eighteen years old, who had had the disease for only three or four days. It came as a great shock to Harold to lose him and the signalman was buried at sea off St Helena in early July. The burial party watched in sadness as the body slipped quietly off the board and swished quickly into the sea.

In September, Harold was called upon to tackle a large but drunk rating. The story is best told in his own words from a letter he wrote on 22 September while sitting in a cool breeze on the quarterdeck and watching the sunset:

> The most exciting thing as far as I'm concerned happened last night. One of our ratings, having, after three months teetotalling, been ashore and drunk Italian Vermouth so-called, came back magnificently fighting drunk and incapable. Later he was bellowing like a bull and appeared to be in great pain and I found he had retention of urine with a bladder up under his chin. So I decided to pass a catheter. He is an enormously big and powerful Irishman called Donohue. Two volunteers sat on each limb and one man on his chest (five in all) whilst I got on with the job. He reared and bit and fought and although he called frequently upon the Almighty and the blessed Virgin and half the saints in heaven, his language could by no stretch of the imagination be regarded as pious. In essays of blasphemy the R-Cs have a distinct advantage over us heretics. But all the invocations of the saints failed to deter me from what I considered to be my duty. When I finished most of the lower deck was gathered in an awestruck way outside the sick bay, no doubt wondering what cold-blooded sadistic orgy of butchery I had been up to.

Like any ship's doctor, Harold was well known. Most of the crew would have cause at one time or another to see him, if only to get a pill for a headache. And his talks on what not to do with the local girls were legendary. Of course, imitation is often the best form of flattery and he was thus pleased one night in early August when the ship's company gave a concert over the ship's radio. It was announced as 'Monday Night at Seven on Wednesday Night at Five: the programme sponsored by the proprietors of prescription No. 9, the safe and gentle laxative' and included a skit on 'Dr Broadrib'. Harold recorded that he found it 'very enjoyable'.

After the *Lothringen* adventure, *Dunedin* spent most of her time patrolling the South Atlantic and going in and out of Freetown, sometimes with *Eagle*, sometimes alone and sometimes on convoy duty. Boredom and the heat remained the main problems, despite the crew's duties and the need to keep a constant watch. It was always on the minds of the men that something might be lurking out there, watching, waiting to strike.

Midshipman Thomas Handley found a mixture of routine and excitement and remembers well the long weeks in the heat of the tropics. He was one of six midshipmen and one sub-lieutenant who shared the gunroom, which had a floor space of some sixteen feet square. It had two leather semi-easy chairs and a round dining table with six chairs and usually they could all dine together. There was no air conditioning to relieve the unbearable heat except for the ammunition magazines. There were punkah louvres but the fan motors became hot and served merely to increase the temperature of the air coming in. The gunroom had no radio, but weekly newspapers came on board with the mail when the ship was in harbour. The midshipmen did have music, but the variety left a little to be desired, with only about a dozen records, including a couple of Vera Lynns, to play on an electric gramophone. Repetition was the name of the game and sooner or later they became unbearable. In any case, the extreme heat twisted and distorted the records and they were soon unplayable.

With a night watch and dawn action stations, seldom did Tommy and his colleagues have a full night's sleep in their hammocks outside the gunroom. It was no wonder that he got into the habit, like everyone else, of taking a rest in the afternoons, a routine he found hard to stop. He recalls now that morale was rarely high in these months, with little shore leave and nowhere pleasant to visit. The only thing that kept people going was the knowledge that there was a war on and plenty of others were worse off.

On the last day of June and the first day of July, *Dunedin* had two successes, both against Vichy French ships. Early on the morning of Monday 30 June, *Dunedin* identified and boarded the SS *Ville de Tamatave*, which had twenty passengers and fifty crew and was bound for Dakar from Madagascar. Since she was running short of coal, she was taken to Freetown, arriving on 4 July.

The next day, *Dunedin* spotted another suspicious vessel and fired a blank warning round. *D'Entrecasteaux*, en route to France, stopped and Captain Lovatt sent out a boarding party for the second time in two days, this time with Lieutenant-Commander Watson in charge. With him were Surgeon-Lieutenant Barrett, Sub-Lieutenant Joliffe, Midshipman Keith Mantell and Sergeant Allen, RM.

Captain Lovatt signaled:

Vichy French ship *D'Entrecasteaux* from Indo China to Castille intercepted in 010 deg 25 S. 017 deg 24' W. Crew 50, passengers 8, general cargo. W/T transmission attempted was swamped. No attempt at scuttling. Guard and navigating party placed on board. Ship has barely sufficient coal to reach Simonstown. Propose sending her direct there unescorted with instructions call for coal Walvis Bay if essential. Her estimated speed 8 knots. Am remaining in company pending your concurrence.

Permission was granted and they set sail for Walvis Bay, some 1,900 miles away. *Dunedin* escorted her through the night but parted company around midday on the 2nd.

The captain of *d'Entrecasteaux* was far from happy that his ship had been taken over. He had served at Verdun in the French army during the First World War and he was reluctant to help work the ship, claiming that the Germans would not confiscate his cargo once he landed it in France and that it would go to the French people to help prevent them from starving. Ultimately, he had no choice other than to help the boarding crew and, reluctantly, he did as he was told. *D'Entrecasteaux* passed St Helena on her way south to Walvis Bay, where she restocked with coal. From there she moved on to Cape Town where she was told that there were too many ships so she would have to proceed to East London.

She reached East London, despite more trouble from the captain, on 21 July. Here the boarding party had completed its mission and began the long journey back to Freetown, taking the train to Cape Town, where they joined *HMS Birmingham* for the last leg to Freetown.

In *Dunedin*, the ship's company could feel very pleased with themselves. Two ships intercepted and captured on consecutive days was a good tally. Harold Broadway sat on the quarterdeck on Saturday 5 July to write home. The weather now was less oppressive and almost pleasant: not too hot, but warm enough for the men to wear only shorts and shirts without feeling the cold. The sea was calm, but with a tremendous swell which gave the ship a slow, soothing roll. The sea had never appeared so blue and the nights never more lovely in the moonlight.

Eager to tell Mary what had been happening in the past few days, Harold was constrained by his own duties as censor and all he could say was that 'this has been a very interesting trip so far and very successful'.

No official shore leave was allowed for *Dunedin*'s stops at St Helena in July and August, which was a pity because those who managed to get ashore on official duties very much enjoyed it. It was very beautiful and much cleaner than Freetown. Harold was looking forward to it:

Just a line to let you know how I am. Apart from the heat below decks, with the cabin like an oven with the ports closed and not much ventilation, I'm thoroughly enjoying it. I haven't been or felt seasick again after that first day and we've been at sea continuously for quite a time now. We've travelled some thousands of miles. Our next port of call most people seem to think is rather a charming spot. I'm afraid I can't let you know where it is. There is a keen yachtsman on board, Sub-Lieut RNVR and I hope to get in some sailing with him. I play chess in the evenings and sometimes deck-quoits in the late afternoon with the engineer-Lieut, who comes from Bebington, but is now living in Colwyn Bay.

Apart from my medical duties, which are not onerous, I am also censor. I'm afraid you're quite right in what you have often said to me. You must be very disappointed in my letters. I just don't let myself go like I might.

Food is good, appetite is healthy, exercise is insufficient, so I am getting fat, unless sweat thins one. I've just come down from lying on the quarter deck sun-bathing.

I believe the mails from our next port of call are atrocious so you may see me before you get this letter.

When *Dunedin* arrived at St Helena, Harold found an excuse to go ashore and stretched his time on the island as much as he dared, pronouncing himself 'enchanted, both with the place and the climate'.

It was mainly a chance, however, to replenish the ship's provisions. The crew took on cabbages, beetroot, onions, bananas, lettuces, tinned food, fresh milk and – for the first time in a month – potatoes. Native women were allowed on board with their trays and baskets and souvenirs. One St Helena woman caused much mirth by proudly boasting that she had royal blood and that her father was a Royal Marine.

Dunedin left St Helena on Thursday 10 July after a short stay of only a couple of days and for the next ten days life resumed its normal monotony. The whole crew seemed to sense that it would be months before they were at home again. In the middle of the great expanse of the ocean, *Dunedin* sighted no ships and had no alerts, her only company a pair of huge albatrosses following the ship and performing a complicated display of aerial gymnastics. The sea rolled in massive waves and washed with spectacular power over the decks.

On the 20th, *Dunedin* had rejoined *Eagle* and the next day they practised a simultaneous throw-off shoot, with *Dunedin* as the 'target'. For the purposes of practice, the gun's direction was altered so that even though the gunner aimed through the sight in the normal way, the shell would fall to one side of the target. In this case, *Dunedin* would appear in the sights, but the shell would miss – at least that was the theory. Captain Lovatt waited on the bridge for the exercise to begin. He stood, binoculars to his eyes, as *Eagle*'s gun flashed in the distance.

Moments later, to his horror and intense annoyance, the splash of the shell occurred not ahead of *Dunedin* but barely a few yards away, dead amidships. Just a little further and huge damage could have been done to her, even by a blank shell. The Captain was not best pleased.

A minor technical hitch had prevented *Eagle* from firing correctly – or rather a protective cover on the training dial of the gun had become stuck and the gun had been fired before this had been shifted. Hence the shell had been fired very accurately (but fortunately not far enough). Not surprisingly, the throw-off shoot was brought to a sudden and embarrassing end.

The day's excitement did not end there. *Eagle*'s Swordfish were up later in the day and reported a mysterious vessel which they had challenged. The vessel had replied with the right codes, but when *Dunedin* came across her, around midnight, the captain established that she was another Vichy vessel – *Dunedin*'s third in three weeks. *Ville de Rouen* was en route to the South of France from Madagascar with fifty-two crew, thirty-two passengers and a cargo of sugar and beans. Although her captain made no attempt to scuttle, he would not succumb willingly, so Captain Lovatt fired a blank at her shortly after midnight, before sending across the cutter with a boarding party.

After the long days at sea, the boarding party was about to get a lucky break. Tommy Handley had watched his comrades board the two previous Vichy ships and now he would get his turn. The boarding party consisted of an RN lieutenant, a sub-lieutenant RNR, a sub-lieutenant (E) RNVR and around thirty-two ratings.

Once *Ville de Rouen* had been secured, it was decided to take her to Cape Town. The prize crew had some difficulty in persuading the French stokers to shovel their coal to keep the ship going, but with *Dunedin*'s guns pointed in her direction and the exhortations of other members of the crew, *Ville de Rouen* eventually succumbed and set sail for Cape Town.

For the prize crew, this was manna from heaven – relief from the general boredom of *Dunedin*'s monotonous existence and the chance to go somewhere other than Freetown. For Tommy Handley, life suddenly became very good. He had a cabin to himself and even a bunk. During the next two months, while *Dunedin* continued her regular patrols, Tommy and his shipmates spent time in Cape Town, East London and Simonstown with nothing much to do except enjoy the local hospitality. Or so they thought. On their return voyage to Freetown on the carrier *Albatross* they were again called upon to form up into a prize crew. Shortly after leaving

Simonstown, *Albatross* received a signal to proceed to Lobito on the Portuguese west African coast where a Vichy French merchantman, *Gascon*, was still in harbour. With Lobito in neutral territory, *Albatross* had to stay at sea and wait for *Gascon* to emerge, which she did after a couple of days. *Albatross* intercepted her and *Dunedin's* prize crew took her over, taking her to Lagos and then to Freetown, where the crew finally met up again with *Dunedin*. They were much envied after their long and eventful absence.

For the most part, the usual life of the ship continued, with no dramatic excitements. And for most of the crew, the prospect of leave, a return to England and the likelihood of mail continued to be major preoccupations. Leslie Russell had persevered in keeping busy and even tried to keep up some studying, but the days of July, August and September brought little relief. He noted in his letter to Jean of 11 July:

> We all feel that it will be months yet before we come home. We have reached the stage of despair when to remark that we will have leave at Christmas is a rather weak joke.

Later, on 21 July, things had not improved:

> I have been following the same routine, like everyone else, day after day. Doing some work, playing solo whist, rummy, chess or reading and writing of course.
>
> Often I want to write about the good old days but I just long for their return and it leads to disappointments knowing that these things are just not going to happen for a long time. The two things I live for these days are leave and mail. I think of leave in almost the same way as the end of the war – some unbelievably happy event in the distant future that I hope we'll both be lucky enough to witness.

Dunedin was now part of Force Z with *Eagle* and *Alcantara*, patrolling as far south as St Helena and on convoy duty. By 10 August she had shifted her patrols further to the north and was back in Freetown, where she stayed for nineteen days, during which time *Dunedin* was inspected by an admiral – 'These Admirals are becoming a bit of a nuisance,' wrote Leslie on 24 August.

By now Freetown held no novelty value for any of the ship's company, even Harold Broadway, who wrote:

> This place is the Devil's private little Hell on earth, and I've never before seen such continuous unceasing rain, nor realised it could be so hot out of hell. I am reasonably happy, chiefly because I am able to take a fairly cynical view of life and anyway I find it quite hard to be unhappy for long at a time and there are a good lot of fellows on board; but in the last 3 months I have spent a total of 8 hours ashore. I haven't seen a white woman since April and I'm not having a gay and giddy time gadding about the world. No virtue in this, however, as I would if I could.

In a separate letter in August, he added:

> This is a pretty poor sort of spot from the point of view of the matelots – nothing whatever to do ashore except get drunk at damnable expense, or fornicate at immense risk and with but little pleasure. So most of them don't bother and stay on board.
>
> Our expert fisherman, the master-at-arms, gave us a nice little diversion yesterday afternoon however, when he hooked an eleven foot shark and what is more, with the aid of much volunteer help and innumerable ropes, blocks and shackles, succeeded in hauling it in-board.
>
> There are so many buzzes as to what our next move is that it's fairly safe to surmise that they're all wrong. I think I'm probably safe in saying that I'll be unlucky again.

September brought a lengthy period at sea but with little action – a lifeboat here, an oil drum there and the occasional unidentified ship in the distance – and then, on 6 September a U-boat was sighted about ten miles away while *Dunedin* was with the oiler *Rapidol*. Captain Lovatt ordered *Rapidol* to turn away from the U-boat at full speed. The U-boat submerged and *Dunedin* did not see it again.

Two days earlier a suspicious convoy had been reported heading for Grand Canary, but nobody could say whether it was an Allied convoy, a French convoy or an enemy force on its way to capture the Canaries. *Dunedin* was therefore dispatched to search for it. By the 8th she had found nothing, having searched south of the Canary Islands and around

Santa Cruz, Tenerife and Las Palmas. The next day she was assisted by Sunderland aircraft based in Bathurst, but still nothing was found.

Finally, on the 10th, *Dunedin* went to action stations when a submarine was sighted on the surface. Captain Lovatt's mid-morning signal tells the story:

> Nothing seen of the convoy but when in position 235 deg Cape Verde 24 miles at 0900Z/10 observed smoke from one possibly more ships close under land to southward Dakar and 2 aircraft patrolling in vicinity. Simultaneously French type of submarine on surface closed *Dunedin* from similar bearing diving when 4 miles distant. At 0938Z sighted French cruiser *Montcalm* class flying flag of SO 4th Squadron, French light forces, who informed me French submarines were present. Another large unidentified warship closer in shore and many general reconnaissance aircraft also sighted.

It had been an uneasy stand-off with *Dunedin*'s guns on stand-by fore and aft in the face of much stronger firepower. Fortunately, all passed off peacefully and *Dunedin* went on to Bathurst, where she refuelled once more. In a sultry and sticky atmosphere it was very difficult to sleep or keep comfortable.

Being at sea for so long gave the ship's company plenty of time to think and to contemplate life. Harold did just this in his letter of 14 September:

> Here I am with nothing to write about and nothing to reply to, trying to write you my usual Sunday letter, though what the hell I can find to put in it goodness knows. That I hope you are well, that I love you, that I hope you and the children are having a nice time and that I wish I were with you there again and that this war were over; you already know and must tire soon of the repetition. Well, I'll try to write something anyway.
>
> I'm once again feeling very fit and well and am in the best of health. The weather, a little on the hot side, perhaps, is none the less glorious and as I write this letter we gallant British sailors are sitting out on the upper deck in our deck chairs, reading or writing or sleeping or just contemplating the glorious blue of the calm sea and the paler blue of the sky, with its fluffy white clouds perpetually on the horizon. It only needs a few kiddies running around

and a few shapely feminine forms in their bathing suits to complete the picture the general public generally gets from the hoardings advertising some steamship company's summer cruise.

We're still at sea you see and likely to be for another week, although the Admiralty keep altering their orders to us. It's been a week of alarums and excursions, but our only casualty has been one of the kittens which fell overboard and got drowned. There are inherent possibilities of excitement yet, but I don't suppose they'll mature.

As we can only provision up with fresh food for about a week and they are now in the habit of sending us off for from 3 to 7 weeks at a time, we get down to iron rations fairly soon, and a diet composed almost exclusively of corned beef, sweet potatoes and beans gets a little monotonous after a while and even, perhaps, inadequate.

But if our bellies and gustatory organs remain unsatisfied, our aesthetic senses have been titillated by the sight, in the evenings, of some of the loveliest sunsets I have ever seen – outside of Bermuda that is.

Our ship's company gave a concert, at least the 'Swing Sextet', now with the addition of a leading stoker who is an absolute wizard on the piano, a swing septet did the other evening, and if not purely aesthetic, the entertainment was thoroughly enjoyable and appreciated by all. These things help to brighten our otherwise monotonously tranquil days. One sees a lot of one's fellow men in ship life, and can't get away, like Greta Garbo, to be alone. It's worse than marriage for that. Especially if you join a ship which only gives shore leave in a place where no one ever wants to go ashore.

It is fortunate for me that I am interested in the things of nature. Of an evening, when the atmosphere in the wardroom becomes barely habitable, I come out on deck and lie on my back and look at the stars and dream. Isn't it lucky for one that it is the happy memories in one's past that one remembers: the unhappiness one relegates to the back of the mind. But it seems that I am sometimes in danger of living in that world of fantasy for which I have in the past chided you.

Passing migrating birds, and even butterflies at least 70 miles from land have been a delight to me as also the whales and porpoises and flying fishes, not to mention, nearer at home, the ship's cat and her playful kittens. For this brown type of cockroach which gets in our food and our drawers and swarms everywhere over the walls, I have not yet learnt the affection I used to have for our lovely black beetles.

The war moves relentlessly on. The tide, I feel, has turned in our favour. May the day come quickly when this senseless destruction of life will cease and once more we can afford to have kindliness and love and beauty. Beauty which I still worship above all things. War is so cruel and ugly, its thoughts and instruments are ugly and it leaves in its trail a path of hideous hate and ugliness.

Life will be very changed after the war. It might be changed a lot for the better.

Well, dear, I seem to have been quite chatty this afternoon after all.

For Leslie Russell, writing to Jean on 14 September, life was also tedious:

Very little happening at the moment – we are wandering up and down the oggin (sea to you). The weather is fine and there are a number of red and raw backs. Life is boring but there is the consolation that some mail may be waiting when we arrive back in harbour.

Midshipman Keith Mantell made similar observations in his log for the same day, but also noted that things might be getting a little more interesting:

Very little has happened during recent days. Sweltering sun and very little wind have made conditions very oppressive. At Divisions this forenoon, the Commander announced that our patrol had been extended, due to the presence of an enemy ship in an area which we reached this morning.

Two days later, while *Dunedin* was still on patrol, two aircraft were seen circling around the ship, apparently keeping well clear of her anti-aircraft guns. Were they from the enemy ship? After *Dunedin* flashed several messages to the aircraft, one came down low and dived across the bows to reveal her American markings, easing the growing tension on board. The aircraft were probably from USS *Nashville*, which was known to be in the area.

Dunedin continued her patrol, but found no enemy ship. Instead she came across a Vichy convoy en route to Dakar, but, since she was escorted, *Dunedin* left her alone. By Friday 19 September, *Dunedin* was back in Freetown and this time mail was waiting. For Midshipman Mantell, this was to be his last day aboard *Dunedin*, as orders arrived for his immediate transfer to HMS *Vansittart*. Within hours of *Dunedin*'s arrival at Freetown, Mantell had joined his next ship.

Dunedin was in for an extended stay in Freetown, with long periods of boredom punctuated by exercises and maintenance, including on fifteen of *Dunedin*'s ageing boiler tubes. The arrival of mail certainly helped to relieve the monotony, but more importantly helped to ease the creeping sense of despair at the lack of prospects of an early return to England. For a few men, however, change was in the air. Some were leaving the ship, either to go home sick or on transfer. Others, like Able Seaman George Wells, were joining *Dunedin*. George had spent some time in the destroyer HMS *Arrow*, but had been at the Portsmouth depot since July 1941. Now he was back on an active ship, having left behind his two young daughters, Olga and Anne. He wrote to his mother and father on 29 September, the day after his arrival:

> I hope you are keeping well these days for the winter is coming, poor Chas would like to see a winter again, he will one day. By the way we shall be having a concert on Wednesday evening or so we are told and I think Wednesday morning and Wednesday afternoon there are other attractions on board. So we look like having a nice time don't we. Nearly all our boys, and there are quite a crowd of us, seem to have somebody or other in the family called Sally. Hope Pop is going along alright and still getting his fags. Bought another tin of tobacco for 2/- so shall be alright. Was very pleased to get a good night's rest last night and will get every night from now on in my hammock. We can get Allsops bottled beer on board, but I haven't troubled about any yet. Hope Edna is keeping better and remember me to Chas when you write. It's no good me writing from here at present but I wrote the other week and will on board when we get cracking.
>
> Olga and Anne will be grown up when I come back I suppose but I know they won't forget their daddy. Send me a snap occasionally. I don't think there is anything I shall want at all from your end except mail. Shall do more

writing out there when I get there, when I get there? eh? We can get Cadbury's bars, ate two yesterday and am on my second now. Am half way through a book, but will be able to have concerts on board and sports of different sorts. Will really look forward somehow to the ship rolling, for it won't be right somehow if she doesn't.

Well, I will close now so will wish you all, all the very best of luck for the future and also a Merry Christmas and brighter and prosperous New Year, your loving son, George.

A few days later, on 4 October, *Dunedin* sailed from Freetown, escorting *Eagle* as far as Bathurst on the first part of her return journey to Liverpool. When *Vimy* and *Wild Swan* took over, *Dunedin* turned back towards Freetown, leaving *Eagle* for the last time.

The next few weeks were not without their tense moments, such as when *Dunedin* was ordered to the Cape Verde Islands, where U-boats were thought to be lying up. Intelligence reports in late October suggested that U-boats might be using the islands as hideouts for refuelling, reprovisioning and recreation, so it was decided to carry out a sweep of the area. 'Operation Corridor', involving *Dunedin*, *Vimy* and *Brilliant* as Force F and some long-range Sunderland aircraft based at Bathurst, took place on 21, 22 and 23 October.

We slipped in at night and I was called to be part of the boarding crew. At last, a chance of some action. Our briefing was short and to the point. We were going to slip silently into the islands to surprise the U-boats and be ready to board. We were issued cutlasses – they were quieter, we were told, and scared the living daylights out of anyone you might meet.

We waited and waited in silence as Dunedin *approached the islands and then picked her way gingerly through them. If it is possible to steer nearly 5,000 tons of steel through a maze of islands without anyone noticing, we did it that night.*

But there were no Germans there and we were stood down an hour before dawn, our cutlasses unused and unthreatening. Throughout the three-day operation nothing was found despite a comprehensive reconnaissance of the area.

For me, it was back to regular routine.

As part of the Royal Marine contingent (of about fifty) I was always on stand-by for action, as a member of either a prize crew or a boarding party, or just about anything else that might arise. In between times I had plenty of other jobs to do. For four hours every day I was part of a team of eight that manned the No. 5 six-inch gun. Not once did we get to fire it at sea in anger, but we would be ready all the time. Much of the time was spent just sitting around the gun, waiting for something to happen, but we also did gun drill and plenty of practice. We must have been the most well-rehearsed gun team in the Marines.

Sometimes I used to think that the non-commissioned officers made up jobs just to make sure we were doing something, and with over 400 men on board most of these blasted jobs did not need doing. How many times did I find myself scrubbing the officers' quarters? And how many times did someone walk right through where I was scrubbing or 'accidentally' kick my scrubbing brush away? But I don't suppose this was different to any other ship of the Navy.

For three months I was 'Corporal of the Gangway', part of whose function was to make sure the officers were called at the right time to go on duty. This made me a sort of back-up alarm clock. If they failed to turn up for duty it was my fault. I was at my most powerful when I was keyboard sentry. Nobody got a key for anything without my permission. I could be a right jobsworth if I wanted.

As Corporal of the Gangway I was also the cocoa monitor. This meant taking the ship's cocoa round in a jug to the other sentries on duty at night. Now, ship's cocoa was a wonder to behold. Sit in your armchair today in front of the fire on a winter's evening clutching a warm mug of chocolate nectar, then feel it caressing your throat and stomach – and you could not be further from the truth of ship's cocoa. Cocoa – or Kia in Dunedin – had a layer of fat on it which stuck to the sides of the enamel mugs and then to the sides of your mouth. The cocoa itself did not so much as slip down soothingly as ratchet down your throat wearing rugby boots. As it lay in your stomach you knew that one day life would have to get better.

'Thank you', the lucky recipients would say, and I would look at them in pity, speechless, and walk on to the next happy cocoa freak.

One night the usual jug was missing so I nipped into the wardroom (sacred territory for a non-officer) and 'borrowed' one. After I had finished the round a *little cocoa was left in the bottom. Knowing how it was made and what went into it, I did not contemplate finishing it off – for fear that it would finish me off – but swished it around and flung it over the side. But the cocoa refused to be parted from the jug and I was left holding the handle as the jug flew silently into the deep. I don't suppose throwing an officer's jug over the side was a court-martial offence but it did not seem worth keeping the handle either. So that went over too.*

My other main task was to be butcher's assistant before meals. My good mate Nobby Hall was the butcher and he was responsible for sharing out the meat rations to the mess cooks every day on the upper deck. I helped him by doing the same for the vegetables.

When we were not doing our usual jobs, we occupied ourselves in a variety of ways during our dogwatches. The centre of attraction was usually in the recreation space, where we played the piano and sang, or played bingo. These were also the times to write letters home, to read, play bridge or just sit around and listen to music on the tannoy.

We could buy soft drinks and cigarettes from the canteen, but we could not buy alcohol. The only booze we ever saw was the tot of rum for those of us over twenty years old.

Even when we were not on duty we had to keep a lookout for U-boats and ships. Sometimes we saw fishing vessels and stopped them to have a look. The saddest sights were the empty boats from sunken ships drifting on the open sea. We would see a small boat in the distance and when we approached we would look anxiously to see whether men were inside. But we never saw any survivors, just the sad emptiness of a vacant refuge. How many men had perished for want of a lifeboat?

In October, *Dunedin* spent much of her time looking for a German surface supply ship, in company with various other ships, including *Dorsetshire*, *Vimy* and *Brilliant*. Once again, nothing was found.

Leslie had found ways to alleviate the longing for home and did his best to enjoy himself when he could. From Bathurst, on 21 October, he wrote:

A good run ashore and a good swim in the sea which was so warm just as you like it. It was a glorious feeling stretched out on the beach in the sunshine. Candy was with me and it was funny to think of England just coming into winter and how many people would pay hundreds of pounds to revel in this warmth. It was ours for nothing. An RAF chap told us the other day that his mob had been sent here for a rest.

We dressed after an hour. A local grandee had set apart a room in his house where we could change. We wandered through the well tended gardens to the house feeling that we were spending a holiday in a luxury hotel. A goodly number of our crew were there and all enjoying it. We were supplied with ice cold water when we had dressed. Later we had tea and Candy and I played table tennis. While we were waiting on the jetty for the boat, we amused ourselves by tossing pennies in the water and watching the small boys dive for them.

A few days later, much to the delight of everyone, mail arrived and with it some early Christmas parcels.

In Freetown on 1 November, the Commander-in-Chief South Atlantic, Admiral Raikes, inspected *Dunedin*. In Harold Broadway's words, the ship had been 'pansied up' and much ceremonial spit and polish was in evidence. He wrote to Mary on 2 November complaining about 'this godforsaken place' and also that there was a general feeling that *Dunedin* would soon move to another station. The C-in-C's visit might have encouraged this thought, but having been away from Britain for almost seven months with seemingly no respite from the constant monotony and drudgery of the Freetown-based patrols, most of the ship's company felt justified in wanting a change.

November would bring a change, but not one that anyone on board wanted.

CHAPTER 8

Enigma and U-124, 30 October–24 November 1941

30 October

U-124 slipped out of Lorient harbour, in north-west France, en route to the South Atlantic. On the bridge was the twenty-five-year-old Johann Mohr, about to set out on his second voyage in command.

Launched in March the previous year, U-124 was already a seasoned and battle-hardened vessel. She was a Type IXB U-boat carrying twenty-two torpedoes and around fifty crew. Submerged, she could make just over seven knots and a steady eighteen on the surface. Dönitz thought the IXB was a little heavy and clumsy for some anti-convoy work, but she was one of the most successful U-boats of the war. Adorning the sides of U-124's conning tower were paintings of an edelweiss, the flower that was the U-boat's emblem.

The original crew of U-124 was made up mostly of the ex-crew of U-64, which had been sunk in a Norwegian fiord in 1940. In a remarkable rescue operation, most of the men had escaped and were picked up from the icy waters by a nearby German Alpine unit, whose emblem was the edelweiss. When the crew were assigned to the brand-new U-124 the edelweiss was the obvious choice of emblem and U-64's captain, Georg-Wilhelm Schulz, was made captain of U-124.

Under Schulz, U-124 experienced the full range of dangers and had many close shaves. On her first patrol, in August 1940, she had been chased from a convoy, having been caught in the searchlight of a British destroyer. Her only means of escape was to crash-dive and sit it out on the bottom, waiting for the depth charges to stop. On the way down, she hit a rock outcrop and suffered bad damage to her bow, but she went very deep and the danger from the destroyer eventually passed. Later on the same patrol, the aft torpedo room flooded and she nearly sank. By the time she limped into Lorient at the end of her patrol, she could nevertheless look back on a successful outing, having sunk three ships.

U-124's second patrol, in October and November 1940, was also successful, but once more she almost paid the ultimate price. Schulz accounted for five merchant ships but had to endure another pounding by depth charges. Her return to Lorient resulted in a triumphant reception yet again.

U-124's third patrol, in December and January, brought only one sinking but also an extraordinary incident that nearly caused her demise once more. In January, she sank the British merchant ship *Empire Thunder*, but Schultz had to fire five torpedoes before she would sink. The fourth torpedo missed the target completely, turned full circle and missed U-124 by just a few yards. This was not unheard of – several U-boats were hit by their own torpedoes in the course of the war.

Between February and May, U-124 produced one of the most successful U-boat patrols of the war, sinking eleven ships, including four in one twenty-one-minute salvo. Again, her luck held out when, on 22 March, her engines failed and she drifted helplessly for ten hours, a sitting target for passing ships or spotter planes overhead. Fortunately for the crew, the engines were fixed and U-124 went on her way again to complete another hugely successful patrol.

One other incident stands out in this patrol. Having sunk the British merchantman *Tweed* in April, U-124 came across a small group of her survivors on an upturned raft. Schulz pulled up alongside and crew members of U-124 helped right the raft, gave the survivors some rations and pointed them in the direction of Freetown. Schultz was not permitted to take them prisoner and it was doubtful whether he should have stopped in the middle of the ocean, leaving his submarine vulnerable to attack.

Dönitz later told Schultz that he had done the right thing and in 1958

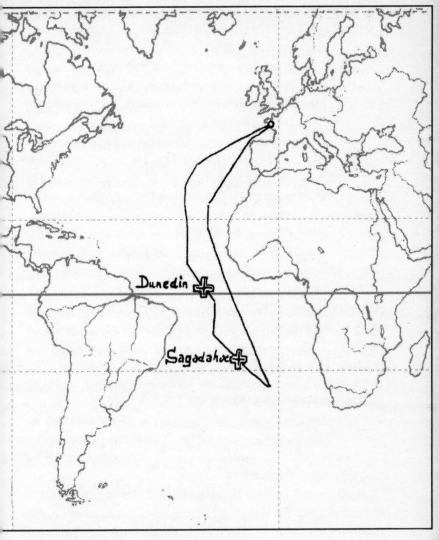

Captain Johann Mohr's sketch map charting the two
successes of his autumn 1941 voyage in U-124

the former third officer of *Tweed* met Schultz to thank him for his humane action. Schultz also submitted a report to the Nuremberg trials in Dönitz's defence against war crime charges.

Schultz's final patrol in command, in July and August 1941, was U-124's least successful. In what must have been a depressing return to Lorient after the triumph of previous homecomings, U-124 brought back all her torpedoes, having sunk not a single ton of shipping.

Johann Mohr took over as captain, but he was not new to the submarine, having served under Schultz already. He was well regarded by Dönitz and earned the respect of the crew. On his first patrol, in September 1941, he sank an astonishing six ships in two separate Gibraltar convoys.

Sent out to intercept the homebound Gibraltar convoy 73, Mohr and U-201 found instead the outbound 74, heavily escorted but nevertheless vulnerable. He sank two freighters late in the evening of 20 September and returned the following day to shadow the convoy to wait for dark.

Three more ships were sent down that day, but not by Mohr this time. He had been about to fire three torpedoes when his targets were hit by U-201, whose captain – much to Mohr's annoyance – was a little ahead of the game.

Among the escort ships was a carrier with Martlet fighters. When Dönitz sent in Condor aircraft to attack the convoy on 21 September, the carrier responded with her Martlets. One Martlet shot down a Condor and another focused on the two U-boats, and neither U-124 nor U-201 was able to make any further attacks in the face of the attention of the Martlets.

The escort carrier was *Audacity*, formerly the *Hannover*, which had been captured in March 1940 by *Dunedin*.

By 22 September, U-124 and U-201 had lost contact with the convoy and were now ordered to find the Homebound Gibraltar convoy 73. With the help of the Condors, Mohr closed on the convoy and sank four more ships, bringing his tally for the patrol to six. He brought U-124 back into Lorient on 1 October with all his torpedoes spent, flying a string of victory pennants.

Lorient was a key submarine base for the Germans. When they took it over in June 1940, it enabled them to bring their U-boats round from Kiel in the Baltic to give Dönitz easy access to the Atlantic, lessening by a week the time taken for the U-boats to get there. Later, Dönitz built huge concrete bunkers several metres thick to protect his U-boats. The bunkers were attacked many times by Allied bombers, but not once was a U-boat destroyed there. Dönitz himself moved from Paris to be near the U-boats and set up his headquarters in a mansion at nearby Kerneval, overlooking the bunkers.

And now, on 30 October, after a few weeks' rest, Mohr and his crew had set sail again, leaving Lorient behind them.

Early November

In Freetown, *Dunedin* and her crew were relaxing after nearly two weeks at sea. As usual, the town was no holiday resort, just its familiar smelly self in oppressive heavy heat. It was a place to leave, not to a place to enjoy. Some of the men tried hard to make the most of it, but after seven months away and weeks without mail, it was a time of reflection, a time to think of families, a time to wonder how much longer this would go on. When, thankfully, mail arrived from home, men all over the ship hunched in corners or on their hammocks, or just lay on deck, the flimsy pieces of paper flickering in the breeze as their silent words drew pictures of home and hearth, children and smiles, wives and girlfriends.

Harold Broadway had three letters from his wife, all dated September. It had been fourteen months since he had seen Bermuda and his family, fourteen months to lose the smell of their skin, the colour of their hair. One of Mary's letters told him how she wanted to dye her hair red and said that she was getting bored with Bermuda – she thought that England must be safer now and she wanted to go back with the children. Harold was convinced, however, that she must stay in Bermuda.

In his reply of 2 November, he wrote:

Whatever happens, I'll not have you coming back to England. I shouldn't mind you crossing the sea in the other direction – to Halifax, New York or Jamaica, but I'm damned if I'll have you risking your life and the children's; don't forget them, coming the other way. Believe me, the risk is still there. I know of course, that if Father isn't well, you'd like to get back of course, but just think once again about your journey outwards from Liverpool.

He remembered very well the stories of his family's voyage with the convoy back in August 1940; he remembered vividly little Christopher's childish enthusiasm and excitement at having seen ships torpedoed by U-boats, an infant's innocence which hid the gruesome reality of life at sea in the middle of a war.

In his mind he saw again Mary's face:

> You sound as if you might be looking rather nice with your hair fairer than ever and long and just turned up at the bottom. I'd like it like that.

Early on the morning of 4 November it was time for *Dunedin* to move again. A distress message had been received from the oiler *Olwen*, en route to New Orleans, saying a surface ship had attacked her. HMS *Canton* and HMS *Dorsetshire*, who were already at sea, were sent to investigate, while *Dunedin* sailed with *Princess Beatrix* and *Queen Emma*. These ships were Dutch cross-Channel ferries that came across to England as Europe fell. They did not have much fighting value and had very poor range, but they were useful in widening a search area. *Olwen*'s attacker was thought to have been at 3 degrees north, 22 degrees 35' west, some 800 miles south-west of Freetown, three hours earlier. *Dorsetshire* and *Canton* were to search south of this point, *Dunedin* and the two others would search to the south-east. In addition, three US ships, the cruiser *Memphis* and two destroyers, who were within six hours, were diverted to the area, but they found nothing.

By the 5th, no fewer than twelve ships had been sent to look for *Olwen*, in the hope of finding either survivors or her attacker. And then came a further message in the morning that said she was steaming undamaged and had not been hit by a raider but had come under a light attack from a U-boat on the surface. This was *Dunedin*'s cue to leave the scene and, together with *Queen Emma* and *Princess Beatrix*, she was ordered to return to Freetown.

As *Dunedin* sailed back to Freetown, some reward finally came from the massive search operation when two US ships, *Omaha* and *Somers,* came across the *Oldenwald*, a German surface raider, near St Paul's Rocks. After attempting to scuttle, she was captured intact.

Meanwhile, *Dunedin* continued her passage back to Freetown and, after five days at sea, she arrived empty-handed on the 9th. There had been no glory for her. In fact, there had been no sightings and no action. But in Freetown, there was little chance for a rest as she was ordered out again the next day on convoy escort duty with *Dorsetshire,* following the so-called 'Operation Bellringer'. This had been a Navy attack on a French convoy on 2 November, in which several French merchant ships had been boarded. The Vichy authorities were none too pleased and – as was heard through the US consul at Dakar – were contemplating reprisals against British shipping. As a precaution, *Dunedin* and *Dorsetshire* were sailed to protect two convoys, SL 92 and OS 10.

And so *Dunedin* found herself at sea again, on one more stage of her seemingly never-ending staccato existence of Freetown and patrols, patrols and Freetown. Commissioned Gunner (T) Harold Lowey, who had so heroically defused the charges on the *Lothringen* in June, wrote to his wife, Maude, and his son, Michael, as *Dunedin* sailed with *Dorsetshire*:

Here we are again at sea, so will just add a bit as I can, until I can post off to you, however, I posted one off to you yesterday when we happened to have a chance for a few hours. I hope you get it soon also the chocolate and everything including my remittance Pet.

How are you and Michael getting along, I do hope you are both well and that it is not getting too cold for you yet, here, it is still as hot as ever, how we could do with a change, I am glad to say I am very well...

Now Darling, I will close for tonight, so with all my fondest love, many kisses and a big big hug, Good night and God bless and protect you and Michael always.

Two days later, life did not appear to have changed for the better as Harold wrote once more while *Dunedin* continued her routine:

Here it is still as hot and uncomfortable as ever and oh so terribly, terribly monotonous, nothing ever for a change or any kind of amusement or diversion.

No trouble was encountered from French warships. The sea was rougher now, a perceptible swell pushing and pulling *Dunedin* against her will. So often the sea was a dirty grey, but this time – as Harold Broadway wrote to Mary on 13 November – it took on a more benign character:

> …a deepest blue with white horses breaking all over the place, and stormy petrels and sheerwaters skimming around the ship and the odd porpoise and school of flying fish breaking away from the bows from time to time. It's lovely on the upper deck except when we turn into the wind, then our eyes and ears and nose get choked with filth from the funnels and we cough and splutter in oil fuel. Between decks it's still too bloody hot for comfort.
>
> I've got a sort of idea that I may be drafted to another ship soon, or possibly to a shore job. I think that that is perhaps why Milligan has been sent here; but I don't want to go until I know where she's going to be sent for her next brush and combing. If I get to England, I should go straight up and see the powers that be and try to get a job on your side of the Atlantic. But this is all entirely guesswork – I've had no official intimation of anything, neither have I heard anything further about my recommendation for promotion. Of course, I'd rather have 2 stripes ashore with you than $2\frac{1}{2}$ afloat out here.

On 14 November, Stoker 1st-class Jack Pitt wrote home to his sister, Kath:

> …I can't say as I'm in the best of things, I don't mean I'm ill or anything, but where we are there's no life at all. It gives you that down in the dumps feeling, when we come in harbour, knowing it's no good going ashore. There's a war on I know, and we can't expect too much pleasure, but we haven't had a break since we left England. How's Bert getting on, I suppose he's saying the same as our lads ('roll on my duration'). Bert Tiller is out here, he has a year and a half to do on the station, I certainly don't envy him. We live in hope of going to some civilised place some time, England preferred. The hands of the clock have reached a quarter past three and I have to go on watch at four, so saying cheerio for the present and hope you and your family are in the best of health, will ring off…

While still at sea, on the 16th, Harold Broadway wrote home with his mind again on England and the contrasts of war:

Well the poor old Ark [*Royal*] has caught it at last! I've seen quite a bit of her off and on, and it seems sad. She certainly did her stuff. Whenever there was a shermozzle, there the old Ark was, right in the thick of it.

I've been reading Gilbert White's Natural History of Selborne, written about 1720. It is the complete antidote to this hot discomfort and the turmoil of war – the peaceful descriptions of the English countryside, the songs of wood warbler, blackcap and thrush, of chalk downs and beech trees form the complete escape from this life. I've also borrowed a Shakespeare and have read several of the plays over again. I am now in the middle of a Midsummer Night's Dream – something very English about it all.

Monday 17 November

Just before dawn, U-124 was sailing south, 600 miles west of Cape Verde, her bow carving through the water. In the radio room the wireless operator was sitting at the desk, the cramped surroundings pressing in on him, the air thick and sweaty. On his ears, the earphones emitted a low hiss and an occasional scratching noise, like a needle on a gramophone.

Then, peep, peep, peep in his ear. The tell-tale signs of an incoming message. It took only a few seconds to complete. The letters were meaningless in their naked form, a seemingly random series, but once the operator had put them through the Enigma machine they would reveal their message and make sense.

First he had to set the three rotors with today's key and then he typed in the letters he had taken down on his piece of paper. As he tapped each letter on the keyboard, an electric current ran through the machine and lit up a letter on the lamp board between the keyboard and the rotors. As each letter lit up, he wrote them down until the message was complete.

Tearing off the paper, he went to Mohr and handed it over. Mohr read it. It was addressed to U-124 and U-129:

Rendezvous with 'Python' altered to a point 35 miles north of point 'Fachinger'. After reprovisioning move off to the east and, when 400 miles distant from the reprovisioning point, report completion. Then proceed via square AR to the 'Kleiderstoffe' area.

Mohr would have to move west pretty quickly. Separately, in U-129, Clausen would be making his necessary course adjustments. *Python* was a German supply ship recently out of France and heading south to reprovision the U-boats in the South Atlantic.

As U-124 and *Python* made their way to their rendezvous, *Dunedin* was heading for Freetown again.

The 'Deadly Dun', as she was apt to be called, would not be in port for long. Men were rushing around, officers were giving orders, small provisioning boats were alongside. Urgency was in the damp, sticky air. *Dunedin* would be back on patrol again very soon.

Leslie Russell too was rushing. He hurriedly completed a letter to Jean and tucked it into an envelope, remembering, as always, not to seal it to allow the censor to read it. He then reached for his biscuit tin, which was crammed full of letters from Jean. Lying at the top of the pile was one he had written a couple of days ago and that he could now send. He took it out of the tin, but before taking it to the mail room he pulled the letter from its envelope and cast his eye over what he had written:

> …I was reading some old ones as I re-packed them and one point I noticed was that although we had a dim idea there might be a time when we would not see each other for a long time we had no idea what it would actually be like – it was inconceivable that it could be so appalling.

Meanwhile, in London, the Admiralty was picking up interesting signs of U-boat and surface ship activity. On the basis of Enigma decrypts, the Admiralty signalled the Commander-in-Chief South Atlantic that U-boats had been told not to attack single ships south-west of a line drawn 500 miles north-west of St Paul's Rocks to a point 250 miles east of St Paul's Rocks until 22 November. This was a possible sign that a German surface ship was in the area and that Dönitz was seeking to prevent his own U-boats from mistaking it for an Allied ship. But C-in-C South Atlantic was not so sure and sent the Admiralty a signal around lunchtime asking for further advice.

Tuesday 18 November

Shortly after dawn, 850 miles south-west of Cape Verde, U-124 came upon *Python* to refuel and reprovision as planned. U-129 was already there, but Mohr needed to be sure of *Python's* identity. She was about the right size but she did not quite look as he had expected. He was not sure about the slanting funnel. Mohr turned U-124 towards *Python* and signalled to her, but she did not reply. This was odd, so he passed her at speed and asked specifically, 'Please – name – answer.' This time *Python* answered, 'Z-ship *Python*,' and Mohr could be satisfied. Before refuelling began, he invited *Python's* Captain Lüders aboard for discussions.

In a modest swell, the operation took longer than expected because of the need to repair some compressor pistons in one of U-124's diesel engines. Mohr's men worked into the night on the pistons while the U-boat was reprovisioned. Then, after a quick test dive, Mohr went aboard *Python* and visited Clausen while U-129 was refuelled.

The Admiralty, in the meantime, had been thinking about C-in-C South Atlantic's signal asking for more details about the protected area and the reasons for it. In reply – nearly twenty-four hours later – the Admiralty said that in its view an Axis surface ship was on a north-west passage and that, although this implied the presence of a U-boat, it did not think that the operations of southern U-boats would be concentrated in this area.

What could C-in-C South Atlantic conclude from this? That a surface ship would appear somewhere in the vicinity of St Paul's Rocks sometime before the 22nd. Admiral Raikes would have to deploy one of his ships to the area.

As Raikes contemplated his options, *Dunedin* was arriving back in Freetown. *Canton* had been there since 13 November and so she was dispatched to an area west of St Paul's Rocks to intercept any northbound German surface ship.

On board *Dunedin*, both Leslie Russell and Harold Broadway had hurriedly finished letters home. Leslie wrote:

> I think we are arriving in harbour soon and I want this letter to leave the ship as soon as possible, just in case there's another ship to take it home.

And Harold wrote:

Now that there's a chance to, I'd better finish this letter and send it off. God knows what new thing there is to talk about. I'm getting very bored with the monotony of this existence and seeing the same faces over and over again. Actually although I have no enemies here that I know of and I like most of the chaps immensely I have formed no really close friendships – actually as a matter of fact there are practically none in the whole wardroom between any two people – that is what probably makes us tolerant of each other and enables us to put up with one another day after day – when neither love nor hate exist.

It doesn't look as if we're getting any incoming mail this time.

It's raining here as usual.

Give my love and a big kiss and a hug to Christopher and Shelagh.

I'll be seeing you some day.

Wednesday 19 November

By the early hours, U-129 had completed her refuelling and Clausen was on his way. Mohr watched as U-129 moved off to the east before disappearing into the darkness. By mid-morning, U-124 had also finished. She and *Python* moved off together before *Python* disappeared away to the south-east.

Thursday 20 November

In London, on the corner of Horseguards Parade, facing St James's Park, beneath the Admiralty offices – the so-called citadel – more decrypts had arrived in the Operational Intelligence Centre from Bletchley Park. Four messages involved communications between Dönitz and his U-boats. The first, sent by Merten in U-68, gave his position as 'grid square 2418' and said that he was proceeding to his rendezvous. What rendezvous could this mean?

The next message, sent on the 10th, was much longer and gave Merten his reply. Bletchley Park had clearly had trouble decoding it, because it arrived in the OIC in two parts, with the second half first. It had five instructions and was a veritable gold mine.

Marine William Gill. One of the sixty-seven survivors, he had signed up in December 1939 and after training at Deal and Portsmouth joined *Dunedin* at Plymouth in March 1941.

ABOVE HMS *Dunedin* at Lyttelton, New Zealand, 22 April 1928. *Dunedin* spent most of her interwar years attached to the New Zealand Navy. (*By kind permission of Madelaine Kirke*)

OPPOSITE LEFT *Dunedin* battling the elements in the early days of the war at sea.

LEFT The original drawing of *Dunedin*'s ship's crest, bearing the date of her completion, 1919.

Submitted

A.A.H.

24th March 1919

Passed as SEALED PATTERN

for the Board

Admiralty 13 Sept 1919

LEFT Scapa Flow, December 1939. As part of the Northern Patrol, *Dunedin* spent the early months of the war in the harsh environment of the North Sea enforcing the blockade on ships attempting to reach German ports. (*By kind permission of Rod Andrews*)

ABOVE Three hundred miles from Bermuda, February 1940. (*By kind permission of Rod Andrews*)

ABOVE LEFT Rough passage to Bermuda, with HMS *Diomede*, February 1940. (*By kind permission of Rod Andrews*)

LEFT *Dunedin* towing the German merchantman SS *Hannover* to Jamaica after capturing her on 8 March 1940. *Hannover* was later converted into the first auxiliary carrier and renamed *Audacity*.

ABOVE The men of *Dunedin* who formed the *Hannover* prize crew.

LEFT HMS *Dunedin* in St Lucia, 1940. She stayed on the West Indies station until September 1940.

BELOW LEFT Captain Lambe greeting the Duke and Duchess of Windsor as they come on board for a visit in August 1940.

BELOW The sinking SS *Heidelberg*, a German merchantman intercepted by *Dunedin* on 2 March 1940 in the Caribbean. *Heidelberg*'s crew scuttled her before she could be captured.

OPPOSITE ABOVE Prisoners from *Heidelberg* under Royal Marine guard and under the fascinated eyes of the ship's company.

OPPOSITE BELOW Crossing the Line ceremony, 28 April 1941. Captain Lovatt, with his back to the camera, stands in front of King Neptune. To Lovatt's right, some of the ship's Marines form Neptune's guard of honour of pirates. The two officers in whites at the far left are Lt-Commander Sowdon (arms folded) and Commander Unwin.

LEFT The Crossing the Line ceremony reaches its pitch with shaving and dunking for the uninitiated, while a group of officers (in whites) look on from atop a lifeboat. To the left, above the mêlée, lie three of the ship's Carley rafts.

BELOW *U-124* and some of her crew. Painted on her side is the edelweiss, the submarine's emblem. (*U-boot Archiv, Cuxhaven, Germany*)

TOP *U-124* Crossing the Line ceremony. (*U-boot Archiv, Cuxhaven, Germany*)

ABOVE *Dunedin* alongside the German tanker *Lothringen*, 15 June 1941. Guided by Enigma decrypts and working with HMS *Eagle*, *Dunedin* captured *Bismarck's* tanker without the German High Command even noticing. Two U-boats turned up two days later hoping to be refuelled, but were forced instead to return home. (*National Archives, London*)

```
ADM

TO  I  D  8  G                        ZIP/ZTPG/18733

FROM  N  S


13768 KC/S                     T O : 1537/24/11/41

             T O O 1551


FROM:   MOHR


''D'' CLASS BRITISH CRUISER SUNK IN SQUARE PE 7985. AM CONTINUING

PASSAGE SOUTH.


(DEPT.NOTE: SQUARE PE = ?).


1423/25/11/41++CEL/LW
```

ABOVE Telex from Bletchley Park
to the Admiralty's Operational
Intelligence Centre (OIC) of the
decrypt of Mohr's message to
Dönitz signalling the sinking of
Dunedin. (*National Archives,
London*)

LEFT Johann Mohr, Captain of
U-124, back in Lorient, France
on 29 December 1941. The
two pennants flying behind him
signify his two successes on only
his second patrol in command.
The top one is for *Dunedin*, the
lower one for an American
merchantman, *Sagadahoc*,
torpedoed on 3 December.
(*U-boot Archiv, Cuxhaven,
Germany*)

ABOVE Possibly the last ever photograph taken of *Dunedin* as she leaves Freetown harbour some time in the summer of 1941. (*By kind permission of Gwen Jackson*)

BELOW In the fading light of 27 November 1941, the US freighter SS *Nishmaha* stumbled upon *Dunedin*'s seventy-two survivors in a ragged flotilla of Carley rafts. Five died before the night was out, but the remaining survivors were taken to Trinidad. The survivors' thank you letter said the crew were 'devoted to the kindness of mankind'.

ABOVE LEFT Leslie Russell, Supply Assistant. Called up in July 1940, Leslie joined *Dunedin* in October the same year and served until *Dunedin* was lost. His letters to his fiancée, Jean, are somehow representative of the feelings of all servicemen far away from home.

RIGHT Surgeon Lieutenant-Commander Harold Broadway. He joined *Dunedin* in Bermuda in August 1940 just before his family arrived from England. *Dunedin* sailed three days after their arrival and Harold never returned. (*By kind permission of Lt-Commander Chris Broadway, RN (Ret) and Shelagh Broadway*)

ABOVE The four known living survivors, 7 April 2001, at the first ever *Dunedin* reunion, at Henley-on-Thames. *Left to right* are William Gill, Jim Davis, Harry Cross and Les Barter. (*Photograph by Michael Gill*)

RIGHT George VI sent many letters of condolence to the families of *Dunedin*'s ship's company. This one is to the wife of Lt Cecil Wright (S) RNVR, who joined *Dunedin* in Bermuda at about the same time as Harold Broadway. (*By kind permission of Mrs Heather Rance, daughter of Lt Cecil Wright*)

BUCKINGHAM PALACE

The Queen and I offer you our heartfelt sympathy in your great sorrow.

We pray that your country's gratitude for a life so nobly given in its service may bring you some measure of consolation.

George R.I.

Mrs. C.J.G. Wright.

First, it made clear to Merten that he would be reprovisioning from an auxiliary cruiser, 'Schiff 16', and that it would be disguised as either a British, a Danish or a Dutch ship. Second, Merten was told to be at the rendezvous from the 13th at 8 a.m. and 4 p.m. Third, the rendezvous was described as 'naval grid square GF 29 middle'.

Merten was also instructed not to report completion of the reprovisioning until Schiff 16 had moved at least 400 miles away and that, until the reprovisioning had been completed, he should maintain radio silence. Thereafter, his orders were to move towards the coast but not to go southwards.

By itself, this meant very little to the OIC. It was already history. If the reprovisioning had gone to plan, then Schiff 16 and U-68 had long since parted company. They could be anywhere.

The next message shed a little more light. Bauer in U-126 had been told on the 11th to expect reprovisioning to take place on the 21st in "square 70". This was a long way north of where U-68 had met Schiff 16. Perhaps Schiff 16 was on her way north, back to France or Germany, and would reprovision U-boats on the way. Was this the surface ship on its north-west passage about which the Admiralty had signalled on the 17th and 18th?

The message to Bauer went on to say that a final decision on the reprovisioning would take place on about the 15th. What did all this mean? Why the 15th?

The OIC concluded that Schiff 16 would have refuelled U-68 at about 24 degrees south, 7 degrees west, about 500 miles south of St Helena, probably on the 15th. Moreover, Schiff 16 was probably the same ship that would be reprovisioning U-126 on the 21st in 'square 70'. This would mean that she would have to travel at about sixteen knots. The OIC decided to take a chance and to pass this on to C-in-C South Atlantic and sent a signal at lunchtime on the 20th. The message read:

Raider 16, known to be disguised, fuelled U-68 in position 24 degs 00' south, 7 degs 00' west on 15th November. Comment: Estimated speed 16 knots. Probably homeward.

U-124 continued her voyage south and was now some 700 miles south-west of Cape Verde, some 1,000 miles north-west of St Paul's Rocks.

Schiff 16 was the German raider *Atlantis*, homeward bound after a long voyage in the Atlantic, Indian and Pacific Oceans. Having passed the Falkland Islands, she had skirted the icy waters of the Antarctic before turning north into the warmer waters of the South Atlantic. For the crew, this meant a welcome move towards home. After their many months at sea, they could finally look forward to seeing their families again.

Any boost in morale on *Atlantis* was quickly dampened by the news that they were to refuel U-68 on their way home. A message from High Command told them to 'Proceed to Flower point Daffodil', between Cape Town and Freetown. *Atlantis*'s Captain Rogge was not happy with this instruction and sought new orders, hoping to be able to switch the rendezvous to a less crowded area away from the busy sea lanes. Merten was similarly concerned and High Command issued a new position, midway between Cape Town and St Helena.

This was the position that the OIC had discovered from the Bletchley Park decrypts, but the rendezvous had not, as the OIC guessed, taken place on the 15th but earlier. Merten had come on to *Atlantis* on the 13th, but the weather had been so bad that he could not get alongside to carry out the refuelling. By the 14th, the weather had improved and Merten finally came alongside to take on oil, food, water, soap, towels, underwear and cigarettes.

The crew of *Atlantis* was happy to get the dangerous operation out of the way as quickly as possible so that they could resume their trip home. But no sooner was the U-68 operation over, than they received new orders to proceed to a point further north to reprovision U-126 – at the rendezvous that the Admiralty now knew something about and had signalled to C-in-C South Atlantic.

Friday 21 November

The teleprinters in the OIC chattered out yet more decrypts from Bletchley Park, mostly dealing with the Baltic area, but just before 3 p.m. the OIC received a decrypt of the message sent to U-124 and U-129 on the 16th, informing them of a new rendezvous with *Python*. Here were two U-boats being ordered to meet *Python* at thirty-five miles north of point 'Fachinger' and told that they should move off to the east for about 400 miles before reporting completion. Then they were to proceed to the 'Kleiderstoffe' area. Mohr had not received this message until the 17th, but it was still four days old. The reprovisioning had probably already taken place. All the OIC knew was that these two U-boats had been heading south.

So, with Schiff 16 heading north and U-boats 124 and 129 heading south, what was going on? The OIC knew that Schiff 16 had refuelled U-68 around 24 degrees south (south of St Helena) and that Schiff 16 was on her way to reprovision another U-boat (126). That made four U-boats and at least two surface ships in the area.

The big frustration for the OIC was that the rendezvous between Schiff 16 and U-126 was expected on the 21st – in other words, that very day – but they were no further forward in finding out where. Had they literally missed the boat?

Just after 6 p.m. another decrypt arrived from Bletchley Park, this time a message from Bauer in U-126, sent on the 17th. He reported engine trouble and wanted to return home after reprovisioning. Nothing was added about the arrangements for the rendezvous, leaving the OIC in the dark and still wondering whether the reprovisioning had already taken place.

And then, at 6.50 and 7.10, two consecutive decrypts from Bletchley Park landed in the OIC that blew open the German plans. The first had been sent on the 12th to UA (commanded by Eckermann). Eckermann was told that he would be reprovisioned in the first week of December in roughly the area Merten was – at that time – about to be reprovisioned. Secondly, and crucially, the message went on to say that 'Thereafter operation near the coast with boats south-eastwards from that point is being planned'.

The mist covering the picture was beginning to lift. The Germans were planning an attack in the Cape Town area. The OIC now had enough information to know that an operation was planned and that it could involve as many as five U-boats. But where were they exactly? And where were their supply ships?

Fifteen minutes after the Eckermann decrypt came in, an intelligence gem arrived. A message sent on the 17th to U-126 gave the exact instructions for the rendezvous with Schiff 16. More importantly, the reprovisioning was to take place on the 22nd, not the 21st. There was still time.

Within the hour the Admiralty had passed on this information to C-in-C South Atlantic, who then ordered HMS *Devonshire* to make for the rendezvous. All eyes were now on Schiff 16.

In the meantime, *Dunedin* was ready to move again. At 10 p.m., *Dunedin* was sent from Freetown. Admiral Raikes, on the basis of the Admiralty's signals and the available ships in the area, had decided to deploy her in search of surface ships. She was dispatched to the St Paul's Rocks area, with *Canton* further west.

As *Dunedin* sailed from Freetown harbour for the last time, Lieutenant Beveridge was standing on the deck of *Edinburgh Castle*, Freetown's depot ship. After taking the German tanker *Lothringen* to Bermuda as head of the prize crew in June, he had finally arrived back in Freetown to rejoin *Dunedin*. But he was just too late to make it back on board. Captain Lovatt told him that his relief was already on board and that he might as well join *Edinburgh Castle* and wait for passage.

At about the same time, Midshipman Tommy Handley was due to leave *Dunedin* to go to HMS *Vansittart* for his destroyer training. As Handley took his formal leave of the captain, Lovatt thought he looked a bit jaundiced and suggested that he report to the doctor for clearance to depart. Harold Broadway examined him and agreed that he was looking jaundiced, but he also knew that *Vansittart* had a good doctor so he signed him off and Handley left *Dunedin*. Unknowingly, Harold had probably saved Handley's life.

Beveridge watched *Dunedin* leave. He looked on with sadness in his eye as she sailed out to sea in the darkness of a West African evening, her sleek profile easing into the tropical night. A bright glow momentarily glared from her funnels as she passed the boom and moments later she was gone.

U-124 was now 500 miles south-west of Cape Verde, 900 miles north of St Paul's Rocks.

Saturday 22 November

Throughout the night of the 21st and into the early hours of the 22nd, *Devonshire* thundered north towards the spot where the rendezvous between Schiff 16 and U-126 was due to take place. At first light, Captain Oliver sent out the ship's aircraft, a Walrus, to scout for the raider. Preserving radio silence, the pilot of the aircraft had to wait until he returned to *Devonshire* to report that he had sighted a merchant ship at approximately 4 degrees 20' south, 18 degrees 50' west, almost exactly where the Admiralty had expected Schiff 16 to be – some 900 miles south-south-east of Freetown. Oliver adjusted his course and steamed at twenty-five knots towards the spot where the raider had been seen.

Ahead, U-126 lay alongside *Atlantis*, the two vessels connected by an oil pipe as *Atlantis* fed the submarine with fuel. The sky was clear, visibility was good and a short, slow swell gently rocked the two stationary craft. The U-boat captain, Bauer, and *Atlantis*'s Captain Rogge sat in Rogge's cabin while the refuelling operation went on outside. In a while, Bauer would go back, U-126 could be on her way south and *Atlantis* would finally head for home.

A little after 8 a.m., *Devonshire* spotted a mast at 4 degrees 12' south, 18 degrees 42' west and the Walrus was sent out again.

On board *Atlantis*, the serenity of the morning was broken by the cry of a lookout who had spotted *Devonshire* and was shouting that he could see a cruiser. All hell broke loose on the ship and the refueling operation was brought to an abrupt halt as the U-boat, its captain marooned on *Atlantis*, pulled away and submerged. Above them, the Walrus buzzed around like an annoying wasp.

Captain Oliver knew that a U-boat would be nearby, so he could not risk going too close to the raider. He therefore stayed at a range of between 12,000 and 18,000 yards, at a speed of twenty-six knots, and frequently altered his course to make life difficult for the U-boat.

The captain of *Atlantis* thought he still had a chance. With the U-boat in the area and with his own armaments, he felt he could lure *Devonshire* in close and make a fight of it. But Captain Oliver had no intention of moving in close. The Admiralty signals had made it all too plain that this was a rendezvous at which to refuel a U-boat. It could be anywhere nearby. Anyway, with his 8-inch guns he had no need to get too near.

Rogge, meanwhile, tried to play for time and swung *Atlantis* around in a complete circle to starboard and then began to make all manner of other course alterations. He wanted to pull *Devonshire* to the south-east and was careful to avoid giving the cruiser a clear view of *Atlantis*'s stern, which would have given away her true identity.

A little after 8.30 a.m., *Devonshire* fired two salvoes, one to the left, the other to the right of the raider. On board *Atlantis,* the crew watched as two 8-inch shells roared into the sea right next to them. Captain Rogge pulled the ship to a stop and considered his next move.

As *Devonshire*'s first shells ripped through the south atlantic air, 1,100 miles to the north-west, Mohr was sailing U-124 east when the radio operator handed him a message from HQ telling him to go direct to the 'Kleiderstoffe area'. This was a change of orders. He was no longer required to go first towards the east coast of Africa but should go direct to his second rendezvous with 'U-611', the code name for *Python*, which was further south. He set his course at full speed with both engines.

From *Atlantis,* Rogge made a last-ditch attempt to fool the British cruiser that the raider was in fact a British ship. He signalled that the ship was *Polyphemus*, which the Admiralty and Captain Oliver knew to have been at Bilbao, Spain, in late September and so could be in this position now. Oliver would have to check. He exchanged signals with the Admiralty and also ordered the Walrus to take a closer look at the ship's stern.

By 9.30 a.m., Oliver had his answers. The Admiralty had confirmed that the raider could not be *Polyphemus* and the Walrus had radioed 'Cruiser stern – hull similar to *Atlantis*'.

Now there could be no doubt. The intelligence reports, the Walrus report, the Admiralty confirmation and the behaviour of the raider herself proved it. This was Schiff 16 – *Atlantis*. Within a couple of minutes, Captain Oliver had ordered *Devonshire* to open fire.

For the next forty-five minutes, *Atlantis* suffered her death throes as *Devonshire* piled shell upon shell into her, firing thirty salvoes in total.

From 17,500 yards, the fourth salvo hit in No. 2 hold, setting it on fire and subsequently blowing up the magazine. *Atlantis*, in desperation, tried one last time to save herself by making a smoke screen and starting up her engines again. She made no attempt to return *Devonshire's* fire but tried to draw her again to the south-east.

As *Atlantis* took the incessant pounding, the crew began to abandon ship, until finally, at 10.16, the raider sank beneath the waves, her long voyage reaching an unscheduled end. All that was left for *Devonshire* was to recover the Walrus, clear out rapidly and head for Freetown. The U-boat lurked somewhere below.

For the OIC, *Devonshire's* report of the sinking would have been cause for huge celebration. But the job was not yet over. At least one other surface ship, *Python*, was in the area and was already heading for her next rendezvous. *Dunedin* and *Canton* would not have to worry any longer about *Atlantis* and could focus their efforts on *Python*.

The OIC could now take stock of what they knew from the decrypts and try to make sense of what the Germans would do next. Later on the 22nd, the OIC was ready to signal to C-in-C South Atlantic the results of its analysis. It reported that two U-boats which had left Biscay ports about three weeks earlier had fuelled from *Python* on or around the 18th in an unknown position and had then moved east. Thereafter, these boats would operate in an area close to the African west coast south of Freetown, before moving off to another unknown area. No information was given about the whereabouts of *Python* after the 18th. The signal did not identify the U-boats, but they were U-124 and U-129.

Furthermore, the Admiralty made plain that a number of U-boats would be operating off the west coast of South Africa after a refuelling operation. Where these boats were coming from and how they were to get there were far from clear.

It was into this uncertainty that *Dunedin* continued her patrol. With one surface raider down, another surface supply ship on the loose somewhere and several U-boats converging at another rendezvous to attack shipping off the Cape, the south Atlantic was getting very busy.

Once *Devonshire* had cleared away from *Atlantis*, U-126 rose to the surface to find the crew of the *Atlantis* bobbing around in lifeboats. Bauer took control of his submarine again and he and Rogge considered what to do. After debating the options, Bauer agreed to take some of the wounded on board the U-boat and to tow the lifeboats with the rest of the crew to Brazil. It would be a long and tricky journey, but both captains thought it preferable to going to Freetown, where they would have to give themselves up.

Late that evening, Bauer sent a message to report that *Atlantis* had been sunk by an English 10,000-ton cruiser and that he was attempting to reach the South American coast with lifeboats and 305 men. In U-124, Mohr received two messages simultaneously, one ordering a change of course for both him and Clausen in U-129, the other rescinding the order. He therefore continued his southerly passage.

Back in the Admiralty building, the men and women of the OIC waited for Bletchley Park to produce more decrypts. With *Atlantis* gone and the refuelling and reprovisioning plans of the Germans in ruins, Dönitz would surely now need to reassess his operation and make adjustments. Having had such a perfect piece of intelligence on *Atlantis*, they now wanted one for *Python*. They knew she had reprovisioned U-124 and U-129, but they could not tell precisely where or when. They also knew that an operation was planned off the coast of South Africa and that reprovisioning would be needed. It would surely only be a matter of time before new decrypts arrived confirming when and where.

Sunday 23 November

All through Sunday nothing came in from Bletchley Park about any of the German vessels. By late afternoon, the Admiralty had decided to send a signal even though no further decrypts had come in, effectively confirming what they thought was happening. On the basis of all the available German messages decrypted up to 4.30 p.m. on Saturday, the Admiralty could be fairly clear that U-124, U-129 and UA would reprovision sometime in the first week of December. This would take place approximately 24 degrees south, 7 degrees west, in roughly the same spot south of St Helena where *Atlantis* had fuelled U-68 on 13 November.

News of the sinking of *Atlantis* had reached Mohr in the early hours with a message informing him that Bauer, in U-126, was attempting to get to South America with lifeboats in tow. He was short of fuel and had 305 *Atlantis* survivors with him. Mohr and Clausen were ordered to slow down to twelve knots and alter their course slightly, presumably to meet up with Bauer. Mohr immediately set his engines to half-speed and altered course. It was not a major course change, but a fateful one for *Dunedin*.

By mid-morning a further message made clear that he and Clausen should head for U-126 once Bauer had reported his location. The rescue mission was now in full swing.

By later that evening, the Germans had decided what to do in the wake of the *Atlantis* disaster. In a series of messages, it became clear what was being planned. Bauer was to steer due west along the latitude which lay 6 degrees 30' south of Point 'Nanking' in order to hand over survivors to *Python*, who had orders to patrol the area on the 24th and, if necessary, the 25th. Bauer was to take on sufficient supplies to return to France. Mohr and Clausen were still to proceed to Bauer, but if the survivors had already been picked up they were to carry on south as previously planned.

Naval listening stations in England intercepted these messages, but Bletchley Park would not decrypt them until more than two days later. The OIC therefore knew nothing on the evening of the 23rd about the plan for U-124 and U-126 to rendezvous with *Python*.

Monday 24 November

Just after midnight on the 23rd, the teleprinter in the OIC punched out a decrypt from U-126. It was Bauer's message of the evening of the 22nd reporting the sinking of *Atlantis* and informing the German High Command that he was making his way to South America with lifeboats and 305 men. The message also said that he would have to reprovision to be able to return to France.

Then, a little over half an hour later, the first of a succession of messages about U-124 arrived. First, U-124 and U-129 were ordered late on the 22nd to change their course. Then, fifteen minutes later, there was a further message, this time from U-124 reporting where she had been at

1200 on the 22nd, and then, a third message three minutes later rescinding the instructions to U-124 and U-129 to change their course. Instead they should carry on with their present task. But what was the task?

Two hours later, the answer came when Bletchley Park teleprinted a further message. This one had been sent before the previous three and instructed U-124 and U-129 to go direct to the Kleiderstoffe area.

It was 3.00 a.m. on 24 November and U-124 had been on its way to the Kleiderstoffe area for forty-two hours. Unknown to the Admiralty, however, U-124 had now been diverted to find the survivors of *Atlantis*.

A map of the Atlantic at this point would have shown *Devonshire* approaching Freetown, *Dorsetshire* further to the south, *Canton* to the west and, between the two, *Dunedin* on her lonely patrol. To the west of *Dunedin* was a small outcrop of land, St Paul's Rocks, in the middle of the Atlantic, some 1,200 miles south-west of Freetown. Uninhabited and desolate, they were no more than markers in a vast open space, barely fifty feet above sea level – somewhere to be avoided.

The OIC needed now to work out what the Germans would do next. They knew that U-126 was low on fuel and was attempting to make it to South America with the *Atlantis* survivors. She had made quite clear that she would need to refuel to have any chance of getting back to France. Her part in the South Africa operation would surely now be over. But where would the refuelling take place? It would have to be with *Python*. Then what? Would *Python* carry on south to refuel the same U-boats, 124 and 129, as well as UA for the South African operation?

Decrypts continued to pour in through the teleprinter. By 8 a.m. a further sixty-eight had come in since the 'Kleiderstoffe' message had arrived five hours earlier, but only two made any mention of the German ships thought to be in the area. And even these were several days out of date. If *Python* was around, and if the U-boats were close by, there were ships already in the area, including *Dunedin*. The Admiralty chose not to send a signal until around 5 p.m. in response to a signal from HMS *Devonshire*. In it the Admiralty speculated that it was likely that *Python* would be ordered to embark survivors (of *Atlantis*) and refuel the U-boat (U-126). It thought that *Python* had been in approximate position 9 degrees north, 36 degrees west on the 20th and was steering to her southerly refuelling point near St Helena. This speculation was very accurate in the circumstances. Bletchley Park had decrypted none of the detailed messages that had reached Mohr on the 23rd about the rescue operation, so it was all guesswork on the part of the Admiralty.

But much would happen before the Admiralty had sent this signal. Would it be too late?

In *Dunedin*, in the early hours of Monday 24th, such strategic thoughts were far from the mind of Captain Lovatt. His job was to continue to look for a German surface ship. He had been instructed where to look and was carrying out the search. For most of the ship's company it was just another patrol, but for the captain it was a painstaking and methodical sweep of a clearly defined area. The orders from the Commander-in-Chief South Atlantic had been quite precise. *Dunedin* was to carry out a search for an enemy supply ship in the area 0–5 degrees north, 25–30 degrees west, an expanse of the Atlantic 600 miles by 600 miles surrounding St Paul's Rocks.

As the first wispy strands of light threaded their way across the dark sky on the dawn of 24 November, *Dunedin* sailed on a slight swell. Soon another day of scouring the ocean would begin. As the sun rose still further, visibility improved rapidly and the chances of seeing something increased by the minute.

CHAPTER 9
Sinking and Adrift,
24 November–27 November 1941

Monday 24 November

Buzzes about a return to England took on as much significance as a drop of sweat in the humid south Atlantic air. All thoughts of home were banished, filed in obscure compartments of our minds. My family was far behind me and only the occasional letter punctuated an otherwise permanent existence on the open sea. Freetown and St Helena were mere blips on an undulating plain of watery nothingness. Sometimes the sea would caress us gently, sometimes she would lash us with her ferocious anger. Her moods and tempers were all we knew of her. Her true identity remained a mystery to all but the officers. Bletchley Park, Ultra, Admiralty signals and the OIC meant nothing to us. We neither knew where we were going nor where we had been. Today was just another day.

A little before noon it was time to get my lunch. I'd finished handing out the vegetables and was feeling hungry. But first I stopped on deck and leaned on the deck rail, drawing on a cigarette and looking out to the calm waters of the Atlantic Ocean. The sun slapped its heat against my face, the sky was sharp blue and a few mountainous peaks of cumulus clouds poked up from beyond the horizon. A gentle swell caressed Dunedin. A soft breeze brushed my face. Only the zigzagging of the ship gave me any sense of disruption to the serenity of the hugeness of the sea. I shifted my weight to go with the patterns of the ship's movement, leaning first to the left then to the right.

Several miles to *Dunedin's* west, U-124 was heading south en route to U-126 and *Python*. The same soft breeze that blew over *Dunedin* hit the faces of the men on the submarine's bridge.

The grey, murky U-boat ploughed through the sea in a straight and resolute course. The sun shone piercingly on the bridge and from the gentle rolling sea spots of surf jumped, splashing against the paintings of the two edelweiss adorning each side of the conning tower.

At 11.56 a.m., the forward lookout on the port side broke the serenity and shouted that he could see a ship. He had spotted, barely visible on the north east horizon, the thin outline of a mast. Soon, four sets of binoculars were trained on the tiny image zigzagging in the distance. When, a few minutes later, Mohr joined them on the bridge, the excitement was spreading through the U-boat. After months of merchants and Americans, could this be an enemy warship?

I took one last drag and flicked my cigarette butt over the rail. It arced a few feet then was whisked away into the white foam of the ship's wash. I turned and went back to my mess, stopping on the way to pick up my lunch at the galley. Nobby had just about finished clearing his meat counter and was almost ready for lunch himself. I waited a few moments for my pal and soon we squeezed into the mess together. We sat side by side and ate what would be our last meal together. Nobby had not long been married and he often told me about his wife and how he would love us to meet. We talked today about what we would do when we got back to England. We were both London boys – from either side of the river, mind, but we knew what London had to offer and looked forward to it, even though it seemed such a distant prospect.

We talked of the buzzes about a return to England and speculated, like we had on many occasions, on how soon we would really get back. We could both tell too that we were on no ordinary patrol. It was clear that we were looking for something specific, but we had no way of knowing what.

In the distance, Mohr was tracking *Dunedin* as she continued her zigzagging on a north-westerly course. By now he had identified *Dunedin* as a light cruiser of the Dragon class. He thought she could have been one of four ships, the *Delphi, Despatch, Durban* or the *Dunedin*, his first real military target and on only his second patrol as captain. The thrill and anticipation on the U-boat grew by the minute. His mind racing to work out the best plan of attack, Mohr turned his submarine to the west. His intention was to keep *Dunedin* in his sights and to pick a spot to wait and fire his torpedoes into *Dunedin's* portside.

On *Dunedin's* bridge, young Harry Cross was Assistant Range Finder, standing over the distance-measuring contraption, a basic piece of equipment mounted on a pedestal with two mechanical arms on the sides. The range finder on duty looked through the viewfinder and it was Harry's job to turn the handle to point it in the right direction.

Below decks Nobby and I finished our lunch. I followed him up to the deck before he went off to his meat store, not far from the wireless room, his quiet cubbyhole where he found some peace and quiet.

Ahead of *Dunedin*, U-124 remained on the surface but far enough away not to be visible. At around 12.40 Mohr cleared the bridge and prepared to dive. This young but already sharp Captain was setting his trap with precision and clever calculation. Now all he had to do was wait for the perfect moment to fire. But within a few minutes of the dive, things began to go wrong. A depth gauge had sprung a leak, shooting water in jets around the sub as the U-boat threatened to lurch out of control. The forward diving planes were not responding. The sub would not stay straight and steady, but jerked violently up and down. Mohr was certain the sub had broken the surface. Surely, they would have been seen.

At 12.50, Harry was jolted into action by the cry of the aloft lookout, Able Seaman Moore: 'Periscope on the port bow!' Harry reached for the handle of the viewfinder and yanked it round to where the lookout was pointing.

Everyone on the bridge was leaning to port, straining to pick out the periscope. The lookout continued to point. Harry had turned the viewfinder round, but he could see nothing to point at. In a while, Harry loosened his grip on the viewfinder. The periscope had gone. No one could see anything, but the captain, who was below decks by now, was informed.

Mohr felt U-124 submerge again, waited a moment, then looked through the periscope once more. *Dunedin* was still there, zigzagging as usual but on basically the same course. Relieved, he continued his underwater pursuit.

I made my way back to the mess. I stayed for a while on deck, having a smoke, unaware of what went on beneath the sea and what had happened on the bridge. I stood, looking out to sea, shifting my weight as usual with the zigzagging. Only this time I felt the ship take a longer lurch to port and I saw the horizon shift. This was more than a zigzag, we were changing course. It looked like we were turning south. 'Where are we going this time? Back to Freetown maybe?' Dunedin *began to shudder as she picked up speed. I tossed my fag end over the side and into the water and went below decks to my mess on the port side. Away from the cooling breeze on deck, the air below decks was, as ever, hot, clammy, sticky and generally unpleasant. Sweat poured from every man. I was wearing only my underpants and a pair of soft shoes, and within seconds wished I had not come down. After a quick rest, I'll go back on deck, I thought.*

Captain Lovatt was back on the bridge now, having ordered a change of course. He had switched from a north-west to a south-west course, in pursuit of what Moore had seen from the mast lookout. Lovatt's pulse must have quickened as *Dunedin* increased her speed to eighteen knots, not quite her best but enough to cause much rattling and shaking. The Admiralty had been right, *Dunedin* was in the middle of something. A boarding party was mustered on the upper deck in readiness. What Lovatt could not know, however, was that his course change was pulling *Dunedin* away from the menace of U-124. As *Dunedin* sailed in a south-westerly direction, U-124 was heading west.

We will never be certain what Able Seaman Moore saw from his lookout position. Was it U-124 or could it have been a different submarine? Or perhaps it was a fast surface ship. Mohr, however, had set his course to lie in wait for *Dunedin* at what he estimated to be the perfect spot. He could see where *Dunedin* was going and he had only to make a simple course calculation. He never knew whether *Dunedin* had seen him. He must have assumed not after seeing *Dunedin* on an unchanged course after U-124 had briefly broken the surface. He did not see *Dunedin*'s change of course. It seems that Captain Lovatt's temporary absence from the bridge coincided with U-124's brief appearance on the surface. By the time Lovatt had ordered the course change, Mohr was back under the surface, below periscope depth. By around 1 p.m. *Dunedin* was unknowingly sailing away from danger. How far Mohr sailed further west after this is hard to tell, but he probably waited no more than quarter of an hour before looking through the periscope again.

By 1.15, Mohr estimated that he would be in a perfect position to meet *Dunedin*, but he could scarcely believe his eyes as he looked again through the periscope. Where was the ship? He was devastated to find that *Dunedin* had gone, changed course. With one more walk round the periscope he saw her, some 4,000 metres away, sailing in the opposite direction, surely out of range.

Mohr was still stunned at what had happened and his sense of loss spread to his men. He pondered his options. He had done everything right. *Dunedin* had been sailing in a north-westerly direction. All he had to do was to haul out to the west, stay in touch with her and wait for the moment. And here he was, exactly where he wanted to be, but the cruiser had done the unexpected. She had changed course.

She was probably too far away, but this could be his only chance to hit a British warship. He ordered a course change due south and began to recalculate his options. He had very little time. He could see *Dunedin* clearly enough through his periscope, but she was getting away and his torpedoes would have to run an incredible distance. Waiting in bow torpedo tubes I, II and IV were three G7e torpedoes, each capable of travelling at around 900 metres a minute at a maximum speed of 30 knots. The U-boat was settled at 12.5 metres depth and travelling at 3 knots. Hurriedly, Mohr continued his calculations. *Dunedin* was sailing at a bearing of 338deg from him, which put her on a course of 223deg. The torpedoes would have to run a good deal further than 4,000 metres - perhaps to their very limits – by the time they reached their target. And, by then, they would have slowed considerably. More calculations. Finally, he was ready. He would send three torpedoes at 2.2 second intervals, 2.2deg apart and at a depth of 2 metres. He would need a 36deg 'aim-off' to take account of *Dunedin's* course and speed and he would have to hope that *Dunedin's* zigzag pattern did not disrupt his mathematical adjustments. At 1.20, he gave the order to fire the three torpedoes. His men waited anxiously in the heat and sweat of their tin tube, listening anxiously. Three minutes passed, then four – surely too long for a hit. Then Mohr raised the periscope again. Five minutes. Surely it was over now.

I lay on a bench by the table, my lifebelt a makeshift pillow, trying to doze in the oppressive heat below decks.

At 1.26 I was shaken from the bench as a massive bang thundered around me and the ship lurched instantly to starboard. The familiar noises of a ship at sea, the humming and vibrating and the clanking of machinery, were stifled by the overwhelming cacophony of explosion and disruption.

The auxiliary lights came on almost immediately as the main lights went out. There were some twenty men in the mess and we all knew instantly what had happened. I was thrown to the deck. Nobody panicked but everyone made for the ladder in the middle of the mess in a rapid scramble.

Shouts and screams filled the room. 'Come on, lads, let's get out of here', 'Bloody hell, we're going down', 'Come on, move it', 'We've been hit', 'Out of my way.' Books, plates, mugs, clothes, anything loose went flying. The relative order of the mess was transformed into chaotic pandemonium as our home was literally being turned upside-down. No one had time for thought, it was simply time to go. I didn't even pick up my lifebelt.

Within seconds the ladder was almost vertical as the ship fell further. It was just a few feet from where I had been lying and I was among the first to reach it. We struggled to pull ourselves up as another loud bang crashed around us as a second torpedo hit, no more than twenty seconds after the first. How many more would hit? We made it to the top of the ladder and into a seaman's mess above ours, then up a second, more crowded, ladder into the recreation space. We tried to move quickly up the ladder, but now it was crowded with men desperately trying to get to daylight. We squeezed into the recreation space.

The piano slammed against a wall in a discordant clang, tables were strewn everywhere, chairs flying around. With the ship now listing violently, the first man in our group to reach the door struggled to wrench it open. We could see a flash of bright blue sky as he heaved it open.

It was now very noisy. Anything loose crashed around us and men were shouting and screaming, some crying out for help. When finally we emerged on deck, the sea was much closer than usual and men were jumping into the sea all around us. Some were covered in blood, others lay on the deck unable to move, probably dead. A fire was raging somewhere and small explosions were now following the initial blast of the torpedo impact.

After the first torpedo had hit, Captain Lovatt made his way from the bridge to the flag deck to order a distress message to be sent. In response, Chief Yeoman Lavington rang the W/T office, but he could get no reply. Then Chief Petty Officer Telegraphist Grant appeared and was told to send a message using the emergency set. Captain Lovatt gave the order to abandon ship.

The ship's joiner, Thomas Moore, had been taking a nap when the first torpedo hit. He had been on the upper deck and was thrown ten feet in the air against the guardrails. Dazed and shaken, he instinctively felt for his lifebelt, but then realised he had left it in his mess. What should he do – take his chances without it or risk going to get it from his mess? Incredibly, within seconds he made his way down the forward hatch and into his mess and found his lifebelt. While he hurriedly fastened it around him, he could see the mess deck had been torn to pieces. And then the second torpedo hit and he clambered up the near-horizontal ladder on to the deck.

As the first torpedo hit, Boy Les Barter, who had joined *Dunedin* in April 1941, was resting in the recreation space after keeping the middle watch the night before. Being small, he scrambled immediately out through a porthole on to the deck, where he could see that some men were already in the water. Hearing the call to abandon ship, he jumped in with a number of others and desperately swam round, trying to find a Carley raft.

As I clung to the sloping and shuddering deck, I knew I had to get to my abandon ships station at the Carley floats stowed on top of the blacksmith's shop behind No. 3 6-inch gun. Someone shouted 'Every man for himself'. While men were pushing past me to get into the sea, I fought against the flow and clambered along the ever-increasingly slanting deck on the port side to the blacksmith's shop. I clambered up to the floats and reached for the fastening clips. I knocked them free and shoved the floats into the sea. With the ship listing violently to starboard they didn't have far to fall, maybe ten feet. I jumped in after them, along with dozens of my comrades.

The water was warm, almost pleasant in the tropical heat. I plunged deep into the sea, the noises of shouting men muffled by the wall of water crushing my body. I opened my eyes as my descent slowed and looked through the clear water to see bubbles rushing to the surface. Beneath me the sea was bottomless and dark, above me the sun glistened through the surface. I kicked my legs and pulled on my arms, my lungs bursting as I held my breath. Beside me another man shot down past me, a dart of bubbles and surf forming in his wake. In a moment I broke the surface and the cacophony of the scene hit my ears once again. People were jumping in all around me, shouting and calling. Debris was everywhere. Furniture, cupboards, everything loose from the ship had either fallen into the water or been blown into it by the explosions. Oil lay on the surface. I breathed deeply to refill my lungs.

I made for one of the floats with several others. Thomas Moore was in the water near me now. He saw Commander Unwin and Lieutenant-Commander Sowdon swimming around near the rafts but refusing to get on until they had found room for as many of the others as possible.

The nearest Carley to me had hit the water upside-down, so we had to struggle to right it before getting on. Without my lifebelt, I struggled to stay afloat and push the raft on its right side. Each time I heaved it up, I went under. Eventually we righted it and clambered on. Someone shouted, 'Grab the paddle, get away from the ship.' We paddled and kicked as hard as we could to avoid being sucked down with the ship. It's amazing how one's training can become reflexive at times of emergency. All those interminable bloody lectures and instruction sessions were paying off now.

On the bridge Harry Cross hung on to a rail, desperately trying to stay on board. After the second torpedo hit, the ship briefly righted herself, giving him the false sense that she was not going to sink after all. If he was quick he could get to his mess and find the money he had been saving ever since he had been on board. He ran into the gangway leading below decks and made for his quarters. Men were pushing in the opposite direction; officers were shouting orders and screaming. He had to get to his money. But it was no use, he turned back with the tide of men trying to get off.

Then, suddenly, *Dunedin* fell further to starboard and Harry went over the side into the water. With *Dunedin* clinging desperately to life, Harry did the same and grabbed hold of a lifeboat derrick before pulling himself back on to the doomed ship. He could see a yellow cloud bellow from somewhere behind him as there were more explosions. He saw men all around him in the sea, clambering for the rafts or clinging to anything that floated, but he gripped still harder and stayed with the ship. Somehow she remained afloat. In fact, she was even moving in a slow but perceptible circle. Perhaps she would stay afloat and Harry could hang on.

Out of nowhere, Commander Unwin had appeared, shouting, 'what are you doing still here? She's going down. Save yourself, man'.

Eventually, Harry fell back into the water, desperately aware that he had plunged into shark-infested waters. He strained to keep as much of his body above the surface as possible, but it was no use. He was prey to his biggest fear – sharks. He called out for help and looked desperately for the Carley floats.

As the sea lapped around his face and came into his mouth, he caught glimpses of the floats sixty or seventy yards away, too far for him to reach. His desperate attempt to stay on the ship had merely lost him precious time. The Carleys were now gone.

All around him the debris of the sinking ship – furniture, clothes, papers, even some vegetables – bobbed up and down.

He now swam for his life away from *Dunedin*'s drag. When he had gone far enough, he floated breathless in the oily water, still among debris but nowhere near a Carley. He could hear men's voices, their shouts and screams, but he could not see them. He thought again of the sharks and looked desperately for something sizeable to cling to. Then, several yards away, he saw a wooden cabinet, probably from the officers' mess. It was about five feet by two. He grabbed it and tried to get on top, to keep his feet out of the water. But it was no good. Every time he heaved his body up, the cabinet tipped over and he slid straight back in.

He had to think fast, otherwise he would never be safe. Clinging to the cabinet, he looked around for something better, but there was nothing he could see that would work as a life raft. Then, as his grip slipped once more, he realised that if he could take out the four drawers, he might be able to get into the cabinet. The cabinet was on its back, so he had to reach up and pull out each drawer with all the weight above his head. With no leverage, he strained every last sinew in his body to pull them out.

When finally he had discarded the drawers, he clambered on to his makeshift raft and lay panting on his back, his feet dangling over the side. At last he could keep his body out of the water. He looked up at the ship and watched as *Dunedin's* bow began to lift.

The first torpedo had struck the starboard side near the seamen petty officers' mess, the second near the wardroom flat. *Dunedin* had listed about 15 degrees to starboard immediately after the first impact, and this list increased to about 35 degrees within five minutes. The explosion from the second torpedo had torn up the quarterdeck, dislodged the No. 6 6-inch gun and blown off the port propeller.

The bare shaft of the propeller was clearly visible as *Dunedin* slowly circled to the port side before finally coming to a halt.

Mohr had moved in closer and had watched from under the sea, his periscope piercing the surface, unnoticed by the men in the water. He and his men waited a remarkable five minutes and thirty-seven seconds for the first torpedo to hit. In a strange quirk of underwater acoustics the first sound that the men of U-124 heard was a dull metallic bump as a G7e thudded into *Dunedin's* starboard side somewhere below the bridge. Then, six seconds later, they heard the explosion, muffled through miles of ocean, but clear enough for them to know that a British warship – their first – had been hit. Eighteen seconds later it happened again, the same metallic clunk followed by the same detonation crack as a second torpedo hit further aft. The third of Mohr's torpedo triumvirate missed. He later reported seeing a massive explosion and a thick yellow cloud when the first torpedo hit, then wreckage flying high into the air as the second one struck. And now Mohr looked on as *Dunedin,* his first British warship, lay helplessly, dying but not ready to disappear. He decided to fire a fourth torpedo. This would be the final kill, the *coup de grâce,* the *Fangschuss* that would put the wounded prey out of its misery. He was closer, only 3,000 metres away and with plenty of time to make his calculations. No need to rush, no need to make last second adjustments, no need to worry about distance or zigzags. The numbers were simple. A 3deg angle, no need for an 'off-aim'. At 1.46, as more men fell into the sea around *Dunedin,* and as many more struggled to stay alive on board the sinking vessel, Mohr fired again. He watched as he heard the torpedo leave his vessel, an echoing fizz sounding in his ears.

Nobody in the water saw the fourth torpedo as it sped towards *Dunedin.* But there were to be no more explosions, no more ripping of metal, for Mohr had missed. Two out of three speculative long shots had done their deadly deed, but the final cruel blow, delivered at point-blank range, had failed to connect. Instead, *Dunedin* made her own decision to slip away gently, wounded and dying, sliding down on her own terms, twenty-five minutes after the first torpedo had struck.

I watched Dunedin's *final moments. We had managed to paddle nearly 100 yards. I saw the ship briefly right herself, then slip back again on her starboard side. Then the bow lifted for a moment before she sank into the depths, stern first, my home of many months falling into the sea. I watched as she disappeared in a white rush of foam, one last shriek of tearing metal piercing the equatorial air, before being stifled by the water. Without a second thought we all gave* Dunedin *three hearty cheers as she slid from view. Some sang 'God Save the King', others just watched in horror and disbelief.*

Someone said she had taken seventeen minutes to sink. Seven Carley floats had got away, each with at least twenty men on board – among them, Thomas Moore on my raft. Many others were in the water, bobbing up and down, shouting, calling, waving frantically, trying desperately to find something to hold.

The surface of the sea was now covered in oil and debris and a last few air bubbles rose from Dunedin *and burst around us.*

Beneath the waves, the creaking and cracking sound became louder as *Dunedin* eased past U-124 on her way to the bottom of the sea. Her ageing and rusting body complained noisily, creaking and cracking under the strain. Water bubbled all around her and rushed into the ship's open cavities. Oil poured through her wounds and into the throng of men on the surface.

Mohr decided to take his U-boat to the surface and have a closer look.

The scene on the Atlantic Ocean that day north-east of St Paul's Rocks was desolate: men bobbing in the sea, not knowing what would happen next, not knowing when or if they would see their homes again, not knowing where their friends were. Where was Nobby? Had he made it? I called out for him but couldn't find him. All around me, men were calling, shouting, screaming. On the open sea, sounds have no resonance, no reference points, nothing to echo from, just a wide expanse in which to get lost, carried away on the breeze, detached from the close-knit intimacy of the ship.

After a few minutes I sat astride the raft's perimeter, struggling to maintain my place among twenty-one other men, the float low in the water under their weight. I was at least afloat, relatively safe, unlike many of the men I could see floating only with the benefit of their life belts, some without even that. Others were clinging to anything that floated by. Some were already dead.

Others swam from raft to raft, trying to find a space. Our raft was already overloaded, there was no more room. We were crammed against each other, unable to shift our position or make any further space. One man swam up to us but he could see that we were already very low in the water and in danger of toppling over. The only way he would be able to get on was if someone got off. Amazingly, this is exactly what happened. Sergeant Allen, RM, slid off the raft to give up his place and swam off to find another Carley. Among the many heroic and tragic acts that filled the next few days, I did not see one to surpass this one.

Some men had made it to the flottanets, pieces of cork tied together in a circle of rope. Men could lie on these, albeit half submerged in water, but at least they were afloat. Marine Dyer had made it to my raft. He told us that he had not been able to reach his action station, the cutter on the port side. He had seen it, crammed with men, sliding down the side of the ship and falling into the water on one end. It was immediately swamped and he did not see it again. All our boats had fared badly. The motor boat and the dinghy were free, but could not be floated off as the ship keeled over.

I was too occupied to be frightened, but fear was in us all, deep down, a fear of the unknown. For the crew of Dunedin, our environment had changed dramatically in an instant. One minute we were all part of a disciplined fighting outfit, governed by rules and protocol, orders and structure; the next we were a floating, scrambling rabble, surviving on our wits and physical strength.

No orders or structure would save us here, we had to make this up as we went along. There was no concept of superiority – no one person assumed charge on my raft. I was a young man of twenty on a small raft with people mostly older than I was. But that didn't matter. We were all bit players in one of the world's great levellers.

As our ship suffered its death throes, the chaos and confusion were punctured dramatically by the appearance of the U-boat, its grey and sinister shape breaking the surface to give us all a new and domineering focus. We were not afraid. Intrigued perhaps and curious, but not afraid. The men's shouting quietened as the submarine manoeuvered around us, stalking us and mocking us. We were silent now, all our gazes fixed on the conning tower and the two deck guns fore and aft, our desperate bids to clamber on board rafts and debris suspended temporarily as we wondered what would happen next.

We watched in disgust as the grey impostor strutted where once Dunedin had sailed. We were close enough to hear the coughing of her diesel engines and our noses filled with her contemptuous exhaust fumes. She passed slowly within fifty yards of us, almost coming to a stop. She was close enough now for me to see a mark on the side of the tower, a painting of something I couldn't quite make out.

No one appeared on the bridge, no one came to man the guns. The men in the water stayed quiet, the tension now unbearable, the chug-chugging of the idling engines and the gentle lapping of the ocean the only punctuation of the silence.

I waited, wet and tired and now not a little scared. The submarine was *barely moving. What did he want? Why didn't he get it over with? I heard a clanking of metal. Something was happening. Was somebody opening a hatch to come on deck? We all seemed to hear it. And then, movement on the bridge. I could sense a tensing of muscles, men straining to sit up straight, standing to attention from the waist up. This was it, the moment we had heard about, when the machine guns would send us down with* Dunedin.

What should we do? To swim away would achieve nothing, we could not possibly swim fast enough. Able Seaman Jim Davis was in the water with a young midshipman, swimming to find a Carley float to cling to. Jim had been on deck, soaking up the sun and reading The Way of a Transgressor *by Negley Farson, when the explosion threw him to the floor. He heard an officer call out from the foc'sle, 'Come on, Davis, let's get these Carley floats over the side.' Now he was trying to find one to cling to. The young midshipman wanted to swim to the U-boat, but Jim would have none of it and held him back. Some men began to shout at the submarine again and a hubbub arose from the sea as we contemplated the awful prospect of being shot. Was this really the end? Had we clambered off a sinking and exploding ship only to be shot in cold blood?*

Then something happened which, if we saw it in a movie today, would be barely believable. Slowly, hardly perceptibly, someone on my raft began to sing. It was hard to understand at first, hard to believe what I was hearing. Within a few seconds others had joined in, tentatively at first, then loudly and defiantly enveloping our tiny band of desperate men. I sang too, the words of 'There'll Always be an England' ringing out triumphantly and rhythmically, our bodies sweating and thrusting with every word, every last breath.

When we were done and our energy spent, we floated expectantly and quietly again, the noise of the submarine's engine audible once more after we had muzzled it with our song. I heard again the shouts of men on other rafts and in the water, the moans of injured men weaving into the cries for help.

I looked again at the painting on the side of the tower as the submarine moved off to the north, then fell willingly into the sea, its grey slatted deck and railings giving way to the white rushing of the sea. It was an edelweiss, a gentle mountain flower. And then it was gone and we were alone. The guns had remained dormant.

Men looked round at each other, wondering what the hell to do next. Our voices seemed to travel so far now without the confines of the ship. Jim Davis had found a Carley raft at last and was clinging to it in the water, unable to clamber on because it already had about twenty-eight people on it. From this raft, Petty Officer Butler called out that we should try to keep the rafts together, so we frantically paddled and kicked once more to get together. Six of the seven rafts that had survived the sinking huddled together on the gently ebbing waves of the vast Atlantic Ocean. We had few means to connect ourselves, but we did what we could to stay together. The seventh Carley had already drifted out of sight.

We scanned the horizon for other vessels, any sign at all that we weren't alone, that help was just a shout away. It was disheartening to realise that we could see very little from our position on the water. From the ship's decks we could see the horizon many miles away. Now, so close to the water's surface, we could hardly see any distance at all. And any moderate wave would itself become our cramped horizon. How ironic that, on such a vast expanse of water, our horizon seemed often no further away than the end of a swimming pool.

By late afternoon we had settled to our fate. The tropical sun was still hot, but thankfully, was beginning to weaken. All around us, men were struggling to stay on anything that floated. The Carleys were hopelessly overcrowded and some men fought to stay on board, especially when waves toppled us back into the sea. I was not immune from this struggle and even found myself grappling with one of my own Marine comrades to regain my tiny patch of sanctuary, such as it was.

Mohr, by now, had turned south again and was back on his original course. He had trouble getting off a signal, but finally transmitted a message to Africa Station:

> To BdU: English Cruiser D-class sunk. Grid Square 7985 ES. Continuing south. Mohr.

The silence of the ocean was too often punctured by the sounds of terror and desperation. Men cried for their families, others called frantically for a doctor. Where was Harold Broadway? Nobody knew.

Huddled together in our ramshackle convoy of rafts as well as in the water *itself, anything up to 250 of us looked around to see who had made it and who had not. The few officers who had made it to the rafts told us what they could about our chances of being picked up. Other ships were in the area on the same mission as ours and a distress signal had been sent. HMS Canton was known to be in the area and would immediately have initiated a search.*

Some of the men wanted to know more and asked questions that could not possibly have been meaningfully answered. 'How far away is HMS Canton, sir?' 'Do we know she got our signal, sir?' 'How long will it take, sir?'

The surviving officers responded as best they could. They didn't know for sure, but it was important that we stuck together and kept a sharp lookout.

I looked desperately among the frightened faces for Nobby. I shouted his name and asked after him. 'Has anyone seen Nobby Hall?' No reply came.

I couldn't help but realise that Nobby must have taken the full brunt of that first torpedo. Nobby's private cubbyhole in the meat store amidships was so private, I doubted he would have stood a chance of opening the watertight doors in time.

But I still looked for him.

In London, it was business as usual at the OIC. If a distress signal had been sent, it had not been received. No one knew that *Dunedin* had gone. For the OIC team, the line-up in the Atlantic was the same as it had been for the last few days, with *Dunedin* still in search of *Python*. In truth, the OIC would have been pretty happy with events. *Atlantis* had been sunk and U-126 had been diverted to rescue the survivors, and all without loss to our own fleet.

It was time, however, to take stock of the situation and to assess what to do next. The decrypts from Bletchley Park had slowed up. Only two concerning this operation had arrived since lunchtime, neither of which had been significant.

The OIC team would have assessed all the available decrypts and any other intelligence coming into the centre, mostly D/F fixes of signals sent by the Germans. Moreover, the OIC was brilliantly skilled at predicting the next moves of the U-boats and surface ships. It was singularly adept at stepping into Dönitz's shoes.

By 5 p.m. they had enough to send a further message to the

Commander-in-Chief South Atlantic. It was not as precise as the intelligence passed on a couple of days earlier which had led to the sinking of *Atlantis*, but it gave some clear indications about the movements of *Python*. It said that a U-boat was making for South America with lifeboats containing 300 survivors and that the U-boat was known to be short of fuel. This information had come direct from the decrypted message received in the OIC just after midnight, some twelve hours before *Dunedin* had been hit.

The message went on to comment that it was likely that *Python* would be ordered to embark the survivors and refuel the U-boat. It gave *Python*'s approximate position on 20 November and its eventual destination further to the south.

C-in-C South Atlantic acted quickly on this intelligence, transmitting a signal to both *Canton* and *Dunedin* to steer south as quickly as possible. The intention was clear – to search for the survivors of *Atlantis*. Both ships were requested to report their position, course, speed and fuel remaining. *Canton*'s response came in three hours later.

Dunedin, of course, could not respond. A second signal was transmitted, repeating part of the first one, and then around midnight a third signal was sent to both ships with further instructions about the search. After completing the search, *Canton* was to carry on in a different area, while *Dunedin* was to return to Freetown. But the messages were no good to *Dunedin* now.

When night fell for the first time it brought with it the realisation that daylight had betrayed us and had not brought us our rescue. As darkness engulfed us we were more alone than during the day. Now we had only each other. We had no chance of being seen until the dawn. We all came crashing down from the relative high of having survived at all to the awful realisation that right now nobody could see us or hear us. No one even knew we were here.

The long hours of darkness were cooler, but we did not get too cold. We talked. Occasionally we sang. Sleep was near impossible, but somehow we could huddle together to grab catnaps. Sometime during that first night two green Very lights filled the sky to the south. We speculated what it could mean. Some shouted optimistically.

Some thought it was HMS Canton. *Hope grew that we would soon be rescued.*

A hubbub of voices arose as the green phosphorescent light faded and we were once more shrouded in darkness. Presently, the sturdy tones of an officer quietened the murmuring with his own sober account of the green lights. Those within earshot heard him say, 'I don't wish to dash your hopes, chaps, but I am rather afraid that our German friends have just found their supply ship. But our boys are in the area and we have a good chance of being rescued.'

No one spoke after this, the excitement of the Very lights now dimmed. Silence again ruled these waves.

Tuesday 25 November

Harry was still alone having never caught up with the Carleys, clinging to his increasingly sodden cabinet and weakened by seasickness. How much more scared must he have been than the men who had made it to rafts. At least they had company, the benefit of numbers. All alone and adrift on the vast ocean, Harry must have thought he was the sole survivor and with only the sharks for company. As his makeshift life raft took on water, his plight became ever worse. In the darkness of the night he faced the prospect of sinking for the second time. He called out for help, but no reply came.

Somehow he stayed afloat, but as the morning light crept into the sky the cabinet had become useless, its wooden frame waterlogged and sinking beneath him. Once more he slipped into the water and again he thought of sharks. He tried to be calm. He knew that if he thrashed his arms and legs, he would attract their attention, but he had to do something, he had to find something else to cling to.

He swam forlornly, seemingly for hours, but probably only for a few minutes, not knowing where he was going or what he was looking for. As the sun rose above the horizon, he could see he was still surrounded by the ship's debris, but he couldn't see any of his comrades. He was still alone. He swam among the debris, desperately looking for something to keep him afloat, to keep his legs out of the water. Was he the only man alive?

Soon he found a mast from a lifeboat, its sail furled tightly around it. He grabbed it and found it was sturdy enough to hold him – not enough to keep his legs out of the shark-infested water, but sufficient to take his weight. The sun was rising fast now and Harry felt a surge of hope that the new day would bring rescue.

Also in the water without a Carley raft was Les Barter, clinging – as he had been all night – to a gangplank.

Our Carley was alone now, adrift from the other rafts. Our little convoy had not stuck together and we could no longer see any of the others.

I had counted twenty-one other men on our Carley soon after the Dunedin *had gone down. Now, in the Tuesday morning sun, I counted again and saw that we had already lost several men. Perhaps I had counted wrong the day before? But no, I had more room on the raft now.*

In the Admiralty, the OIC continued its assessment of the available intelligence material. No new decrypts had come through during the night that might shed light on the movements of the U-boats or *Python*.

On the other side of Horseguards Parade, in the Cabinet Office in Downing Street, a group of senior naval personnel were assembling for their regular Battle of the Atlantic Committee meeting. The First Sea Lord, Sir Dudley Pound, was in the chair for this, their twenty-sixth meeting. They were in good heart.

After the First Sea Lord brought the meeting to order, the Director Anti-Submarine Warfare addressed them. He reviewed the past week and said it was the first time he could report that no ship had been sunk by a U-boat. Later, the Assistant Chief of Naval Staff said it had been an unexpectedly exciting week. Three raiders had appeared after about eight weeks' inactivity: one off Australia, either from the Pacific or Indian Ocean, which was presumably the one *Sydney* had met; one in the North Atlantic which had probably got home; and one in the South Atlantic which the *Devonshire* may have accounted for. All in all, the committee must have felt rather pleased.

Unknown to them, the remaining members of *Dunedin*'s ship's company were not so happy. And in the Mediterranean that day HMS *Barham* was torpedoed with the loss of 862 men.

From Freetown, a further message was sent to *Canton* and *Dunedin* warning them to give the *Atlantis* lifeboats a wide berth if they sighted them because a U-boat would probably be accompanying them. By now *Dunedin* had failed to respond to the last four signals transmitted by C-in-C South Atlantic and fears began to grow for her. At 10.41 a.m. *Dorsetshire* and *Canton* were asked whether they had intercepted any signals from *Dunedin* since 6 the previous evening. Two hours later, the first reply came in. It was from *Dorsetshire* and it said simply, 'No'.

I looked again at the diminished group of men around me. Of those no longer with us, some had drowned, sharks probably took some, others just swam away and never came back. Hysteria and delirium took over on occasions, even on the first night. Some were convinced they had found a canteen with plentiful supplies of water and tea. Others said they had found the ship just below the surface.

As the numbers dwindled on my raft we disciplined ourselves as best we could. The sailors aboard the raft kept telling us to 'trim the dish', keep the raft balanced. The daytime sun was unbearable. I wore only a pair of shorts and, as the time ground on, the urge to drink seawater became stronger and stronger. I doused my face with water, desperately telling myself, 'Don't drink it, don't drink it.' Not once did I succumb to the temptation, as others surely and under-standably did. To have drunk the water to quench our thirst would merely have dehydrated us more and led to certain death.

Sharks threatened us constantly. Many swam close by, mostly in curiosity, but they were frightening nevertheless, bull-nosed, some at least twelve feet long. Once, one of my comrades, Marine Rose, had slipped off the raft and attracted the attention of a shark, which nosed all around his body as he hung over the side. As he tried to scramble back on board I hit the shark with a paddle and frightened it away.

Many times, the silence of the men was violently shattered by the shrieks of pain caused by the bites of barracuda, and other vicious fish, which nibbled away at a man's fleshy parts, his legs, arms and even his balls, and the stings of Portuguese men o'war, virulent jellyfish that washed into the raft on the crests of waves. Worst of all were the black durgons, about a foot long, blunt-nosed, with razor-sharp teeth. Mostly they attacked at night, sometimes even jumping from the water, biting wounds an inch or more deep.

Out of the blue, the pain would grip the victim with stabbing, flesh-tearing agony and panic would fill the raft as men thrashed violently and desperately, trying to keep their limbs out of the sea, to shake off the fish. Even the grating and netting of the raft could provide no defence against their penetrating reach. The flesh of my legs were ripped by the tiny but deadly teeth.

I was one of the lucky ones. While my legs were bitten and torn and while the salt water stung my wounds, others suffered more deadly blows and were struck in their arteries. Blood poured out relentlessly and messily and those so hit died a painful, slow and horrible death. Comrades vainly tried to stem the bleeding, but out there, on the ocean, this could buy only a few precious moments of lingering life. Unceremonious burial would follow. A body launched over the side, perhaps a prayer, perhaps a tear. More room on the raft. More blood in the sea for the sharks to smell. More death among friends.

Having survived his first night alone Harry spent the early part of Tuesday morning trying to stay afloat on his mast. Likewise, Les Barter was still hanging on to his gangplank, hoping to spot a Carley in the morning light. They were very tired, thirsty and hungry. As the sea lapped around their faces they resisted the temptation to drink and concentrated instead on trying to see around them and desperately to stay awake. Sleep would be fatal.

It was not long before Les spotted a Carley some distance away. He swam towards it and was lifted aboard, exhausted and immensely thankful. Harry's world, meanwhile, continued to be confined to the ocean's surface, for what seemed like hour after hour, his horizon stretching for miles one second, then diminishing to a wall of sea a few feet away the next. Each time he rose to the crest of a wave he looked frantically for something to comfort him – a ship, his comrades, a Carley float, anything but this loneliness and despair.

As the sun climbed still further, its equatorial intensity began to sear his skin and blind his eyes. But then, as he rose to the top of yet another wave, he caught a glimpse of a dark object in the distance. In a flash it had disappeared as he fell back again. He strained his neck as the wave receded and his vision was again unimpeded. Yes, there was the dark object. And then once more it disappeared from view.

Twenty or more times he bobbed up and the object flashed into view, each time slightly nearer. Now he could see its outline, some fifty yards away. Heads, arms, men. It was the group of Carley floats. He yelled out, 'Over here, over here', and immediately swallowed a mouthful of sea water. The next time the floats came into view he couldn't shout because he was choking on the water. He paddled frantically with his arms, edging closer to the Carleys.

Soon the men on the floats could see him as he struggled to pull himself and his makeshift raft alongside him. He managed a smile and shouted, 'help me on, help me on.'

Harry reached a raft containing perhaps twenty men, but he soon realised that this was no welcoming committee. Some of the men on the raft did not want to let him on and shouted at him to go away. Could he really have floated alone all night, only to find that he couldn't get on the raft? He pleaded with them to make room, but the men kept resisting.

Harry hung on to the Carley, clutching the rope with one hand and his mast with the other, but he couldn't get on. He scanned the faces, looking for a friendly expression, but to no avail. And then one man spoke up. Harry knew him as the 'Chief' – Chief Petty Officer Francis. At last, a friendly face. 'Come on, let him on. Move up, make room there.' Slowly the men acquiesced and Harry was pulled aboard.

The Chief was tired. He had seen comrades slide off in the night and during the day. He had struggled to stay awake, to stay alive, and now he was reaching out to save Harry.

Harry let go of the mast and was soon sitting astride the sides of the raft. He looked around him and could see four other rafts, packed closely together. His mast bobbed up and down beside the Carley, reluctant to float away. Someone leaned over, grabbed it and unfurled the sail.

After half an hour, the burst of activity had subsided and the men had dropped back into sagging-shouldered slumps.

Just after 2.20 p.m., two hours after *Dorsetshire*'s curt 'No', another flimsy slip of paper carrying the latest decrypt from Bletchley Park chattered off the teleprinter in the OIC. It was the 317th decrypt since the Kleiderstoffe message had arrived in the early hours of Monday morning, but it was the first really significant one since then.

The 'teleprincess' on duty would have taken hold of the message, as she had done with so many hundreds of others and glanced at its few words. She could not possibly read all the messages that came into her hands and, anyway, it wasn't her job, but this one might have caught her eye as she placed it in the out tray. Amidst all the technical, tactical and strategic messages that passed through her fingers, occasionally one would touch her heart and make her realise that the lifeless pieces of paper carried news of real people and real events. Sometimes the messages were very personal. Only a few days earlier one had conveyed news to a U-boat crewman that his wife had given birth to a daughter. But this latest one carried a more sinister tale. It was Mohr's victory message:

D-class British cruiser sunk in square PE 7985. Am continuing passage south.

Within the hour, the OIC had passed this on to C-in-C South Atlantic. It was a risky decision, since the message repeated virtually word for word what Mohr had said in his. Every time the Admiralty used Enigma intelligence to direct its ships, it risked giving away to the Germans that their messages were being read. The message sent by the Admiralty about *Dunedin*'s sinking was one such example, and it showed also that the Germans' grid references were understood, because the OIC had stated clearly that the D-class cruiser had probably been sunk at 2 degrees 30' north, 25 degrees 54' w. This was 275 miles east of St Paul's Rocks and over 900 miles from Freetown.

A risk indeed, but it was on the basis of this message that British ships in the area could be alerted to *Dunedin*'s fate. The armed merchant cruiser *Bridgewater* was the first to learn that *Dunedin* might have been hit by a U-boat and was sent in search.

HMS *Canton* was patrolling some 350 miles to *Dunedin*'s west and had been sailing first north, then south, in its patrol area. By late Tuesday afternoon she had been diverted into *Dunedin*'s patrol area and was sailing east close to St Paul's Rocks.

In the Admiralty a decision was taken to send a further message based on Bletchley Park's decrypts. The OIC was now pretty sure that the

Kleiderstoffe area was the place where *Atlantis* had refuelled U-68 on 15 November and that Mohr in U-124 and Clausen in U-129 were to rendezvous there with *Python* on 5 December. This information, including a repeat of the news that a D-class cruiser had been sunk, was sent just after 4.30 p.m. on Tuesday.

Canton finally replied at 5 p.m. to Freetown's request for information about *Dunedin*. She had not intercepted any signals from *Dunedin*, but had picked up an earlier one that had given the ship's position. But the message had not been received clearly and the references were garbled.

As the remainder of the crew of the D-class cruiser drifted slowly to the north-east, the U-boat and surface raider operation was moving south, away from them. Even *Canton* was too far south. By 10 p.m. *Canton* had been ordered to search the St Paul's Rocks area before proceeding towards Freetown in a wide sweep.

Two rain showers brought some relief late in the afternoon and for all of us it was an opportunity to lift our mouths to the sky and let the rain ease our swollen tongues and parched throats. Some even licked rain water from each other's skin. We had no water supply on our raft. The stone jar of fresh water provided in our Carley had salt water in it because the Carley had entered the sea upside-down when the ship was going down.

Sometime during the afternoon, Thomas Moore and the Chief Ordnance Artificer saw a rum barrel floating about fifteen yards from the raft. They swam out to it and pushed it back to the raft amid great excitement and anticipation. Our hopes were dashed when we found that the barrel was full of nothing but sea water.

Soon, a second night beckoned. Far away, Morse code messages peep-peeped into the ether. To the south-west of the dwindling band of survivors, HMS *Canton* was moving into the area *Dunedin* had been searching, but now the tiny fleet of rafts was merely a needle in a haystack.

As the sun went down, the men took scant comfort from the relief from the heat. Now they would have to face the long dark hours trying to stay awake for a second night, fighting against the will to sleep and the inevitability of falling into the sea. The barracuda did not let up and soon the men realised that those who were bitten died within an hour or so.

Nobody spoke much. Each man was locked in his own thoughts, his own private way of keeping sane and maintaining hope. Jim Davis prayed a lot on his raft; Harry conjured a vision of his mother, warm and embracing.

Early during this second night, Harry noticed that the sail quickly got damp. This had nothing to do with the sea, because between them the men had kept the sail dry when trying to shelter from the sun. No, this was the equatorial dew. After a while, he realised that this was drinking water. He took the sail in his mouth and sucked on it, but there was not enough to quench his thirst. Chief Petty Officer Francis saw what he was doing and told the rest of the men to make sure the sail stayed out of the water. During the night it also rained on and off.

'Keep the sail up, out of the water boys, and by the morning we might have collected enough water for a little drink,' said the Chief. The weary and sceptical crew of the Carley reluctantly held up the sail, not believing the Chief Petty Officer but too weak to argue.

As the night wore on, Harry saw their numbers reduce a little further. A couple of men simply slid off, either asleep or dead. Another swam away from the raft and never came back.

At some point in the depth of the night, he looked up at the horizon and saw passing lights in the distance. At first he did not know what he had seen. He was tired and cold and his eyes would not focus properly. His comrades were slumped in the raft, barely able to hold themselves up, but he nudged one of them and said, 'Look, lights over there.'

The man looked up, his head seemingly too heavy for his neck to bear. He also saw the lights and suddenly a surge of adrenalin and energy coursed through his body. He waved his arms and shouted out, 'Over here, over here.'

The others on the raft stirred from their semi-slumber and began shouting too, half of them not knowing why they were doing it. They waved their arms and yelled with all their remaining strength, and some even toppled into the water. But Harry knew it was no use, the ship couldn't possibly see them. In a few moments, the lights had gone and the men fell back to their positions, silently, morosely, but very angry inside.

Soon the Carley had returned to its sense of gloomy abandonment, the crew barely able to speak, just capable of fighting the desperate urge to sleep. Harry again thought of his mother. He could not bear the idea of her receiving a letter to say that he was missing. It would break her heart and he had to prevent it. He would not let her down.

Beside him sat a man, his head hanging, tears falling down his cheek. Desolation and helplessness hung over the pathetic little raft, the calm lapping of the night ocean accompanied by the gentle sound of the sobbing of a young sailor many miles from home.

Wednesday 26 November

By morning, men on every raft were in a bad way. Some lay back, half in their raft and half out of it, their heads resting limply on the side of their Carley. Occasionally they would stir, perhaps muttering to themselves incoherently, until they finally fell silent and were slid lifelessly into the sea in yet another impromptu funeral.

The urge to drink sea water overcame a number of men, the temptation too much to resist. Desperate, they drank from their cupped hands, half mad with thirst, but within only a few minutes they began to feel unwell and to moan and shout. They couldn't drink any more but they could feel a burning in their stomach and a surging in their throat. Others would watch horrified as their comrades deteriorated during the following hours, descending from pain to numbness to delirium and finally to wide-eyed exasperation. Salt is a killer. The bladder excretes salt in a 2 per cent solution, whereas sea water is about 3.5 per cent salt. The excess salt is deposited in the tissues under the skin, pickling victims alive. Their brain cells desiccated, men died raving and mad, perhaps having made one last dash for freedom over the side, lunging into the sea, thrashing in the waves and then disappearing from view.

HMS *Canton* was east of St Paul's Rocks, just above the equator, some 200 miles from the remaining survivors. By 10 a.m., she had launched her seaplane. As she sailed in a northerly direction, the plane was in the air for more than three hours before returning to *Canton* at 1.40. In the afternoon it was up again, for another three hours.

No one in the water saw it.

The persistent threat of sharks was probably the biggest single factor that kept us all awake. More bodies now floated in the sea for the sharks to feed on. We saw many fins and even felt their coarse rubbery skin rub against us and cut us as their curiosity brought them ever closer to our tiny raft.

Our numbers had dwindled still further by this time. We spent another whole day burning in the equatorial sun and I watched more of my comrades sink into oblivion and some literally into the sea. Some just slid over the side, at first hanging on to the rope around the edge, their heads dropping under the surface, then reappearing again momentarily as the last vestiges of the strength in their hands kept them afloat. Those left on the raft tried to hold them up out of the water. But this became too big a task for most of us and the desperate men clinging to life would simply slip away, their heads disappearing for good under the surface as their fingers limply fell from the rope.

Others swam away looking for Dunedin. One man came back and told us he had found a canteen with plentiful supplies of food and tea. No one listened to him.

During the morning, a lad of eighteen jumped over the side, saying he was going back to the ship. Barely had he entered the water when a shark's fin appeared around him. Thomas Moore, a tall man, leaned over the side while others held on to his legs. Thomas desperately reached for the boy and managed to grab hold of him and pull him back towards the raft. But the shark would not give in and Thomas felt a terrific shudder as the shark attacked. Thomas managed to pull him aboard, but the boy was so badly torn by the teeth of the shark that he became hysterical, screaming and crying in terrible agony, and he jumped back in again. This time there would be no rescue, only death, as the shark approached once more.

Our raft fell silent again, no comprehension, no logic finding a home with us.

Later, another man – I don't remember his name – seated at the opposite end of my raft grabbed the distress torch and started swinging it wildly at us. 'Get away from me,' he shouted as he lashed out at us. A string of expletives and insults rang out, and for the first time I felt very frightened and very vulnerable. I was so weak. I needed comfort and security, the sort that only your mother can give you. As the man continued his ranting, I found myself grabbing Colour Sergeant MacAuley around his waist, clinging on to him, my only solace on the lonely and hostile sea.

The man carried on his tirade into exhaustion. Finally, he sat quietly, slumped in the water, until later he too drifted over the side, never to be seen again.

Throughout the afternoon and into the evening, a flurry of messages between Freetown, *Canton*, *Bridgewater* and *Devonshire* signalled the frantic efforts to coordinate a search.

Wednesday night was dry and warmer than the previous night, but we lost still more men. Desperation and delirium truly set in. Men swam away from the rafts in search of Dunedin, *some hailing taxis, some returning from drinking tea in the mess. They showed no willingness to return to the safety of the rafts. They had a better place to go, to* Dunedin, *to her warmth and comfort.*

'Come on, boys. She's only over here. Just follow me.' And off they would swim again, struggling with reality and with the waves, sinking a little more each time they took a stroke, each time they reached for Dunedin, *each breath one nearer their last. They drowned easily and gracefully, muttering and gliding into oblivion. We watched in silent resignation as once strong men and eager boys destroyed themselves pitifully and painlessly. At times it was hard not to wonder whether it was true, whether they really had found water, or a taxi. One half of your mind wanted it to be true; the other half knew it to be a betrayal.*

All through the night, the dead left the raft.

Thursday 27 November

Three of us were still alive as the sun rose again: Colour Sergeant MacAuley, Thomas Moore and myself. A fourth man lay in the centre of the raft, having drowned sometime in the night. It was a while before we realised that he was dead. I suggested we put him over the side and between us we managed to bundle him over and give him a burial of sorts, one more committed to the deep, one more lost for ever. We watched as his body floated away, gently undulating with the waves, only its back visible to us. Soon sharks approached and his body disappeared in a brief splashing and flailing of fins and tails. Nobody spoke.

Despite getting weaker and weaker we continued to scan our near horizon, still hoping for rescue or maybe even to see land. We had no idea where we were.

For all we knew, we could have been half a mile from Freetown. We only knew that we were horribly hot and alone.

With our numbers dwindling and our cause seemingly hopeless, did I think we would be rescued? Did I have faith that we would be saved? I like to think that I did, that I had the confidence that I was living an aberration, that I would wake up and it would all be over, that I would be back at the barracks in Eastney, or at home with Mum and Dad in Swinley House. But did I?

By the fourth day, I had come to accept this as my lot. I would be on this raft for the rest of my life. I would still be here in six months' time. We all look forward in life, we all have ambitions, but at the precise moment in which you exist, that is all you have, that is your complete life. This is my life. Until I stop, it will be all I do.

The raft had become my life. That was it.

Beyond our tiny band of desolate men and our bobbing raft, all I could see were the sea and the sky. There were no trees, no mountains, no rolling fields, no buildings – nothing but nothingness. I lay in the raft, half submerged, hardly able to lift my head, able only to gaze up at the sky, blinking to keep out the sunlight, following an occasional cloud. My mouth was dry, my eyes burned, my legs were ripped. I tried to remember faces. My mother, my father, my brothers, Nobby. I tried to find some inspiration, some comfort, some guidance.

But I saw only sky, its vastness above me. And then it occurred to me that I was also looking to God. He would help me, He would tell me what to do.

I didn't know what I wanted to say to Him, to ask Him. But it didn't matter. I knew that He was there. I knew that He was watching. I wasn't really alone. But was this it? Was this how I would end my life? I had watched men fall into the sea. I had willingly pushed others overboard who had died among us. I had seen hysteria in once sane eyes.

And then, above me, I sensed the sky change its mood. The sun dipped towards the horizon, beginning its slow descent into the sea for a fourth time and the sky gave its first hint of a slide from deep blue to wispy pink. I looked at my two remaining comrades and I knew I would not last another night. Soon it would be my turn. I was hot, burning, my skin red raw, my hair matted with salt and Dunedin's oil. My legs were ripped, my throat was a sheet of sandpaper, my stomach empty and aching, my tongue swollen. I was near to tears and near to death. I was tired and wet. I wanted to sleep. My eyes kept closing and I kept falling into the raft. My head kept dipping into the sea, bringing me round sharply, forcing me to stay awake, to stay alive. A voice inside cried, 'Leave me alone. I've had enough. Let me go.'

I could hear only the lapping of the water against the raft and the splat of water against my ears. The voices of the others had grown quieter each day, but now there were even fewer words to hear. How many others were still alive? How many others were like me, lying in wait for nothing? The images of my family passed before me now, their silent faces trying so hard to make themselves heard, trying to reach me. My eyes kept closing, then opening, blotting out the images and then conjuring them up again.

With darkness threatening its arrival once more, I heaved myself upright in one last effort and gazed around to find the other rafts. They had grown so quiet that I wanted to reassure myself we weren't alone. I needed the comfort of knowing that the other rafts were still with us, that we still had the Dunedin connection. If we could at least stay in the same vicinity, then we might still have hope. But now, seventy-two hours after we first hit the water, the scene was very different from those early moments. Then it had been noisy and frantic, crowded and chaotic. Now the scene was almost peaceful, almost serene. No one was shouting, no one was screaming, no one was talking. As I pulled myself up with seemingly the last ounce of my strength, I could see no others. We were still alone. I had not seen the rafts since the first night. The sea was empty.

Moore, MacAuley and myself lay in the bottom of the raft waiting our turn, not caring for each other. It would be a happy relief to join our comrades. We had no worries and almost hoped for the darkness to end our peril.

And then I sensed that Moore was awake, struggling to raise his head, straining to look into the distance. I lifted my weary and expiring body and half turned my head. And there, out of the corner of my eye, I saw what he was trying to see. A ship. A bloody ship. 'O my God, o my God, look, look. For Mercy's sake, look.' I raised my head to the sky and thanked God.

I waved and screamed with every last fit sinew in my body. Moore and MacAuley were both shouting too. Somewhere from deep within ourselves, we found our last reserves of strength and determination. The ship was very close, barely 200 yards away, smoke billowing from her funnel.

'Over here! Over here!' we called.

Anything we could wave we waved – arms, clothes, flashlight. And we shouted as loud as our bodies would allow us, not realising in our frantic panic that either the ship had seen us, or it had not. No amount of shouting would penetrate the crashing sound of a moving ship. My brain worked painfully to calculate whether the ship was moving too fast to have seen us. Was it stopping? Would this prove to be only a cruel temptation that was taken away?

But as we waved and screamed, each of us knew that we had been saved. The ship was slowing down and men were leaning over the sides and pointing at us.

Soon the ship had stopped and we relaxed our contortions. Slumped in our raft, we awaited rescue, the grey hulk a welcome blockage on our horizon. After four days on the open ocean, with nothing to hear but the sounds of our own voices and the rushing of the sea, and nothing to see but our own faces and the swelling of the vast ocean beneath a blue sky and a fierce sun, now we could hear other men, machinery, activity – life.

Within a few moments of the ship stopping, a cutter was lowered over the side. And as it hit the sea its three crew members manoeuvred in our direction and our miracle was about to take place.

What was I thinking as we waited for the cutter to reach us? Did I contemplate the lives of those who had not made it? Did I wonder who had made it and who had not? Did I think of my home and family, of Mum and Dad? This was all there in some sub-stratum of my brain, but all our attention was on the job at hand, on getting to safety and, above all, on making sure our rescuers knew we were not the only ones.

The cutter moved closer until I could see into the faces of our rescuers.

'The others, the others, there's more,' we kept saying, over and over.

'Yeah, we know. It's OK, pal, just take it easy. Come on, easy does it.'

And suddenly we were being hauled into the cutter. Someone gave me cold fresh water in a stone jar. I gulped it clumsily and feverishly, pouring more over my face than down my throat, feeling its cold relief flow over me. Then the jar was snatched away from me by Moore or MacAuley. I tried to grab it back, but my body wouldn't allow it. I lay slumped on the bottom of the boat, exhausted, drained, but alive.

As the cutter drew up alongside the ship, a rope was thrown over the side to us, some ten or twelve feet down. At the end of the rope was a webbing loop, which we each slipped over our head and round our back. I felt the searing pain *on my sunburnt back as the webbing bit into my skin. In the midst of exhaustion and pain, the swell of the sea sent the cutter and the ship up and down in opposite directions and I found myself hanging from the end of the rope, the webbing biting deep into my red-raw skin. I screamed out in agony but somehow managed to scramble on board. Two crew members helped me out of the loop and I lay on the deck, panting and hurting, but murmuring still, 'There's more. Get the others. There's more.'*

Once again came the reassuring answer that the others had been seen and that they too would be picked up. As I lay on the deck, I could feel the swell of the ocean beneath me. Only now it was different to the hostile tossing and throwing of the last four days, when we could feel the ebbs and flows in our bones, when the slightest wave would topple us all back into the sea. Now I could feel it again, but it was a long way down, through tons of steel, comforting and caressing me. I lay, exhausted, and wondered again if Nobby had made it.

I could barely lift my head, but I could see a man who looked like he was in charge, directing men, pointing, looking over the side for more men. A sailor came to me and bent over me with a cup of water. 'Here you are, buddy. Take some of this.'

I muttered a thank-you and took in what I could. The water spilled down my face and onto my chest. It felt good, refreshing, salt-less.

In the gathering darkness, I heard the crew shouting about more rafts. The cutter was lowered again and I knew that others would be saved. Soon the little ship became crowded with more men dragged from the rafts. In two hours everyone afloat had been pulled aboard, the darkness now pierced by the rescue ship's arc lights shining on the last desperate group of survivors. I looked around at the human flotsam and I tried to see Nobby as more and more weak and exhausted men appeared on the deck. But all I saw were the sunken eyes and sun-dried flesh of once familiar faces. There was an eerie quiet as the men settled onto the solid deck of the ship, the only voices coming from the crew, their language comforting but strangely foreign, accents from another land.

'I can't find my friend Nobby. Can you ask about him, see if he made it?' I said to one of the crew.

'Sure. I'll look around. There's quite a few of you,' the sailor replied. He had a kind face and a warming smile. I didn't want to let him go.

'Where are you from? You're not English. What ship is this?' I asked.

'You're on the *Nishmaha*. *We're American, on our way to Philadelphia, but we've had engine trouble and drifted way off course, which is how we came to find you. I tell you, this damned ocean is crowded with Navy ships and German U-boats and yet it took this little thing to see you. You're a bunch of lucky guys. Now, just lie where you are a bit longer, I've gotta see to your pals. What d'ya say your buddy's name was? Nobby?'*

'Yes, that's right. Nobby.'

The sailor rose, but before I could ask his name he had gone. I lay back and stared at the darkening sky and felt again the gentle rolling of the ship. In a while I was placed in a bunk in a cabin on the upper deck. The rest of the night faded into a blur of fitful sleep. After three nights in the water, the bedclothes were rough against my reddened skin. Any movement sent burning tears across my body. My body cried out for water, my mind craved the warmth and softness of the bed.

That night, Dunedin's *survivors, seventy-two men, thanked God for their deliverance. In my bunk an American crew member leant over me with a cup of water and asked me what day I thought it was. I didn't know, it could have been any day of the week, I was not even sure what month it was.*

He looked at me and smiled. 'It's Thanksgiving Day.'

CHAPTER 10

Rescue,
28 November–7 December 1941

Friday 28 November

I awoke to a morning I had not expected to see. My bed was full of flakes of skin, like cornflakes. I was still very weak and now confused. The two others in the cabin with me managed to raise their heads to see what was going on in my bunk, but they quickly realised that they too had 'cornflakes' in their beds. Slowly we understood that our bodies had been so burned in the sun that our skins had peeled overnight.

The three of us looked at each other and began to ask questions. What happened to you? Where were you when we were hit? How many of us do you think made it?

We chatted slowly, painfully, trying too soon to relive the agonies of the last four days. I told my story as best I could. 'I was in my mess having a lie down. I just ran up the ladder and out as fast as I could. I didn't even have my life-jacket.'

But none of it made any sense. We were still in a dream world, somewhere between normal ship life and the awful realisation that it was all over, that we had survived while hundreds of others had not. We fired off names to each other, trying to find out who had made it and who was missing. Our minds held the fresh images of drowning and death, pain and agony. In mine a line of a song drifted in and out.

The conversation ceased within a few moments and we lay on our backs in our bunks, confused, tired, alone.

The silence was broken by a crewmember squeezing into the cabin clutching a bowl, a shaving brush, and some razors.

'How are you doing boys?' he asked cheerily. 'I thought you guys would like to freshen up, get that oily matted grime off your faces.'

He was quite right, we looked dreadful, with four days' growth on faces splattered with oil and bathed in salt water.

No one outside of the crew of the *Nishmaha* knew about the rescue. HMS *Canton* and her own seaplane continued to search for the next few days, helped by the armed merchant cruiser, *Bridgewater*. By the time the survivors were being hauled on to the decks of the *Nishmaha*, *Canton* had turned north-east, and on Saturday 29 and Sunday 30 she passed very close to where *Dunedin* had gone down and to where the *Nishmaha* had come across the survivors. On Sunday morning, the seaplane also passed very close to the point where *Dunedin* had been sunk, if not directly over it, an oil patch the only sign that anything might have happened there six days earlier. No rafts, no men, no debris.

By Sunday afternoon, HMS *Devonshire* had appeared on the scene to take over the search from *Canton* and *Bridgewater*. How different this mission was from *Devonshire*'s last one. Only a few days earlier, she had triumphantly sunk *Atlantis* and must have still been in the flush of glory when she was ordered from Freetown to look for *Dunedin*'s survivors. How disheartening it must have been for the captain and crew to search for days and find nothing.

In the early hours of Monday 1 December, the Commander-in-Chief South Atlantic officially accepted *Dunedin*'s fate. The signal to the Admiralty read as follows:

Regret to report that *Dunedin* has failed to return from patrol in Area H.34.C and must be considered lost. U-boat presumed in view of German claim to have sunk 'D' class in Atlantic.

(2) *Dunedin* failed to answer signals PM/24 and 25th. *Bridgewater* who was on patrol 300 miles from Freetown was ordered to search probable area which she reached on 28th.

(3) *Canton* was also ordered to search NE from St Paul's Rocks Area commencing on 26th then to R/V with *Bridgewater* in position 2 deg N. 26 deg 55' W. PM/28 and to continue search till PM/30. Nothing has been sighted.

(4) *Devonshire* continuing search in conjunction with her patrol of Area H.34.C for enemy surface units.

Many miles south, later that afternoon, between St Helena and Cape Town, the denouement of the Admiralty's plans was being played out. HMS *Dorsetshire* had found *Python* and two U-boats, just as the OIC had predicted. *Python* scuttled, the U-boats tried unsuccessfully to attack *Dorsetshire*, and the Admiralty's objective had been achieved.

Devonshire, meanwhile, with the help of her Walrus aircraft, searched for *Dunedin*'s survivors in the right place, but by now they had long gone. All she found was another oil patch, in position 2 degrees 35' north, 26 degrees 24' west, 275 miles east of St Paul's Rocks, and later an oil track further northeast, probably from the wreck of the *Dunedin*.

News of the rescue reached the Admiralty on 2 December after the captain of the *Nishmaha* had signalled his own authorities. In a message from Washington that evening, the Admiralty read the following:

US merchant ship *Nishmaha* picked up 72 men on 27/11 from *Dunedin* which was torpedoed and sunk on 24/11. Five died since. *Nishmaha* has been directed to land survivors, some of whom require medical attention, at Trinidad.

Nishmaha position 007 deg 30' W. at noon 2/12. Course 283 deg speed 9 knots.

The news reached *Devonshire* on Thursday 4 December that *Dunedin's* survivors had been picked up and the following day she was given the position of the rescue – 3 degrees 30' north, 21 degrees 30' west (400 miles from where *Dunedin* went down). By Saturday morning *Devonshire* had begun searching the area.

As Saturday slipped into Sunday, *Nishmaha* approached Trinidad, 2,700 miles from where the survivors had been rescued and where *Devonshire* was about to abandon her search.

The five who died were buried at sea on the 28th. These were William

Francis, Chief Petty Officer; Oswin Towndrow, Mechanician 1st-class; Robert Macintyre, Leading Signalman; Robert Suttle, Leading Signalman; and Boy Robert White. A short burial service was held and the last rites were read over each body in turn as it was placed on a hatch cover before being consigned, with great solemnity and reverence, to the ocean depths.

The nine and a half day cruise to Trinidad was a time of recovery and reflection, a time to wonder when we would be home again and a time to wonder whether our other friends and comrades had been picked up by other ships. It was a time too to hear from others what had happened to our shipmates. Slowly, small pieces of the jigsaw began to fall into place.

We heard many terrible and courageous stories. Horace Tall, Chief Engine Room Artificer, had somehow made it to a raft with both his legs broken. With the water's every ebb firing pain through his body, Horace lay in a Carley with terrible injuries in need of urgent help when none was at hand. He had kept up a stream of jokes throughout the first night in a gargantuan effort to hold his pain at bay, but as the night drew to a close, so too did poor Horace.

Others, myself included, were luckier to have survived without injury and did what they could to help the wounded. Boy McCall and Boy Morris, plunged at a tender age into the abyss of war, also made it to Carley rafts and both responded brilliantly to their plight. They showed cool and courageous spirit and cheerfully did everything asked of them, never uttering a single complaint.

Able Seaman David Fraser had volunteered to swim to the assistance of a drowning man knowing that the water was full of sharks and barracuda. He reached the man just as he died.

One of my Royal Marine shipmates, Sergeant Harry King, nursed a fellow marine who had been badly wounded when the torpedoes hit. Harry, immersed up to his shoulders, held him without complaint for forty-eight hours, patiently encouraging him. But by Wednesday afternoon Sergeant King's comrade in arms had run out of time and had died.

Able Seaman Moore, who seemingly knew no bounds to his energy and did whatever was required of him, kept up the spirits of everyone around him, but he reached the point when he himself could not keep going and he died.

Within a few days, I had regained enough strength to walk around the ship to see who else had made it. I recognised many faces, but I didn't find Nobby. Jim

Davis had made it, along with only five or six left on his raft. So too had Harry Cross. Lieutenant Milner came round to count up who had survived and those who were well enough helped the wounded as much as possible. Lieutenant-Commander Watson was the senior surviving officer, but I did not see him on Nishmaha. Having refused a place on the Carley rafts, Lieutenant-Commander Sowdon had been seen hanging on to a large spar, but he had not made it to Nishmaha.

Another survivor was Electrical Artificer Ernie Stevenson. He had been by the port wing of the bridge when he heard the sharp crack of an explosion that he thought was the sound of one of our 6-inch guns. He realised quickly, however, that we had been torpedoed and he felt the ship shudder and surge forward in leaps. When the second torpedo hit, he grabbed hold of the guardrail and looked aft to see that the forward funnel had toppled over the starboard side. He could also see large sections of the ship's plating hurtling through the air, spinning far away from the ship and smacking into the sea amid huge columns of spray. The aft 6-inch gun and its mounting too were blown away and flew high into the air before plummeting into the sea.

Stevenson had seen the barrel of the 4-inch AA gun bent like a banana and a marine sergeant, the Captain of the Gun, had had his clothes torn off in the blast. He had seen the terrible fate of the cutter too. Loaded with men, some of them terribly wounded, it had scraped down the side of the ship before dropping into the water. He had watched helplessly as it slithered along the ship's bottom plating towards the shattered stern of the ship. Worse, he had seen it cut to pieces by the port propeller, which had carved through the men in the boat. Stevenson himself had followed a boy into the water by sliding down Dunedin's port side. The boy had cut himself badly on Dunedin's barnacle-encrusted bottom, but Stevenson had managed to leap clear of them into the water.

In the sea, Stevenson had clung to a wooden spar with four other men before finding a Carley raft. Like all of us, he saw terrible things. Many men in his raft were wounded from the torpedo blast. In his arms he held a man who had been horribly burnt by the blast. He held the man's head above water until he became aware that he was no longer breathing. The man's scalded skin had come away from his body in long semi-transparent strips, exposing large areas of raw flesh. Four hours after Stevenson had taken him in his arms, a sick berth attendant, who had also made it to the raft, confirmed that he was dead. He and Stevenson lifted him over the side and let his body drift away.

Stevenson contemplated his lucky turn of fate as he recalled standing alongside the man moments before the first torpedo had struck. Something had compelled him to walk away, leaving the other man alone by the galley hatch. The shock of the explosion had thrown boiling water in the tanks of the galley range upwards through the hatch. Wearing nothing but a pair of tropical shorts and sandals, the man had suffered terrible scalds to his body.

Also on Stevenson's raft were ERA Tom Brunton, both of whose legs had been blown off below the knee, a boy seaman with a broken arm and a Royal Marine with a compound fracture of his left thigh. Tom Brunton had realised from the moment he had been lifted into the raft that he would not survive. Tourniquets around his legs had kept him alive for a few hours, but he knew what would happen to him. He shook hands with those around him before lapsing into a coma and dying. He had faced death calmly and courageously, remaining cheerful up to the point where he lapsed into unconsciousness.

The boy seaman on Stevenson's raft had lived for two days before he too had succumbed, having refused all offers to splint his arm. Eventually he swam away and disappeared into the sea, his good arm raised above his head as he slid below the surface. There were many such stories of men seen but not identified, men who had struggled beyond endurance, men who had left the rafts never to return. The boy on Stevenson's raft could have been one of many, possibly Boy Seaman Jackie Lamb, who was known to have broken limbs and was last seen on the rafts by his friend Ed Longmuir, who survived to tell the tragic tale to Jackie's family.

Les Barter had made it too, but only just. After being hauled up the side of Nishmaha he had been carried to the mess hall, where he had been given iced tea and laid down to recover. He was very weak and within a few minutes he either passed out or fell asleep. On waking sometime later, he was confused and disoriented, lying in the dark in a strange place with people around him. He felt very stiff and extremely tired, but he crawled away and into the shower room, where he stumbled on the feet of a crew member, who took him to his cabin. Once more, Les was laid down to recover. He learned later that the crew had thought he was dead and he had been laid out with the other five Dunedin crew members who had died within a few hours of the rescue.

And what of Captain Lovatt? Someone had spotted him on the hull of *Dunedin* as she circled shortly before sinking, another had seen him give up his place on a raft, and another saw him clinging to a large box, perhaps his last refuge before slipping away.

And Harold Broadway and Leslie Russell? Their last known thoughts are recorded in their last letters, written on 18 November, just before *Dunedin* left Freetown for the final time. Where would they have been when the torpedoes hit? Harold might have been in his usual spot on the quarterdeck, writing another letter, or in the sickbay attending to an ill sailor. Quite possibly, he would have been in his cabin, roughly where the second torpedo had struck. He could not have survived the blast and was almost certainly spared what followed. Leslie could have been any-where – in the storerooms, or eating his lunch. Fate probably put them amidships or aft, where the two torpedoes struck; fate might have put them both in the water; fate did not bring them to the *Nishmaha*.

I now began my slow recovery. I could not walk very easily. I had been lucky not to have been injured in the blast, but I was very weak. I tried to get round to see as many of the others as possible in search of Nobby, but it was to no avail. I recognised a few faces, but most of them were faces in a crowd, some unrecog-nisable now, their faces burnt by the sun, their eyes sunken and dark.

I rank the crew of the Nishmaha *among the most wonderful of men. Captain Olsen and his crew did everything possible to make our lives bearable. They gave us clothes, cigarettes, food, water, and what medical assistance they could muster. We outnumbered them by two or three times, but they could not possibly have done more to help us.*

We learned that Nishmaha *had found us purely by chance. En route from Takaradi on the west coast of Africa, loaded with tungsten ore and bound for Philadelphia, she was making her way across the Atlantic at a steady ten knots. On Wednesday 26 November, she had developed a mechanical defect. To fix it, the engines had to be turned off and* Nishmaha *drifted on the Atlantic currents.*

By the time the repairs had been completed, she had been drifting for eight hours and needed a course correction. In her path – miraculously – lay six Carley rafts, a flottanet and seventy-two men, surrounded by sharks and spread out across the sea. At around 5, Nishmaha's *fourth officer noticed something on the port horizon. Captain Olsen altered the ship's course to have a look and, when she was closer, a lone Carley raft could be seen through binoculars. In Captain Olsen's official report later, he reported that four men were in this first raft, but in fact there were only three, myself, Moore and MacAuley. As* Nishmaha *circled round, officers came to the bridge and other rafts were spotted. In all, she deployed three lifeboats. In one of them, a* Nishmaha *officer spotted a torch light in the growing darkness and directed the ship towards it. There she found the two remaining rafts and the rescue operation was completed.*

And now, in the aftermath of the miracle, we began to cope with everyday life again, doing our best to get on our feet. It was impossible, however, to walk barefoot on Nishmaha's *all-metal decks, which, under the intense strength of the sun, became unbearably hot. Chief Electrical Artificer Stevenson and Fred Manning, though they were both very weak, set about making wooden sandals for each of us who could walk. In the carpenter's shop in the forecastle they gathered tools and canvas and made outlines of our feet. They got the wood from packing cases and crates and somehow produced sandals that allowed us to walk on deck. I cannot say these were the most comfortable shoes I ever wore, but they enabled us to shuffle around.*

With the sun rising behind us on the morning of Sunday 7 December, Trinidad came into view, its palm trees and white-fronted houses welcoming us in from the wide-open space of the sea. We had been at sea for eighteen days, barely five of them in Dunedin. *I looked at the land as it edged closer and, as a gentle breeze brushed my face, I thanked God once again.*

I thanked Captain Olsen and his crew too. I was sad to leave them, sad to leave the safety and comfort of their overwhelming and breathtaking hospitality. After much shaking of hands and emotional farewells, it was time to go, but not before we had given 'three cheers' for the captain, officers and crew of the Nishmaha, *the men who had saved our lives.*

As we left Nishmaha, Dunedin's *chief shipwright, W.C. Thomas, handed Captain Olsen a letter written in pencil:*

Dear Captain:

How jolly thankful we felt when we saw your ship in the distance, and I think that everyone of us must have offered up a prayer that you would see our small Carley floats – one minute visible on top of the waves, and next out of sight.

I suppose no one can imagine the ordeal of being three days and three nights on a raft, with your shipmates constantly passing to another world – the endurance too much, or that God had something better in mind for their spirits.

May God comfort those dear wives and dear children, Mothers, and sweethearts of those brave shipmates that were taken from us.

Captain, what a task your Officers and men performed, not forgetting your very kind remarks from time to time were very much appreciated. For myself, I must mention the Second Engineer – his hospitality and kindness I can never forget.

Captain, Officers and men, THANK YOU! Just a HUMBLE THANK YOU for all you have done for us all. THANKS from the Officers and 64 men of HMS Dunedin. May God bless you all, may your kindness be returned to you a thousand-fold. To all of you we wish a Very Happy Christmas and a Prosperous New Year. You are Americans, never to be forgotten; THANK YOU one and all from those on board your Good SS Nishmaha. THANK YOU AGAIN!

(signed) W. C. T

PS Lykes Bros. Lines can be proud of such wonderful, untiring seamen, devoted to the kindness of mankind. When this World War is over, may that wonderful nature prevail.

W. C. T

A few moments later I was standing on the jetty.

CHAPTER 11

Recuperation and Return to England
December 1941–January 1942

I walked unsteadily from Nishmaha. *The ulcers on my legs and my skin were very sore, but I had come through the worst. I was taken to the small hospital, with about ten other survivors, at HMS Benbow, the shore establishment not far from the quay at Port of Spain, where I was given a bed in one corner. Thomas Moore lay opposite me. Of the sixty-seven of us still alive, eighteen were stretcher cases.*

Most of the other survivors were sent to HMS Goshawk, a Fleet Air Arm station some fourteen miles inland at Piarco. There the injured were placed in the hospital, while others were allocated to messes, issued with tropical uniforms and given a little pay.

At HMS Benbow I continued my slow recovery in the pristine white surroundings of the hospital, with little to do except receive the attentions of the nurses and the doctors and try to come to terms with what had happened to me. The crisp sheets, soft pillows and quiet humming of the ceiling fan were a far cry from life in Dunedin and the awfulness of the aftermath of the sinking. I had entered an in-between world, far from home and far from the horror of the sinking and the days adrift, almost as if the whole thing had been a bad dream and I had woken in an antiseptic waiting room before returning to normality – whatever that was. I didn't know any more.

Some time during the first day, as I lay in my bed, I heard for the very first time Glenn Miller's 'Chattanooga Choochoo' playing through a loudspeaker. Unlike the muffled and distorted music played in Dunedin, this was loud and clear, rhythmical, and induced my feet to move in step under the sheets. It was fresh, crisp and vibrant and made me smile, perhaps for the first time in weeks. It was new and somehow, because it was American, it represented in my mind a symbol of hope and daring and a release from the terrible things which seemed to have engulfed as all. And then news came in of what had happened that very morning on a different island in a different ocean. The Japanese had attacked the US fleet at Pearl Harbor, inextricably bringing the Americans into the war.

Until now the war had barely touched Trinidad. In fact, it hardly existed at all, despite the presence of the British military and many US naval personnel. Our arrival was therefore something of a novelty for the islanders and we were given wonderful treatment by the locals. In the first few days, a number of the women from the island visited us and made sure we were comfortable. One asked me what I had most craved while on the raft and I rather feebly replied that, apart from water, I would have loved a cup of tea. But since I had been plied with gallons of the stuff since arriving on the island, my visitor insisted that I choose something else. I would like, I said, an apple.

The next day a large barrel of apples appeared in the ward. And after that we were given almost anything we asked for. Life had become good.

My most memorable visitor in those first few days was Ellen Walker, a British woman married to an American, Gus Walker, who ran General Motors' office in Trinidad. Mrs Walker was infinitely kind to me and was the chief architect of the wonderful attention we all shared. By an amazing coincidence she, like me, used to live near Regent's Park. She lived in an expensive house on the other side of the park, but we enjoyed our times together reminiscing about London. It made me think increasingly about home and about my family. The more we talked, the closer they became and the more I needed to get home.

When I had recovered sufficiently to move into a billet on the island, it was obvious to me that I should stay with the Walkers, since they had been so kind to me. I stayed with them in their small bungalow, which had a dining room, a veranda, one bedroom, an office, a lounge area and a kitchen. Gus set up a camp bed for me in his office and even took me to a department store to choose some clothes.

For some of the survivors, their stay on the island was a short one. Those who were fit enough were shipped out in the troopship Duchess of York after only *four days. These men made it home for Christmas, but for most of us left behind Christmas would be in the heat of the Trinidad sun.*

In the coming days I became the luckiest man alive. The sun shone every day, I had no work to do, I went to parties, lunches and dinners. I met the governor and mixed in company that, as a young man of twenty, I could only have dreamed about.

On Christmas Day I walked out from the Walkers' bungalow and imagined what my family would say if they could see me. With the sun beating down on my back, I strolled around in tropical clothes, barely able to comprehend my change in fortunes.

I was ready to leave in early January and was told I would be going home on the next available ship to England. I was assigned to the Awatea, a New Zealand passenger liner converted into a troopship for the war. The day we left was one of the saddest of my life. Yes, we were going home and, yes, we would see our families again, but it was with tears in my eyes that I said my farewells to the Walkers. And, as Awatea pulled out of the harbour, two Fleet Air Arm Swordfishes swooped down in a fly-past.

I felt strange being back at sea and not a little wary after the Dunedin experience. We had little to do except pass the time and think of home and what had happened to us. The habit of scanning the sea for submarine periscopes stayed with us and took on a deeper sense of purpose after our experience. Despite the vast expanse of sea, we now knew what could have been lurking beneath us. Sleeping below decks became a more nervy experience especially on the first night, when all I could remember was the last time I had been below decks on 24 November. I made certain I knew the quickest way off the ship. Fortunately, the Awatea was a fast ship and within a few days we were back in the Northern Atlantic waters and approaching England once more.

When the shores of England came into my view for the first time since April the previous year, we were approaching Liverpool. I thought about the times I had imagined how our return in Dunedin would feel – triumphant perhaps, weary certainly and with a huge sense of euphoria even. This was nothing like it. England's welcome was a cold affair, with a thin shroud of mist and a grey demeanour. With my tanned skin and wearing clothes suitable only for the tropics, I felt like I had arrived in a foreign land. The people's faces revealed a tiredness but also a resoluteness. Something about them told me that I had *returned to a country wearied by the war but that somehow could find the will to carry on, knowing that it would one day end. The looks on people's faces were ones of quiet determination to get on with the job and to make the best of it. No one would be interested in what I had been doing and no one would stop to ask.*

Once ashore, my orders were to return to Eastney barracks. I made the long train journey to London and then took a connection at Waterloo for Fratton station in Portsmouth. I arrived at Eastney barracks cold and tired. I heard the familiar barking of orders and the crunch of boots on marching men's feet. Nothing appeared to have changed. An occasional familiar face slid by and one or two people looked at me a second time as if they thought they knew me but could not quite place my face. Arriving at the barracks at the same time was a small group of new recruits who looked at me as if I were as fresh-faced as they were. I could barely remember my own first day in the Marines, it seemed so long ago.

My only welcome back to the fold was £1 compensation for the loss of my personal belongings, a pair of boots and a greatcoat. Other than that, I was told to get on with it. The paymaster sergeant said, 'Here you are, here's your pound. Aren't we generous?' It was hard to know what to say in reply.

Within a few days, I was given leave and I travelled back to London to see my mother and father for the first time in nearly a year. I knocked on the door of our flat at 17 Swinley House and found no one at home, so I waited with the Westcotts, our neighbours. We got word to my mother that I was back and she rushed home to see me, but my father came later, after he had finished work.

When my mother arrived she said very little but looked at me intently, examining me for changes, trying to read my eyes. We hugged, we kissed, but mostly we looked and let the relief of our reunion flood over us. My father too was unusually lost for words, but as the evening drew on we talked more and I told them a little of what had happened. My brothers, Eric and Jack, were impatient to know what I had been up to, but it all had to wait. This was a time of brittle emotion and it was clear to me from the look in her eyes that my mother had suffered terribly by my absence. To make matters worse, news of Dunedin's sinking had reached her before she was convinced that I was safe. I had arranged with my mother and father before I left that I would not send telegrams directly to them but to friends of ours, who would pass on my news and – if necessary –

break bad news gently. Unfortunately, a telegram I had sent from Trinidad had gone directly to my home address. Even though its message was reassuring, the mere arrival of a telegram was enough to unnerve her badly and – convinced that I had been killed – her hair turned white overnight. Sent on 12 December, the telegram said simply, 'All well and safe', which should have reassured her. But when news of Dunedin's sinking hit the newspapers a few days later, she convinced herself that the telegram had been sent first and that I had been killed later.

For the sixty-seven survivors, similar scenes would have been acted out in homes across the country. Emotional reunions with parents, wives, brothers, sisters and friends and a chance to start again. For all of them, the anguish of not knowing what had happened to their loved ones would have been short-lived and with a happy ending.

For more than 400 other families, the pain never stopped, first through not knowing what had happened and then through the long and awful wait for good news, news that would never come. For most the wait lasted many months. Within two days of the survivors arriving in Trinidad, the Admiralty had written to the families of all the men who had not been rescued to explain that they were missing in action. It would not be until May 1942, however, that Jean and Mary received confirmation of Leslie's and Harold's deaths. Months of anguish and denial, despair and disbelief, ended by a letter. And so it was for the relatives of all the men who lost their lives.

Tragically, Harold's father clung forlornly to the hope that Harold had survived and that he had been taken prisoner. He could not accept that another of his children had gone. His eldest son had died as he finished his training as a doctor and his only daughter had died of complications following childbirth. He maintained the hope until after the war that Harold had made it to the seventh raft. When that hope died, so too did Harold's father, one more casualty of HMS *Dunedin*.

For young Jim Davis, rescue and survival would be followed by a return to the sea on the corvette HMS *Stonecrop*. Jim only ever encountered a U-boat twice, once on 24 November 1941 and once on the night of 2 April 1943, when *Stonecrop* was escorting convoy OS 45 en route to

Sierra Leone. One of the other escorts, the sloop HMS *Black Swan*, picked up a stray radar echo and then saw the conning tower of a U-boat disappear beneath the waves no more than 100 feet away. *Black Swan* dropped a salvo of depth charges and then called in *Stonecrop* to help. *Stonecrop* made a sonar connection and she too dropped a depth charge salvo. Then she lost contact and the U-boat was seen no more, sunk with the loss of all her crew. It was U-124, the fourth most successful U-boat of the war.

Several years later, with the war long behind her, Jean was unpacking a box of books in her home. Among them were several that Leslie had sent her in 1941. Thumbing through the dusty books, she remembered fondly how Leslie would ask her to look after them until the war was over. Sometimes he would mention in his letters specific passages that she might enjoy and as she leafed through the pages she read again what Leslie had pointed out with his familiar circled crosses in the margins. She could remember every piece and every implied message and was about to put the box away when she picked up one last book, a collection of Robert Burns's poems. As she turned it over in her hands, it fell open at a page marked with a silk ribbon. She saw his familiar pencil marks around a short poem, but she had never read it before because Leslie had not mentioned it in any of his letters. When she read the poem, she realised why:

> Tho' cruel fate should bid us part,
> Wide as the pole and line;
> Her dear idea round my heart
> Should tenderly entwine.
>
> Tho' mountains rise and deserts howl,
> And oceans roar between;
> Yet, dearer than my deathless soul,
> I still would love my Jean.

It was Leslie's – and *Dunedin*'s – last message.

POSTSCRIPT
Dunedin and Enigma

After *Dunedin* was sunk, U-126 successfully embarked *Atlantis*'s survivors to *Python* and set sail for France. *Python* steamed on to her rendezvous further south, reaching it on 30 November and meeting UA and U-68. While *Python* refuelled UA, the final pieces of the Admiralty's plan were put in place when *Dorsetshire* opened fire with her 8-inch guns on 1 December. Neither U-boat was able to attack *Dorsetshire* and *Python* scuttled.

U-124 had sailed south in search of U-126 and *Python* after sinking *Dunedin*, but U-126's successful meeting with *Python* meant U-124 could carry on to the Cape Town area to proceed with the attacks on shipping there. On her way south, U-124 came across a US merchant ship, the SS *Sagadahoc*, and sank her. When *Dorsetshire* intercepted *Python*, U-124 and U-129 were recalled from their Cape Town operation to help rescue the survivors of *Python* (who, of course, included survivors of the *Atlantis* sinking). The two U-boats came across UA and U-68 on 5 December and together the four vessels made for home with the survivors, the Cape Town expedition abandoned. U-124 arrived in Lorient on 29 December, having disembarked survivors to an Italian submarine.

The Admiralty could rightly feel very pleased with itself – two supply ships down and the end of the Cape Town operation before it had really begun, thanks largely to the breaking of the Enigma messages. In the grand scheme of things and in the map room calculations of strategy and tactics, the loss of an ageing light cruiser would have been considered regrettable but worthwhile. *Dunedin* was part of this mission due to the brilliance of British intelligence operations. Ironically, her part was terminated because that very intelligence did not quite reach the even higher standards it had attained just a few months earlier. Why is this?

Dunedin's movements after 21 November – that is, after she left Freetown for the last time – are not recorded other than in her deck log, which went down with her, and briefly in the official record of the events surrounding the sinking. She was sent from Freetown on the evening of the 21st in search of a surface ship in an area around St Paul's Rocks. This would have been on the back of intelligence reports that U-boats had been ordered not to attack single ships in an area south-west of St Paul's Rocks until after the 22nd. This was because U-boat Command was planning to use a surface ship on her northbound passage to resupply U-boats. When *Dunedin* left Freetown, she most likely made straight for the area where she was eventually hit by U-124.

On the 21st, when the OIC knew for sure – through Enigma decrypts – where *Atlantis* would reprovision U-126 the following day, all eyes in the OIC would have been on this operation. The other refuelling operation, to take place in early December a long way to the south, was also known about by now, and by the 24th the OIC knew that this second operation would involve *Python*. With over a week to go before the second operation was due to take place, the OIC would be confident that it could wait for further decrypts with more details of the reprovisioning, just as had happened with the *Atlantis* intelligence. The Admiralty would be able to plan very carefully how it would intercept *Python* and – crucially – which ship to deploy.

If *Dunedin* came across *Python* in the meantime, all well and good, but she was only an old light cruiser. Better that something like *Devonshire* or – in the event – *Dorsetshire* should be on hand at the right time and place further south. It is reasonable to assume, therefore, that – at this time – *Dunedin* was not expected to play any part in the apprehension of *Python*, except if she came across her by chance. The 'real' *Python* action would take place a long way south nearly two weeks later.

However, the sinking of *Atlantis* changed everything. Both the Admiralty and U-boat Command had to think again. When Bauer, in U-126, signalled to U-boat Command that he was attempting to reach

South America with *Atlantis*'s survivors, German Naval High Command immediately ordered *Python* to pick up the survivors. At the same time, Dönitz, at U-boat Command, ordered U-124 and U-129 to change course and assist in the towing of the survivors. This change of course was to prove fatal to *Dunedin* because it took U-124 directly into her path.

The Admiralty also acted. The passage of *Atlantis*'s survivors in lifeboats towed by U-126 was discovered (by Bletchley Park) and transmitted to the OIC at midnight on the 23rd. Someone in the OIC and/or Bletchley Park made the connection between U-126's westerly passage and *Python*'s southerly passage and hazarded the guess that U-126 – which was running out of fuel – would meet up with *Python*, hand over the survivors and take on supplies and fuel.

This advice was not passed to the Commander-in-Chief South Atlantic until 5 p.m. on the 24th, after *Dunedin* had gone. The signals made directly to *Dunedin* after she was sunk contained orders based on the OIC's intelligence. On receiving this intelligence, C-in-C South Atlantic acted very quickly and ordered *Dunedin* (and *Canton*) to search for the *Atlantis* survivors at its estimation of the rendezvous between *Python* and U-126. It was not difficult to guess approximately where the U-boat and the supply ship might meet. It was known that U-126 was heading for South America, and *Python*'s position on 20 November and her destination in the south were both spelt out in the OIC's signal. It would have been possible simply to draw two lines on a map of the Atlantic and see where they crossed – one joining *Python*'s position on the 20th with her expected position in the south, the other joining U-126's position at the time of the *Atlantis* sinking and the nearest point in South America.

By the time these signals had been transmitted it was too late for *Dunedin*. U-124 had sunk her several hours before her new orders containing her course change were sent.

The fate of *Dunedin,* therefore, rested on two changes of course, both a consequence of the sinking of *Atlantis* and the subsequent rescue operation: the first, by U-124, which brought her into line with *Dunedin*; and the second, which *Dunedin* was ordered to make but never received.

Two questions arise. First, why did it take around seventeen hours for the Admiralty to pass on its assessment that *Python* would be brought into the rescue operation? And second, could Bletchley Park have produced the 'rescue' decrypt any quicker?

In the absence of clear evidence, the answer to the first question must remain mostly speculative and probably just raises more questions. There were probably several reasons for the delay. The OIC had finite resources and the *Atlantis* rescue operation was not the only show in town. The key decrypt (at midnight on the 23rd) giving details of the rescue, was the 138th decrypt since 4.30 p.m. on the 22nd, very few of which bore any relation to events in the South Atlantic. A further 224 decrypts had arrived in the OIC by around 5 p.m. on the afternoon of the 24th. Each and every decrypt would have been examined for its intelligence value, especially in relation to other decrypts and other sources. The 'rescue' decrypt was crucial principally in relation to the known intelligence about the movements of *Python*. Someone would have had to connect the two. In the midst of all the other work going on in the OIC, it is possible that this connection simply went unnoticed until well into the afternoon of the 24th.

Might this connection have been spotted more quickly if the rescue decrypt (and others) had been passed directly to the Commander-in-Chief South Atlantic for interpretation? Very probably, yes, but this was never a practical proposition. The Admiralty (and Churchill especially) was acutely sensitive to the need to limit the use of Enigma-derived naval intelligence for fear of compromising its source. It was very important, therefore, that its use should be closely controlled centrally by the OIC. Signals were issued by the Admiralty strictly on what might be called a 'need to use' basis.

It is this aspect that partly answers the second question, whether Bletchley Park could have produced the rescue decrypt more quickly.

The key decrypts produced by Bletchley Park for the *Lothringen* operation in June had taken - at most - four to five hours to reach the OIC. The *Lothringen* intelligence was therefore of a very high quality – good content and very timely. In November, Bletchley Park decrypted all the relevant messages, but the key decrypts reached the OIC sometimes thirty hours after they had been intercepted, substantially diluting their intelligence value. No matter how good a piece of intelligence, the older it gets the less useful it becomes, especially in a fast-moving situation.

One can only wonder whether *Dunedin*'s fate would have been different had Bletchley Park been reading German messages with the same speed as it had been in June. The key information about the *Python/* U-126 hook-up – the rescue decrypt – would have been available as much as twenty-four hours earlier for the Admiralty to plan an ambush and – possibly – to deploy *Dunedin*. Instead of sailing north-west in her patrol area, she would have been searching further south – which was not necessarily any safer (given that any one of three converging U-boats could have found her), but possibly with a view to engaging *Python* and with very clear knowledge about the proximity of U-boats.

Why did Bletchley Park take so long? The answer, ironically, lies in their very success in June and July, when German messages were being read concurrently by Bletchley Park. *Dunedin* herself had participated in this when she captured *Lothringen*. In fact, the wiping out of the German supply fleet at that time was such a spectacular success that the Admiralty feared that its intelligence gathering would be compromised. In addition to the brilliant cryptanalysis of the brains in Bletchley Park, the intelligence hauls in May and June – for example, from the weather ships and U-110 – had given Bletchley Park the documentary material to be able to read the German messages almost as quickly as the Germans themselves.

Fearing that the Germans would smell a rat, the Admiralty decided that no further pinches would take place after the end of June. The last such pinch was on 28 June with the capture of a trawler, *Lauenburg*, from which the settings for July were acquired. This nervousness probably also partly explains the Admiralty's reluctance to take up Bletchley Park's suggestion to ambush the U-boats heading for the rendezvous with *Lothringen*. The lack of new material meant that, from 1 August, Bletchley Park would have to rely on cryptanalysis alone to read German messages, increasing the time taken to send translated decrypts to the OIC. After the luxury of concurrent reading in June and July, the average delay in reading Enigma in August rose to fifty hours. By November, things had improved, but the times taken to decrypt the messages varied considerably throughout the month, with some messages taking several days to be decrypted.

Curiously, the messages sent by the Germans on the 22nd (including the rescue message) were decrypted the fastest, but none of the key messages was decrypted in less than twenty-eight hours.

Even if there were good reasons why it took the Admiralty seventeen hours to pass on the intelligence about the rescue, one is left to speculate how *Dunedin*'s fate might have been affected if the OIC had been given a further twenty-four hours to assess the intelligence.

None of this is intended as a criticism of Bletchley Park and the OIC. The success of the overall operation is not in doubt – the Germans lost two surface ships and were forced to abandon their planned operation in the Cape Town area. And yet, having seen in June how exceptionally good British intelligence could be, one is left to wonder whether the hitherto obscure but tragic events of 24 November 1941 might have been different.

The fate of *Dunedin* rested, ultimately, on two course changes – one that happened and one that didn't.

Appendix 1
HMS *Dunedin* Specifications

Displacement	4,850 tons
Length	472 ft 3 in
Beam	46 ft 3 in
Draught	14 ft 6 in
Machinery	2-shaft geared turbines
	6 boilers
Speed	29 knots
Bunkerage	1,060 tons oil
Range	6,700 nm at 10 knots
Armaments	6 6-in AA guns
	2 3-in AA guns (replaced in 1927 by 3 4-in guns)
	12 21-in torpedoes
Complement	450 (increased in wartime)

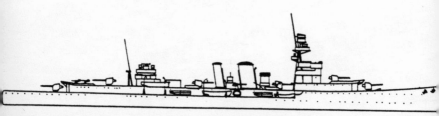

Appendix 2
U-124 Specifications

Displacement	1,051 tons (surface)
	1,178 tons (submerged)
Dimensions	252.45 x 22.308 ft
Speed	18.2 knots surfaced (diesel)
	7.2 knots submerged (battery)
Torpedoes	22
	4 bow tubes
	2 stern tubes
Deck gun	105-mm canon
	37-mm flak
	2 20-mm flak
Complement	48

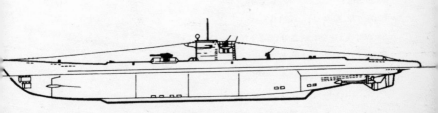

Appendix 3
HMS *Dunedin* Casualty List

KEY

MPK = Missing Presumed Killed

K = Killed

DWS = Died on War Service

Royal Navy

Allen, L. H., Ord. Seaman, MPK

Andrews, D. R., Supply Petty Officer, MPK

Ardley, G. W., Ldg Signalman, MPK

Armstrong, B. B., Ordnance Artificer 4th-class, MPK

Arnold, E., Boy 1st-class, MPK

Arnold, W. G., Shipwright 4th-class (RNSR), MPK

Baird, D., Able Seaman (RNVR), MPK

Balchin, H. P., Chief Engine Room Artificer, MPK

Ball, T. O., Able Seaman, MPK

Bamford, E., Ldg Supply Assistant, MPK

Barber, E., Able Seaman, MPK

Barnes, A. G., Stoker 2nd-class, MPK

Barry, J. M., Stoker 1st-class, MPK

Beasley, K. J., Able Seaman, MPK

Beauchamp, R. J., Able Seaman, MPK

Benjamin, J. N., Stoker 1st-class, MPK

Bennett, A. G., Stoker 1st-class, MPK

Berry, E. R., Able Seaman, MPK

Beven, R. L., Able Seaman, MPK

Billings, T. E., Ord. Signalman, MPK

Black, J. S., Ord. Seaman, MPK

Blower, W., Able Seaman, MPK

Blythe, G. S., Stoker 1st-Class, MPK

Boggit, J. W., Able Seaman, MPK

Bolt, C. R. W., Commander (E), MPK

Boucher, D. H., Boy 1st-class, MPK

Bowyer, G., Ordnance Artificer 4th-class, MPK

Brackstone, J. C., Able Seaman, MPK

Bray, W. J., Shipwright 4th-class, MPK

Brennan, H. G., Boy 1st-class, MPK

Brewer, A. C., Ord. Seaman, MPK

Broadway, H. T. L., Temporary Acting Surgeon, Lt-Cdr (RNVR), MPK

Brown, D. N., Able Seaman, MPK

Brown, W. A., Engine Room Artificer 3rd-class, MPK

Brown, W. H., Telegraphist, MPK

Brunton, T. J., A/Engine Room Artificer 4th-class, MPK

Bull, F. W., Able Seaman, MPK

Burden, F., Steward, MPK

Burns, T., Stoker 1st-class, MPK

Burton, J. A., Able Seaman, MPK

Byford, K. J., A/Engine Room Artificer 4th-class, MPK

Campbell, J. A., Cook (S), MPK

Candy, C., Supply Assistant, MPK

Carson, W., Stoker 2nd-class, MPK

Castledine, W. A., Stoker 1st-class, MPK

Caws, T. B. N., Paymaster, Lt (S), MPK

Cheney, F. T., Chief Stoker, MPK

Clark, C. E., Stoker 1st-class, MPK

Clark, G. W., Boy 1st-class, MPK

Clay, S. J., Ord. Signalman, MPK

Cobbett, J., Ldg Seaman, MPK

Codd, W. E., Sick Berth Attendant, MPK

Collins, J., Boy 1st-class, MPK

Collins, P., Petty Officer, MPK

Commons, W. D., Ord. Signalman, MPK

Compton, C. G., Coder, MPK

Condie, J. M., Asst. Steward, MPK

Connery, J. G., Ord. Seaman, MPK

Cooper, G., Stoker, MPK

Coote, C. J., Petty Officer Cook (S), MPK

Cope, L., Stoker 1st-class, MPK

Copp, A. W., Telegraphist, MPK

Covington, A., Supply Petty Officer, MPK

Coxwell, P. L., Able Seaman, K

Crawford, W., Able Seaman, MPK

Cubitt, E. J., Able Seaman (RNVR), MPK

Curtis, I. D., Ord. Seaman, MPK

Davis, G. D., Petty Officer, MPK

Dawson, J., Able Seaman, MPK

De Guerin, J. F. C., Able Seaman, MPK

Denman, L. A., Petty Officer Cook (O), MPK

Denton, W. E., Shipwright 5th-class, MPK

Dobson, A. J. R., Ldg Stoker (Ty), MPK

Donaldson, C. D., Petty Officer, MPK

Doney, A., Ord. Coder MPK

Dunn, A. P., A/Ldg Stoker, MPK

Dutta, K. R., Midshipman, MPK

Dyer, L., Leading Seaman, MPK

Eastabrook, R. E., Plumber 3rd-class, MPK

Eccles, A., A/Ldg Seaman (Ty), MPK

Edwards, C., Stoker 1st-class, MPK

Elliott, A. J., A/Engine Room Artificer 4th-class, MPK

Ellis, S. J., Stoker 1st-Class, MPK

Ellis, V. K., Able Seaman, MPK

Evans, A. J. L., Stoker 1st-Class, MPK

Farrar, S. B., Coder, MPK

Fedrick, F. L., A/Ldg Stoker (Ty), MPK

Fender, A. C., Stoker Petty Officer, MPK

Fenner, A. R., Leading Supply Assistant, MPK

Fishlock, D., Steward, MPK

Folds, W. E., Stoker Petty Officer, MPK

Forster, A. E., Able Seaman (RNVR), MPK

Fountain, W. J., Ldg Signalman, MPK

Francis, W. G., Chief Petty Officer, DWS

Franklin, G. H., Stoker Petty Officer, MPK

Freer, T. F., Chief Mechanician, MPK

French, E. M., Sub-Lt, MPK

Frost, W. R., Boy 1st-class, MPK

Gaisford, W. G., Stoker 1st-class, MPK

Gane, H. E. J., Chief Petty Officer Steward, MPK

Garton, H. T., Able Seaman, MPK

George, R. C., Petty Officer Steward, MPK

Gibbs, D. E., Able Seaman, MPK

Gibson, E. E., Lt, MPK

Godber, S. F., Telegraphist, MPK

Goldfinch, E. M., Gunner, DWS

Graham, R., Stoker 1st-class, MPK

Grant, A., Chief Petty Officer Telegraphist, MPK

Grantham, D., Ord. Seaman, MPK

Gray, A. J., Able Seaman, MPK

Gray, J. H., Stoker 1st-class RFR, MPK

Green, W. R., Ord. Seaman, MPK

Greenaway, N. V., Able Seaman, MPK

Greenley, T. F., Able Seaman, MPK

Grunnill, A. D., Wireman, MPK

Hamblin, W. G., Ldg Stoker, MPK

Hamill, C. W., Stoker 1st-class, MPK

Hanlon, J. C., Stoker 1st-class, MPK

Hanson, D., Sub-Lt (E), MPK

Harcombe, G. D. L., Temp. Instr. Lt, DWS

Harkins, R. W., Wireman, MPK

Harper, P. G., Able Seaman (RNVR), MPK

Harris, J. R., Ord. Seaman, MPK

Harris, M. L., Writer, DWS

Hartley, T., Stoker Petty Officer, MPK

Harvey, J. W., Stoker 1st-class, MPK

Hawkins, R. W., Boy 1st-class, MPK

Hawton, A. W., Electrical Artificer 1st-class, MPK

Hay, C. J., Engine Room Artificer 4th-class, MPK

Haymes, A. E. R., Stoker 1st-class, MPK

Hayward, P. A., Able Seaman, MPK

Hayward, W. J., Chief Petty Officer, MPK

Hearne, L. B., Able Seaman, MPK

Hemingway, W. E., A/Engine Room Artificer 4th-class, MPK

Hemsley, A. E., Able Seaman, MPK

Herridge, P., Wireman, MPK

Hewett, E. R., Chief Petty Officer Cook (O), MPK

Hewson, A. R., Stoker 1st-class, MPK

Hickey, E. W. J., Acting Warrant Eng., DWS

Hill, A. A., Able Seaman, K

Hockney, D., Boy 1st-class, MPK

Hodge, D. E., Steward, MPK

Holdaway, R., Telegraphist, MPK

Holford, R. F., A/Petty Officer Writer, MPK

Holland, R., Able Seaman (RNVR), MPK

Hollinshead, J. G., Sub-Lt, MPK

Holloway, H. C., Stoker Petty Officer, MPK

Hook, R. E., A/Ldg Seaman, MPK

Horner, W. H., Telegraphist, MPK

Howell, B. D., Able Seaman, MPK

Hudson, A. C., Able Seaman, MPK

Hughes, A. R., Schoolmaster Warrant Officer, DWS

Hughes, A. W., Temp Acting Lt-Cdr (E), DWS

Hurrell, C. B., Coder, MPK

Hurst, S. C., Chief Stoker, MPK

Hutfield, A. F. T., Ord. Seaman, MPK

Jackson, J. W., Telegraphist, MPK

Jackson, P. T., Ldg Telegraphist, MPK

Jackson, W., Able Seaman (RNVR), MPK

Jacques, J. E., Ord. Seaman, MPK

James, H., Stoker 1st-class, MPK

James, M. F., Able Seaman, MPK

Jamieson, D., Boy 1st-class, MPK

Jennings, J. A. A., Signalman, MPK

Jerrard, D. C., A/Petty Officer, MPK

Jervelund, J. M., Lt, MPK

Jones, I. B., A/Ldg Seaman, MPK

Judge, R., Ord. Seaman, MPK

Kearley, C., Able Seaman, MPK

Kendall, L. C., Able Seaman, MPK

Kenna, A., Able Seaman, MPK

Kinsella, P., Chief Ordnance Artificer, MPK

Kittle, J. E., Stoker 1st-class, MPK

Knight, J., Ldg Seaman, MPK

Kossick, L., Ord. Seaman, MPK

Lamb, A. T., Petty Officer, MPK

Lamb, J. C., Boy 1st-class, MPK

Laney, S. B., Able Seaman, MPK

Lee, D. A., Engine Room Artificer 4th-class, MPK

Lester, J., Stoker 2nd-class, MPK

Ling, R., Stoker 1st-class, MPK

Linton, J., Able Seaman, MPK

Loft, J. F., Signal Boy, MPK

Lovatt, R. S., Captain, MPK

Love, H. W., Chief Yeoman of Signals, MPK

Lowey, H., Commissioned Gunner, MPK

Loy, J. R., Able Seaman, MPK

Mackay, E. B., Lt (RNVR), MPK

Macintyre, R. H., Ldg Seaman (RNVR), DWS

McCahon, R. G., Stoker 1st-class, MPK

McCaigue, J., Able Seaman, MPK

McDiarmid, M., Able Seaman (RNVR), MPK

McFauld, J., Ldg Seaman, MPK

McGeachie, E., Engine Room Artificer 4th-class, MPK

McIver, W., A/Ldg Seaman, MPK

McLeod, D. M., Wireman, MPK

McWilliams, G., Able Seaman, MPK

Manners, J. A., Chief Petty Officer, MPK

Manock, J., Able Seaman, MPK

Marsh, J. W. C. S., Able Seaman, MPK

Martin, W., Ord. Seaman, MPK

Maskrey, W. T., Ord. Seaman, MPK

Masters, K. J., Sick Berth Attendant, MPK

Mathieson, R., Wireman, MPK

May, L. G., Wireman, MPK

Meek, A. H., Ord. Signalman, MPK

Miller, J., Ldg Seaman (RNVR), MPK

Milligan, C. J., Temp. Surg. Lt, MPK

Mills, A. W., Able Seaman, MPK

Moffat, R. L., Able Seaman, MPK

Moore, J. W. C., Able Seaman, MPK

Moran, L., Ord. Signalman, MPK

Morgan, L. J., Stoker 1st-class, MPK

Morrell, B. C., Boy 1st-class, MPK

Morton, P., Able Seaman, MPK

Mullan, J., Able Seaman, MPK

Murray, A. W., Stoker 1st-class, MPK

Mursell, N. H., Petty Officer, MPK

Napier, A. W. H., Chief Stoker, MPK

Nevett, A., Ord. Seaman, MPK

Noakes, R., Able Seaman, MPK

Oliver, C. H., Stoker 1st-class, MPK

Owens, G. A., A/Petty Officer, MPK

Page, H. W. C., A/Ldg Stoker, MPK

Palmer, A. W. F., Ldg Stoker, MPK

Parker, J. A., Mechanician 2nd-class, MPK

Payne, N., A/Ldg Telegraphist (RNV[W]R), MPK

Peachey, R. H., Ord. Seaman, MPK

Pettitt, C. H. C., Petty Officer, MPK

Pike, M. E., Boy 1st-class, MPK

Pitt, N. J., Stoker 1st-class, MPK

Plummer, H. J., Chief Petty Officer Cook, MPK

Polain, V. G., Telegraphist, MPK

Poore, E. A., Stoker 2nd-class, MPK

Potts, H., Ldg Seaman, MPK

Powell, P. J., Stoker 2nd-class, MPK

Pratt, R. A. S., Temp Acting Sub-Lt, MPK

Pritchard, F., Able Seaman, MPK

Pugh, E. A., Able Seaman, MPK

Pugsley, D. I., Able Seaman, MPK

Quinton, E., Stoker 2nd-class, MPK

Quinton, J. H., Stoker Petty Officer, MPK

Rasmussen, V. J. S., Ldg Telegraphist (RNVR), MPK

Reading, P. J., Stoker 1st-class, MPK

Reeley, W. E., Ldg Cook, MPK

Ritchie, G. W., Boy 1st-class, MPK

Robinson, J. A., Boy 1st-class, MPK

Rodger, W. A., Stoker 1st-class, MPK

Rolf, H. F. S., A/Petty Officer Telegraphist, MPK

Ross, A., Able Seaman (RNVR), MPK

Routledge, A., Able Seaman, MPK

Russell, L. B., Supply Assistant, MPK

Russell, O., Stoker 1st-class, MPK

Rutland, V. A., Sick Berth Chief Petty Officer, MPK

Salmon, J. R., Ldg Telegraphist, MPK

Samways, J., A/Blacksmith 4th-class, MPK

Saunders, W., Stoker 2nd-class, MPK

Scott, A. E., Petty Officer, MPK

Searle, W. A., Boy 1st-class, MPK

Senior, B., Ldg Steward, MPK

Sharp, W. J. T., Stoker Petty Officer, MPK

Shaw, L. E., Able Seaman, MPK

Shearer, K. W., Signalman, MPK

Shelvey, B. Q., A/Ldg Seaman (Ty), MPK

Shepherd, F. G., A/Electrical Artificer 4th-class, MPK

Shepherd, W. H., Electrical Artificer 1st-class, MPK

Sherrick, A., Able Seaman, MPK

Shevlin, H., Able Seaman, MPK

Siddle, H. T., Able Seaman, MPK

Simmonds, S. E. E., Stoker 1st-class, MPK

Simmonds W. A., Chief Petty Officer Cook (O), MPK

Skinner, R. M. P., Lt-Cdr (S), MPK

Slack, J., Stoker Petty Officer, MPK

Smith, A. E., Ord. Seaman, MPK

Smith, A. S., Able Seaman, MPK

Smith, J. A., A/Engine Room Artificer 4th-class, MPK

Smith, L. A., Able Seaman, MPK

Smith, S. S., Stoker Petty Officer, MPK

Smith, T. H., A/Ldg Stoker, MPK

Smith, W. D., Telegraphist, MPK

Smithies, J. H., Ord. Seaman, MPK

Snell, K. P., Boy Telegraphist, MPK

Soal, L. E., A/Ldg Seaman (Ty), MPK

Solivon, D. I., Engine Room Artificer 4th-class, MPK

Southwell, H. J., Ord. Telegraphist, MPK

Sowdon, R. M. H., Lt-Commander, MPK

Spencer, S. J., A/Petty Officer, MPK

Stainer, V. H., Ord. Seaman, MPK

Standen, J. E., Able Seaman (RNVR), MPK

Stead, F. H., Able Seaman, MPK

Stebbings, J. G., Able Seaman, MPK

Stephenson, C. E., Engine Room Artificer 4th-class, MPK

Stewart, A. P., Able Seaman, MPK

Storer, H., Able Seaman, MPK

Sturrock, A. G., Ord. Seaman, MPK

Sullivan, T. G., Ord. Coder, MPK

Suttle, R., Ldg Signalman, DWS

Sutton, E. J., Supply Assistant, MPK

Swalwell, G., A/Ldg Seaman, MPK

Sweett, J. G., Petty Officer Writer, MPK

Tait, H. F., Coder, MPK

Talbot, E. R., Able Seaman, MPK

Tall, H., Chief Engine Room Artificer, MPK

Taylor, A. D. H., Boy 1st-class, MPK

Temple, A. J. P., Ord. Signalman, MPK

Thompson, B., A/Petty Officer Telegraphist, MPK

Thomson, T., Stoker 1st-class, MPK

Till, E. H., Able Seaman, MPK

Timms, R. M., Boy 1st-class, MPK

Tinkler, A., A/Ldg Seaman, MPK

Towndrow, O. A., Mechanician 1st-class, DWS

Tragheim, A., Chief Petty Officer Telegraphist, MPK

Tribe, E. G., Ord. Telegraphist, MPK

Trott, I. J., Asst Cook, MPK

Tunstall, C. A., Stoker 2nd-class, MPK

Turnbull, H. J., Stoker 1st-class, MPK

Tyler, W. F., A/Ldg Seaman (Ty), MPK

Unwin, E. O., Commander, DWS

Vicars, T. G., Able Seaman, MPK

Wade, J. A., Cook, MPK

Wainwright, G. D., Able Seaman, MPK

Waller, H., Able Seaman, MPK

Walters, W. L., Temp Sub-Lt, DWS

Warrin, J. E. L., Master at Arms, MPK

Watkins, G., Stoker 1st-class, MPK

Watkins, J., Stoker 1st-class, MPK

Weate, L. A., Ord. Seaman, MPK

Webb, A. F., Stoker 1st-class, MPK

Webb, H. C., Stoker 1st-class, MPK

Webb, W. S., A/Stoker Petty Officer, MPK

Weeks, W. H. A., Ordnance Artificer 1st-class, MPK

Wells, D. P., Ord. Signalman, MPK

Wells, G. E., Able Seaman, MPK

West, F. Q., Ord. Seaman, MPK

Wheeler, C. G., Able Seaman, MPK

White, B. C., Able Seaman, MPK

White, J., Able Seaman, MPK

White, R. E., Boy 1st-class, DWS

Whiteley, L. T. G., Able Seaman, MPK

Whittaker, R. A., Able Seaman, MPK

Wicken, R. L., Cook (O), MPK

Wicks, A. F. S., Chief Stoker, MPK

Willacy, K., Ord. Signalman, MPK

Williams, A. J., Engine Room Artificer (RNR), MPK

Williams, G. R., Able Seaman, MPK

Wilson, C. H. S., Midshipman, MPK

Wilson, E., Wireman, MPK

Wilson, J., Ldg Stoker, MPK

Wilson, T., Stoker 1st-class, MPK

Winsborough, S., A/Petty Officer, MPK

Wood, W. A., Electrical Artificer 5th-class, MPK

Worsley, A. G. H., Ordnance Artificer 4th-class, MPK

Worth, J. K., Ldg Cook, MPK

Wright, C. E., Stoker 1st-class, MPK

Wright, C. J. G., Temp. Pay. Lt, MPK

Wright, J. M., Ord. Seaman, MPK

Wyatt, G. T., Chief Petty Officer Cook, MPK

Young, A. G., Painter 4th-class, MPK

Young, A. V., Able Seaman, MPK

Young, F. C., Ldg Stoker, MPK

Royal Marines

Allen, S. W., Sergeant (Ty), MPK

Blackburn, A. E., Musician, MPK

Bowyer, W. F., Musician (Pens), MPK

Bracey, F., Marine, MPK

Britcher, C. W., Marine, MPK

Callaghan, C. C., Marine, MPK

Clapham, C. H. G., Musician, MPK

Court, C., Marine, MPK

Cox, G. D., Marine, MPK

Crago, R. P., Musician, MPK

Dale, N., Marine, MPK

Dodd, J., Marine, MPK

Dyer, J. J., Marine (Pens), MPK

Fletcher, E. B., Marine, MPK

French, E., Marine, MPK

Frost, R., Marine, MPK

Garthwaite, E., Sergeant (Pens), MPK

Hall, A., Marine, MPK

Hardy, B. W., Marine (Pens), MPK

Irving, D. T., Marine, MPK

Jacklin, K., Marine, MPK

Jenkins, G. O., Marine, MPK

Jones, E. S., Marine, MPK

Jones, J. H., Band Corporal, MPK

Joughin, E. W., Marine, MPK

Kemp, W. A., Corporal, MPK

King, A. F. C., Marine, MPK

Laurence, H. A., Marine, MPK

Leith, R., Marine, MPK

Lloyd, E. H., Marine, MPK

Maul, R. H. L., (RM) Lt (Captain), MPK

Meakins, H. D., Marine, MPK

Mills, D. G., Marine, MPK

Moody, T., Musician, MPK

Moore, A. F., Musician, MPK

Moyle, C. W.,Marine, MPK

North, J. H., Marine, MPK

Pacey, T. H., Sergeant, MPK

Peacock, G. H., Corporal, MPK

Penney, G. L. R., Musician, MPK

Pickard, R. A., Marine, MPK

Riddleston, W. W., Musician, MPK

Robertson, P., Marine, MPK

Robins, F. J., Marine, MPK

Rose, F., Marine, MPK

Salway, E. H., Marine, MPK

Sargeant, J. M., Bandmaster 1st-class, MPK

Smith, C., Marine, MPK

Steer, A. L., Marine, MPK

Sunter, J. E., Corporal, MPK

Symonds, H. A., Marine, MPK

Wandless, J., Marine, MPK

West, C. R. M., Band Corporal, MPK

Worthington, C. A., Band Boy, MPK

Young, D., Marine (Pens), MPK

NAAFI Staff

Matthews, L. W., Canteen Assistant, MPK

Rowett, L. W., Canteen Manager, MPK

Traviss, A. E., Canteen Assistant, MPK

Yardley, D. M., Canteen Assistant, MPK

Appendix 4
HMS *Dunedin* Survivors List

Royal Navy

Baker, G., Shipwright

Ballard, R., Able Seaman

Barter, L. D., Boy

Bellboy, L., (not known)

Binley, C. A., Able Seaman

Bradbury, E., Stoker

Brown, H., Able Seaman

Butler, R. D., Petty Officer

Christie, T., Able Seaman

Clarke, H., Ldg Seaman

Cooke, A., Able Seaman (RNVR)

Cooper, C. T., Ldg Seaman

Cross, H., Able Seaman

Davis, R. H., Able Seaman

Davis, W., Able Seaman

Fleming, A. P., Engine Room Artificer

Fraser, D., Able Seaman

Greenslade, R., Stoker

Garlick, (F?) C., Able Seaman

Gubbins, P. R., Boy

Hawks, F. L., Ldg Telegraphist

Hicks, A. H., Engine Room Artificer (RNR)

Jarrad, E. F. G., Stoker Petty Officer

Jeffery, R. A., Ldg Seaman

Jolliffe, E. F., Sub-Lt

Jefferies, B. E., Able Seaman

Knight, J. H., Able Seaman (RNVR)

Lavington, E. T. H., Chief Yeoman of Signals

Longmuir, A. E. A., Boy

Lea, N. E., Able Seaman

Legg, E. J., Able Seaman

Lelliott, D. H., Stoker

Lowe, G. H., Stoker

Manning, M. F., Engine Room Artificer

McCall, A. S., Boy

Miles, J. G., Able Seaman

Milner, G. E., Lieutenant

Moore, R., Able Seaman

Moore, T., Joiner

Morris, C. A., Boy

Pavis, J. J., Stoker

Peterson, H., Stoker

Pring, C., Chief Engine Room Artificer

Quinn, A., Stoker

Rainbow, R. H., Ord. Seaman

Rogers, A. C., Navigation Petty Officer

Sharp, J., Steward

Shinn, R., Able Seaman

Starley, C., Ldg Seaman

Stevenson, E. J., Electrical Artificer

Thomas, W. C., Chief Shipwright

Titheridge, C. B., Commissioned Gunner

Turner, F. J., Petty Officer

Watson, A. O., Lt-Cdr

Wills, G. W., Stoker

Wilson, J. J., Stoker Petty Officer

Woodley, H. G. J., Able Seaman

Wood, S. R., Yeoman of Signals

Ward, R. M., Able Seaman

Royal Marines

Allen, W., Marine

Collins, A. (E), Musician

Dunkley, D. A., Marine

Gill, W. J. J., Marine

Harper, J., Musician

King, H. M., Sergeant

MacAuley, R. J., Colour Sergeant

Mullane, D. J., Marine

Appendix 5
HMS *Dunedin* Awards List

The following appointments and awards were approved by the King on 3 August 1942:

For good service, resolution and endurance after HMS *Dunedin* was sunk, through which a number of men were eventually rescued after great privations.

Officer of the Order of the British Empire (Military)
Lieutenant Commander A. O. Watson, RN

Member of the Order of the British Empire (Military)
Lieutenant G. E. Milner, RNR

Mr C. B. Titheridge, Commissioned Gunner

British Empire Medal (Military)
Sergeant King, RM

Able Seaman Fraser

Mention in Dispatches (Posthumous)
Chief Engine Room Artificer Tall

Engine Room Artificer Brunton

Mention in Dispatches
Chief Yeoman of Signals Lavington

Engine Room Artificer Hicks

Yeoman of Signals Woods

Petty Officer Butler

Able Seaman R. Moore

Boy McCall

Boy Morris

Appendix 6
Sources

Books

Beesly, P. *Very Special Intelligence*, Greenhill Books, London, 2000

Blair, C. *Hitler's U-Boat War*, Vol. I, Cassell, London, 2000; Vol. II, Cassell, London, 2000

Brice, M. *Axis Blockade Runners of World War II*, B. T. Batsford, London, 1981

Churchill, W. *Memoirs of the Second World War*, Bonanza Books, USA, 1978

Dönitz, K. *Memoirs: Ten Years and Twenty Days*, Cassell, London, 2000

Gasaway, E. B. *Grey Wolf, Grey Sea*, Arthur Baker, London, 1972

Herrick, T. D. *Into The Blue*, Parapress, Great Britain, 1997

Hinsley, F. H. *British Intelligence in the Second World War* (abridged), HMSO, Great Britain, 1993

James, Admiral Sir W. M. *Portsmouth Letters*, Macmillan, London, 1946

Kahn, D. *Seizing The Enigma*, Arrow Books, London, 1996

Morgan, Daniel *EOU: The Naval Career of Commander E. O. Unwin RN*, London, 2001

Mohr, U. *Atlantis: The Story of a German Surface Raider*, London, 1955

Sebag-Montefiore, H. *Enigma: The Battle for the Code*, Weidenfeld & Nicolson, London, 2000

Smith, P. *Eagle's War*, Crécy Books, Great Britain, 1995

Warner, O. *Admiral of the Fleet*, Spottiswoode, Ballantyne, Great Britain, 1969

Whitley, M. *Cruisers of World War Two*, Arms and Armour, London, 1996

Documents held at the Public Record Office, Kew

Doc Number	*Details*
ADM 1/10626	Report by Captain Lambe, HMS *Dunedin*, of events of 23–28 November 1939
	Report by Captain Lambe, HMS *Dunedin*, of events of 28 November–2 December 1939
ADM 1/12272	Letter confirming award of British Empire Medals (BEMs), dated 23 July 1942
ADM 53/40428–40433	HMS *Dunedin*, Deck Logs, September 1919–December 1920
ADM 53/76345–53/76351	HMS *Dunedin*, Deck Logs, September 1920–April 1930
ADM 53/102664–102679	HMS *Dunedin*, Deck Logs, March 1937–December 1938
ADM 53/108413–108417	HMS *Dunedin*, Deck Logs, January 1939–November 1939
ADM 53/112064–112070	HMS *Dunedin*, Deck Logs, June 1940–December 1940
ADM 53/114156–114165	HMS *Dunedin*, Deck Logs, January 1941–October 1941
ADM 53/114104	HMS *Devonshire*, Deck Log, November 1941
ADM 53/114139	HMS *Dorsetshire*, Deck Log, November 1941
ADM 53/113801	HMS *Canton*, Deck Log, November 1941
ADM 116/3071	Report, dated 22 January 1934, of HMS *Dunedin* activities on New Zealand Station, 1 October–31 December 1933
	Report, dated 16 July 1934, of HMS *Dunedin* activities on New Zealand Station, 1 May–3 July 1934
	Report, dated 4 May 1934, of HMS *Dunedin* activities on New Zealand Station, 1 January–30 April 1934
	Report, dated 15 October 1934, of HMS *Dunedin* activities on New Zealand Station, 3 July–30 September 1934
	Report, dated 12 February 1935, of HMS *Dunedin* activities on New Zealand Station, 3 October 1934–31 January 1935
ADM 179/159	Report by Captain Lovatt, HMS *Dunedin*, of events of 23–24 November 1940

ADM 199/394 – 395	South Atlantic Command War Diary, June 1941–December 1941
ADM 199/725	Report, dated 17 February 1941, by Commanding Officer, HMS *Berwick*, of *Hipper* incident
ADM 199/736	Report, dated 26 November 1941, by HMS *Devonshire* of sinking of *Atlantis*
ADM 199/809	Report, dated 21 June 1941, by HMS *Dunedin* and *Eagle* on *Lothringen* capture
	Report, dated 9 June 1941, by HMS *Eagle* of destruction of *Elbe*
ADM 199	Report, dated 7 December 1941, of proceedings of HM Ships *Dorsetshire* and *Canton*, 4–13 November 1941
ADM 199	Report, dated 5 January 1942, by HMS *Devonshire* of search for *Dunedin* survivors
ADM 199/2067	Report of sinking of HMS *Dunedin* by Lt-Commander A. O. Watson, RN, dated 28 January 1942
ADM 199/2225–2234	Admiralty War Diary, 26 March 1941–7 December 1941
	Also, in earlier series, Admiralty War Diary, 28 August 1939–16 March 1941
ADM 223/103	Admiralty signals, November 1941
ADM 223/150	Admiralty weekly intelligence reports, April–June 1941
ADM 223/321	Operational Intelligence Centre Special Intelligence Summaries:
	11 June 1941
	23 November 1941
	26 November 1941
	28 November 1941
	7 December 1941
DEFE 3/66-69	Teleprinted translations of decrypted German naval radio messages, 2–26 November 1941
DEFE 3/1–4 and 3/20–21	Teleprinted translations of decrypted German naval radio messages, 13 May–3 July 1941

HW/92	Naval Section Naval Headlines for June and November 1941
HW 11/38	The Battle of the Atlantic – Operational Intelligence Centre Special Intelligence summary
CAB 86/1	Cabinet Minutes, 26th meeting, 25 November 1941

National Archives and Records Administration, Washington

War diary of U-124: Microfilm roll 2973, T1022

Bibliothek fuer Zeitgeschichte, Stuttgart

Dunedin Torpedo Report (Schussmeldung U124 24.11.41/1521 and U124 24.11.41/1546)

Naval Historical Branch, Ministry of Defence

I am indebted to Kate Tildesley, Curator, for guidance and assistance in the search for relevant documents in a number of sources.

Unpublished Documents

Broadway, H. T. L., letters, 29 August 1940–18 November 1941

Ellis, S. J., diaries, 24 August 1939–23 September 1940

Gaines, A. G., 'A Long Way From Home', 1989

Grant, A., letter, 18 June 1940

Handley, T., 'The Life And Times of Thomas D. Handley'

Harris, R., diary, 21 August 1939–27 January 1940

Hughes, A. W., *Hannover* anti-scuttling report, March 1940

Lowey, H., letters, November 1941

Mantell, K., midshipman's journal, 20 October–19 September 1941

Moore, T., 'The End of a Great Ship: The *Dunedin* Drama', 1971

Morgan, D., 'The Naval Career of E. O. Unwin, RN', London, 2001

Pitt, N. J., letter, 14 November 1941

Russell, L. B., letters, 5 October 1940–18 November 1941

Sowdon, R. M. H., letter, 22 May 1941

Stevenson, E. J., 'HMS *Dunedin*'

Wells, G. E., letter, 29 September 1941

Wood, S. R., notes

The following members of the ship's company gave me first-hand accounts of their time on board HMS *Dunedin*, either in writing or in interviews:

Les Barter

Harry Cross

Jim Davis

Charles Emburey

William Gill

Tommy Handley

Raymond Harris

Harry Hunt

Alan Jarvis

Keith Mantell

Andrew Prideaux

In addition, Lt-Commander Chris Broadway passed on information to me gleaned from correspondence and interviews with Richard Beveridge (now deceased). Daniel Morgan passed on information and photographs obtained from Johann Mohr, the son of the captain of U-124.

Newspapers and magazines

Evening Standard, 16 September 1941

Evening Standard, 19 December 1941

Daily Mirror, 20 December 1941

Fleet Flashes, February 1942 (company magazine of Lykes Brothers)

Kriegsmarine, March 1942, article by Harald Busch, 'Meisterlich Getroffen' ('A Master Stroke')

Bremer Nachrichten (Bremen News), 1942, article by Kreigsberichter Hans Dietrich, 'Mit rotem Siegeswimpel am Turm' ('Red Pennant Flying from the Tower')

INDEX